June 5, 1998

To Meg,
  Happy Birthday!
This book was meant for
you. Have lots of fun with
Kate and Gavin

Basic Nature
Projects

Basic Nature
Projects
101 FUN EXPLORATIONS

Priscilla M. Tucker
with illustrations by David Besenger

STACKPOLE
BOOKS

Published by
STACKPOLE BOOKS
5067 Ritter Road
Mechanicsburg, PA 17055

Printed in the United States of America

Cover design by Tracy Patterson
Front cover illustration by John McNulty
Back cover illustrations by David Besenger

First Edition

10 9 8 7 6 5 4 3 2 1

To Jim, for his love, patience, advice, and help.
He is truly my strongest supporter and best friend.

In all things of nature
there is something of the marvelous.
—Aristotle

Library of Congress Cataloging-in-Publication Data

Tucker, Priscilla.
    Basic nature projects : 101 fun explorations / Priscilla M. Tucker. — 1st ed.
        p.   cm.
    ISBN 0-8117-2511-1
    1. Natural history projects.   2. Nature study—Activity programs.
3. Natural history.   4. Nature.   I. Title.
QH55.T83   1995
508—dc20   95-3821
                                                                       CIP

CONTENTS

Foreword   vii

Introduction   ix

A Word about Names   xi

Mountains, Meadows, and Woods

Der Fledermaus: The World's Only Flying Mammal   3

Seeing with Their Ears   9

Homeward Bound   14

Egg Rolls   20

Happy Trails   28

Nightlights   34

Nature's Plow   42

Tap-Dancing Turtles   48

Treasure Hunters   53

Don't Get Rattled   57

Taking Root   65

Branching Out   70

Green Blood   77

Following the Leader   83

National Champion Trees   89

Butterflies on the Move   97

Five Useful Wild Plants   103

An Underground Monarchy   109

The Ways of the Ant   116

Marshes, Rivers, and Oceans

The Rise and Fall of the Ocean   127
The Well-Balanced Lobster   133
The Living Lie   141
The Crustacean with the Custom Home   147
Living Skeletons   152
Snails Dextral and Sinistral   156
Of Gills and Air Bladders   162
Bubbles   166
The Eyes Have It   174
There's No Such Thing as a Sea Gull   178
Big Birds with Special Bills   182
Otters: Streamlined and Friendly   186
Hide-and-Seek   191
The Animal That Somersaults   195

Air, Sky, and Space

Fireworks in the Sky   201
The Sun: Our Closest Star   205
The Moon: Stepping-Stone to Space   211
Between Earth and the Sun   216
Three More Bright Stars   222
The Unknown Planets   229

Glossary   239

ONE OF THE MORE DIFFICULT ASPECTS OF TEACHING ELEMENTARY SCIENCE is finding supplementary reading material that will engage and hold young learners' interest in their environment. The natural curiosity of the young is quickly diminished by material that is either too difficult or too simplistic. Priscilla M. Tucker has produced a book that goes a long way toward meeting the needs of the conscientious parent or teacher who wants to build upon the initial desire to learn that the typical youngster possesses. She has drawn from her wide experience with the natural world to present a multifaceted picture of that world, filled with interesting imagery and careful exposition of some key concepts in the important field of science, a subject that is increasingly vital to the well-being of both students and their nation.

Among the innovative features of this book is the introduction of original activities that the learner can enter into with enthusiasm as an adjunct to the more abstract aspects of the basic reading material. Hands-on tasks are among the best learning techniques for the incorporation of real meaning into—and thus retention of—new concepts. The activities generally use common, inexpensive household items; thus the acquisition of significant new ideas is accomplished with little expense and in a manner that is fun as well as educational.

Adult readers with an interest in nature will also find a great deal of provocative content in these bite-size essays.There is a rather astonishing breadth of variety in the topics discussed, with entertaining approaches taken that enhance our understanding of natural processes we thought we had mastered. Once again we are reminded that there is always something to be learned, a new way to conceptualize ordinary events that blasé adults tend too much to take for granted, without experiencing that spark of understanding that illuminates the natural wonders all around us. It is a good example of the old idea that "The more you know, the more interesting a topic becomes."

This book is one of those rare gems that can be recommended wholeheartedly to parents and other educators who desire to give the children in their care the best start in attaining true understanding of the world around us.

Hugh Willoughby
Audubon Society of Rhode Island
Riverside, Rhode Island

INTRODUCTION

All things in this world must be seen with the morning dew on them, must be seen with youthful, early-opened eyes.
—Henry David Thoreau

I REMEMBER GETTING A JAR, DROPPING HALF A DOZEN CLOVER BLOSSOMS inside, punching holes in the lid, and going out to catch bees: I wanted to be able to observe them gathering nectar and to hear their amplified buzzing when I held the jar up to my ear. I remember watching anthills, searching under rocks for salamanders, and wishing that my mother would let me keep the mouse that our cat had caught for her kittens.

In those days I would pick up worms without feeling squeamish and would gather lady's slippers with no idea that someday they would be endangered. It was a time to enjoy and to discover—even to fear a little bit—the wild things around me.

This book is written for the child in all of us who feels wonder and apprehension at the same time and who wants to know more about the world but isn't sure how to start.

This book is written for naturalists of any age: anyone who has ever wondered how much dirt a worm chews in one day, ever tried to identify a dozen species of birds, or ever found joy in watching a family of rabbits playing leapfrog.

This book is written for parents and children, teachers and students, Scout leaders and Scouts, and everyone who is even slightly curious about what happens every day on land, in water, and in the sky.

And this book is deliberately designed for grown-ups and children to learn together. The adults can read and share the chapters with the children, and then the children can follow the instructions for the projects. In some cases, adult supervision is needed for the activities.

As you read, you'll notice that most of the names of the plants and animals are capitalized. The common name (for instance, the Herring Gull) has two parts: a genus name that categorizes the plant or animal with its close relatives, and a species name that usually refers to its discoverer or typical habitat. Everything also has a Latin name (for instance, *Larus argentatus*), in which the genus name is always capitalized and the species name is not.

The underlying message of this book is that we can appreciate our world just by being aware of it. We don't need to—and shouldn't—adopt wild creatures to learn about them. We don't need cages, pens, or elaborate terrariums. We do need to understand that the natural world is a well-balanced place where misinformation or lack of knowledge about the lowliest worm and the ugliest horseshoe crab denies their importance and threatens their survival.

Through short write-ups and simple activities, this book offers ways to observe, explore, and get to know the world around us.

Mountains,
Meadows, and
Woods

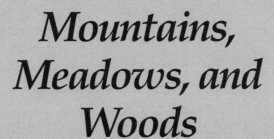

Der Fledermaus: The World's Only Flying Mammal

Fillet of fenny snake,
In the cauldron boil and bake;
Eye of newt, and toe of frog,
Wool of bat, and tongue of dog,
Adder's fork and blind worm's sting,
Lizard's leg and howlet's wing,
For a charm of powerful trouble,
Like a hell-broth boil and bubble.
　　　　—William Shakespeare, *Macbeth*

THE SPIKE-FLOWERED CENTURY PLANT OF THE AMERICAN SOUTHWEST IS so dependent on the Longnose Bat that it deceives the little animal into carrying out an important mission. To attract the bat, the Century Plant emits the scent of tyric acid, the hormone that attracts the male Longnose Bat to the female. When the bat uses its long tongue to get nectar from deep inside a flower, pollen clings to its furry face. Then when the bat probes the next plant, it pollinates it. This is a symbiotic relationship—one that benefits both parties— for the bat also depends on the plant. The Century Plant's nectar contains two essential amino acids: proline, which helps to produce the skin of the bat's wings, and tyrosine, which is secreted with a nursing mother's milk and stimulates growth in infant bats.

Most of us probably don't picture a bat sipping nectar from flowers and pollinating plants. More than likely, we think of *der fledermaus*, the "flying mouse," as a peaceful insect-eating creature at best or a blood-sucking vampire at worst. But because it couldn't be neatly defined as a bird or a mammal and because it flew only at night—when, as everyone knows, all evil events take place—the mysterious bat was an easy target for superstitious minds.

Certainly, Shakespeare's three witches believed in the bat's supernatural powers. Right in there with various parts of venomous reptiles and amphibians, the filthy owl, and the loyal but often cruel dog is a bat's fur, one of the features that makes this flying mammal an oddity—and therefore an essential ingredient in any good witch's brew. Of course, this vile stew did nothing but smell awful.

Throughout European folklore, the bat was a symbol of doom; if a bat entered a house or flapped against a window, people believed that death would come soon to someone living there. Sooner or later, someone in the household would die, thereby "proving" the belief. In Mayan mythology, the bat's connection to death went one step further, for the bat god was thought to control the underworld. Chinese legend, however, contradicts the sinister image of the bat in other cultures; for the Chinese, the bat represents happiness and long life. Sometimes the appearance of a bat has contradictory meanings even within the same country; for example, depending on where in Great Britain you live, if you see a bat during the day, it may be a bad sign or a good one.

Because of its conflicting physical characteristics—its fur and its wings—the bat often was portrayed as having a dual nature that eventually caused its banishment to darkness. Aesop described the bat as a coward and an opportunist; it was always ready to change sides from bird to mouse to bird again to avoid danger, so it was permanently driven from the honest light of day. This lack of loyalty also is found in ancient Latin writings, but the following Nigerian folk tale tells the story best.

During a war between the birds and the animals, the bat joined neither side until it saw that the birds were winning. Then, using the excuse that it had wings, it joined the birds. When it seemed, however, that the animals were going to be the victors after all, the bat tried to defect to their side, showing them its teeth as proof that it really belonged with them. But the animals refused to accept the bat, and the birds refused to take it back. Forever an outcast, the bat still leaves its home only at night.

Although fuel for folklore, the bat is in truth a highly specialized creature. Unlike gliding animals such as the flying squirrel, which uses flaps of loose skin to sail downward from limb to limb, the bat has fully formed wings. The bones that give shape to the hands and arms in primates and the front paws and forelegs in most other land animals are, with some modifications, wing supports in bats. The bone of the bat's upper arm is short, the bone of the forearm is longer, and the finger bones are extremely long. The

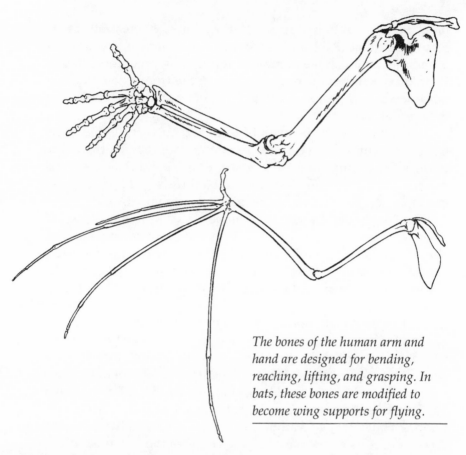

The bones of the human arm and hand are designed for bending, reaching, lifting, and grasping. In bats, these bones are modified to become wing supports for flying.

thumb, free of the wing, ends in a claw that the bat uses when walking, climbing, and handling food.

The bat's wing is webbed with a thin, leathery membrane, or skin, that stretches over and between the bones of the hands and fingers. The membrane then extends to the forearm and upper arm and along the sides of the body to the hind leg. The membrane is puckered, not smooth, so that when the bat folds its wings, the skin contracts instead of falling into folds or pleats, and it expands when the bat opens its wings. Most species of bats also have a membrane connecting the legs and tail.

To fly well, the bat must keep its wing membranes and tail membranes flexible. Because the creature is nocturnal, it easily avoids the drying effects of the Sun's heat on the delicate skin. To keep the wing and tail membranes extra supple, the bat regularly smears them with a lubricant secreted by a gland between its eyes and nose.

Thirty-nine species of bats live in North America, picking millions of beetles, mosquitoes, gnats, and moths out of the air every night. Some types of bats roost in large groups, whereas others prefer to roost alone. All bats roost upside down, hanging by the claws of their feet high above the threat of prowling predators. Because their knees bend to the back rather than the front as ours do, this head-downward position is more comfortable for them than perching upright.

Some bats dangle beneath bridges and culverts. Others hang from the ceilings of caves, mine tunnels, or attics. Still others cling to the sides of buildings or rock ledges or spend their days suspended inside the hollow trunks of dead trees. A few hang from tree branches. To take off, a bat simply releases its grip and flies.

The twenty-eight species of plainnose bats form the largest category of North American bats. They range from the southern United States northward throughout Canada almost to the Arctic Circle. Some of these little brown bats are easy for amateur naturalists to identify by sight, but others are difficult to tell apart, even for experts.

Unlike most bat species, the tail of a freetail bat extends well beyond the tail membrane. The most famous of North America's six species is probably the Mexican Freetail. Each day at dusk, crowds of people watch millions of these bats pour out of Carlsbad Caverns, New Mexico, and Nye Cave, near Bandera, Texas, to feed.

Only one species of vampire bat can be found in North America. The Hairy-legged Vampire Bat strays to Texas from Mexico, where it uses its razor-sharp teeth to cut open the skin of large animals. When it has licked up about an ounce (28 g) of blood, it's satisfied. Contrary to the Dracula legend, the bloodthirsty little creature rarely attacks humans.

The most unusual North American bats are the four species of leafnose bats of the American Southwest. A leafnose bat has a triangular flap of skin extending upward from the tip of its nose. Two species, the Hognose Bat and the Longnose Bat of Century Plant fame, supplement their insect diets with nectar and pollen.

Although bats mate in fall, the female doesn't produce eggs until the following spring, when fertilization takes place. Most species bear only one baby each year, although a few have twins. The naked and blind infant clings to its mother for the first weeksof its life, even when she goes in search of food. When the growing youngster is too heavy to carry, the mother leaves it hanging upside down at the roost site while she feeds. Eventually, the young bat follows its mother on her nightly forays, learning to catch insects for itself. Unlike birds, young bats take no practice flights but fly well on the first attempt. Clearly, the world's only flying mammal deserves lots of attention—not as the subject of superstition, but as a unique member of the animal kingdom.

Notable wildlife

Hairy-legged Vampire Bat, *Diphylla ecaudata*
Mexican Freetail, *Tadarida brasiliensis*
Hognose Bat, *Choeronycteris mexicana*
Longnose Bat, *Leptonycteris nivalis*
Century Plant, *Agave palmeri*

DISCOVERY

1. Hanging Around. Bats hang upside down for hours as they wait for the Sun to set. Yet they don't seem to be affected by the fact that the "blood is rushing to their heads,"as we are. Hang upside down by your knees. Feel the uncomfortable sensation in your head. Then get down!

2. Make a Bat Mobile. When the bats leave their roosts to feed at night, they do so by the millions—and not just at Halloween. Make a mobile of bat shapes, but you can stop short of a million, if you want to.

ITEMS NEEDED

graph paper, eight squares to the inch	black construction paper
	black thread
pencil	paper punch
scissors	wire coat hanger
glue	cup hook
cardboard	

PROCEDURE

1. Trace the bat shape on the next page.
2. Cut out the shape.
3. Glue the bat shape onto the piece of cardboard, and cut it out. This is your pattern.
4. Trace around the cardboard bat pattern onto the construction paper, making as many bats as you want
5. Cut out the bats.
6. Punch a hole in the center of each bat, as shown, and thread with a twelve-inch piece of black thread.

Use this full-size pattern
for your bat mobile.

7. Tie the thread, being careful not to rip through the hole.

8. Tie the other end of the thread to the coat hanger. Tie the bats at different lengths, and slide them along the hanger until the hanger is balanced.

9. Suspend the coat hanger from a cup hook screwed into the ceiling of your room.

Seeing with Their Ears

*If you wish to see anything submerged and deep in
the night, and that it may not be more hidden from
thee than in the day, and that you may read books in
a dark night—anoint your face with the blood of a
Bat, and that will happen which I say.*
—Albertus Magnus

IMAGINE YOURSELF IN A DARK, DIM WORLD. IT'S NIGHT, AND OBJECTS ARE
barely visible. Yet you are moving fast, whipping around houses
and tearing between trees at breakneck speed. Nothing fazes you.
Just for fun you rush headlong toward a moving obstacle—it's a
person!—and wait until the very last moment to change course,
avoiding disaster by the merest fraction of an inch.

Fun! Easy, too—if you're a bat.

Bats aren't sightless, despite what the adage "blind as a bat"
implies. They see very well, and a few fruit-eating species find food
by looking for it. Of course, that doesn't mean that smearing your
face with bat blood will improve your night vision. (Bat blood is
only valuable when it's circulating inside a bat.) Yet even though
bats generally have acute vision and see well in the dark, most of
the world's several hundred species locate insects by sound rather
than sight.

To prove that the world's only flying mammal didn't depend
on sight to navigate, in 1793 Lazzaro Spallanzani, an Italian naturalist, covered the eyes of several bats. Then he released them. The
blindfolded bats easily navigated the darkness without crashing
into solid objects. Spallanzani then crisscrossed a room with strung
silk thread. The bats easily avoided the strands of that irregular
web. What was their secret? Spallanzani conducted one more
experiment: He plugged the bats' ears. Now they were helpless.

Those early experiments clearly showed that bats "see" with
their ears. But how?

More than a hundred years after Spallanzani did his research, Harvard scientist Donald R. Griffin proved that bats use sonar to fly unerringly through the night. They produce high-pitched beeps, wait for the beeps to hit a solid object, and then interpret the returning echoes as navigational information. The echo that bounces back tells the bat what lies ahead. Using its sonar, the bat can distinguish the smallest soft-bodied gnat from the tallest concrete-and-iron skyscraper, and it can calculate how far away it is.

The bat knows that the farther away an object is, the longer the echo takes to return, so it allows for distance variations when it sends out its signals. As it patiently hunts, the beeps are lower pitched and slower, about 10 per second. But when it picks up the echo of a moth or other insect, the beeps come faster and faster, accelerating from 250 beeps every second to 3,000 every second. This rapid-fire staccato sounds like a scream in recordings of bat sounds. The bat fields its food in its cupped tail, then retrieves it with its mouth.

Bats live in a noisy world. At close range, a bat's sound pulses are twenty to sixty times louder than the jarring noise of a jackhammer. (Fortunately, the beeps are too high pitched for us to hear

Scientists estimate that ounce for ounce and watt for watt, the flying mammal's sonar is a billion times more sensitive and efficient than any man-made device. Echolocation works so well that a bat can locate and eat five thousand gnats in less than two hours. The average total time that passes between the detection of prey and its capture is less than half a second.

The bat almost always nets the insect in its cupped tail, then bends to seize it in its teeth. Although there is photographic proof that bats can catch insects directly by mouth, they rarely use this method because it is much less reliable.

them!) Each species has its own sequence and pitch of beeps, and each bat has its own sound. As a result, every bat can sort out the transmissions and echoes of every other bat from the various night sounds. In some species, specialized nose leaves amplify the sound as it is emitted. The large size and cupped shape of bats' ears amplify the returning echo.

Leafnose bats emit sounds through the nose, and the "leaf" directs the sound outward. All other bat species emit sounds in the throat, then form their mouths into the shape of a megaphone to direct and amplify the sounds.

Bats can't fly as fast as swifts and hummingbirds, the speed-sters of the bird world, but what they lack in speed they make up for in maneuverability. At ten to twenty miles per hour, they can make precise right-hand turns to avoid collisions with trees, build-ings, and other bats as they home in on tiny flying insects. They don't even slow down to make a landing. Still operating at full speed, a bat approaches the roost, flips over, and grabs for a well-deserved rest after a job well done.

DISCOVERY

1. Catching Moths. Since you don't have a net-shaped tail, you'll have to improvise to catch moths.

ITEMS NEEDED

> piece of heavyweight
>   cardboard, about
>   four by five inches

> paper cup
> craft glue
> table tennis balls

PROCEDURE

1. Glue the cup to one end of the cardboard. This represents the bat's cupped tail, used for netting insects.

2. Have a partner throw the balls—the moths—into the air, one at a time. He gets twenty-five throws in all.

3. As the Bat, you have to catch the balls in the cup. You get a point for each ball that stays in the cup.

4. Now change places. The person with the higher score after twenty-five throws each is the better-fed Bat.

2. Play Bat and Gnat. How good is your hearing? Can you pick up a gnat at twenty paces? At ten? Okay, how about five?

ITEMS NEEDED

> blindfold

PROCEDURE

1. One player, the Bat, is blindfolded.

2. Four or more other players, the Gnats, stand in a loose circle around the Bat, at least six feet away. The players should be unevenly spaced and at different distances from the Bat.

3. To begin the game, all the Gnats call out "gnat, gnat, gnat, gnat . . ."

4. The Gnats continue calling out "gnat," using both loud calls and soft ones and remaining at all times in their original positions.

5. Based on sound only, the Bat must walk up to and touch each Gnat.

6. The last Gnat to be found by the Bat becomes the Bat for the next game.

Variation: The Bat must walk between two lines of Gnats without touching any of them. The Bat must use the "gnat, gnat, gnat" signals to avoid the insects. Players take turns as the Bat.

By the way, bats accelerate from 250 beeps every second to 3,000 every second. Compare that to the world's fastest rapper, Tung Twista, who can rap out only 597 syllables in 55.12 seconds.

3. Look, Ma, No Hands. Bats catch moving insects in their mouths. Can you catch moving food?

ITEMS NEEDED

string	yardstick
scissors	plain doughnuts, one per person
masking tape	blindfolds

PROCEDURE

1. Have an adult tape lengths of string hanging down from the top of a doorway, one string for each player. The lower ends of the strings should be six inches below mouth level.

2. Tie a doughnut to each piece of string.

3. Put on the blindfolds.

4. Now, without using your hands or your eyes, eat the dangling doughnuts.

4. "Seeing" Sound. Ships use sonar to avoid underwater hazards. (If the *Titanic* had had sonar equipment, it wouldn't have hit that iceberg.) When sound hits a solid object, it echoes back to its source. "See" for yourself how sonar works.

ITEMS NEEDED

flashlight

PROCEDURE

1. On a dark night, shine the flashlight across an open field or down a long road. The beam seems to disappear.

2. Now shine the light on a tree or building. What happens? The beam of light bounces back to you, just as the "beam of sound" bounces back to the bat.

Homeward Bound

Mid pleasures and palaces though we may roam,
Be it ever so humble, there's no place like home.
        —John Howard Payne, *Home Sweet Home*

IF YOU HAD TO CHOOSE THE ANIMAL THAT HAS CONTRIBUTED THE MOST
to fighting wars, which would it be? The cow that fed the soldiers?
The mule that carried the supplies? The horse that formed the cal-
vary? Or the pigeon that carried messages of positions, maneuvers,
and help? The bird wins over the mammals. From racing to soldier-
ing and back to racing, the history of the world may have been
much different without pigeons.

Pigeon racing began thousands of years ago. Looking for a
readily available and trainable animal to use in competition,
ancient sportsmen began to train Rock Doves, the common pigeon
that in the modern world nests under highway bridges and begs
for food in parks. Common throughout the world, Rock Doves
were the ideal choice. The ones that could fly the fastest and farthest were bred to develop a race of superpigeons called homing
pigeons, homers, or racing homers.

The Greeks soon saw the value of putting these birds, with
their swiftness and endurance, to work. So, in addition to racing,
the speedy pigeons carried names of the winners of the Olympic
contests all over Greece. Later, European merchants and bankers
recognized the practical value of the birds and created a sort of
pigeon express to speed general correspondence from one town to
another. The pigeons carried letters and stock-market reports
throughout the continent.

Racing pigeons served in wartime as well as during times of
peace. The armies of Phoenicia, Egypt, Assyria, and Persia used
homers to serve as military couriers. With news of maneuvers and
orders strapped to their legs or backs, these dependable birds flew

During World War I and World War II,
homing pigeons carried messages to and
from headquarters in tubes harnessed to
their backs or strapped to a leg.

directly from battlefield to headquarters. When the birds were flying, they looked like ordinary wild pigeons and often made it
across enemy lines that no foot soldier could penetrate. Because of
their speed and stamina, homers helped to build the empires of
Julius Caesar and Genghis Khan. A homing pigeon carried the welcome news to the people of England that the British army had
defeated Napoleon at Waterloo. Later, in the Franco-Prussian War,
the French continued to use homers as messengers. Recognizing
the importance of the pigeons, the Germans retaliated by training
hawks to catch them.

Homers served as couriers in Europe and the United States
well into the twentieth century. The birds' modern uniforms were
harnesses with message-carrying tubes attached. During World
War I, World War II, and the Korean Conflict, homing pigeons were
kept in mobile lofts, traveling with the troops until needed to carry
news to headquarters when telephone and telegraph lines were
disabled. The record flight for a U.S. Army Signal Corps pigeon
stands at twenty-three hundred miles, but flights of one thousand
miles or more were common.

During World War I, a remarkable pigeon named Big Tom flew
twenty-four miles in twenty-five minutes to save the men of New

York's Seventy-seventh Division. The bird was the last resort for these Allied soldiers, who were pinned down by the crossfire of enemy guns and their own artillery. Two pigeons had already died trying to cross enemy lines with the message that help was needed, but Big Tom made it—with a bullet in his breast and one leg shot off. The pigeon recovered from his wounds. Another feathered hero, Mocker, carried a message that gave the locations of the enemy batteries decimating American forces. Although Mocker lost an eye during his journey, he completed his mission, and the enemy troops were defeated. When he died, Mocker was buried with the full military honors that he deserved.

During World War II, spies carried pigeons when they parachuted behind enemy lines; then they released the birds with valuable information that would help their side. Advance foot patrols used them in the same way. And when a German submarine attacked a British fishing boat, one of the crew members released his pet homer with this message: "*Nelson* attacked by subs. Send assistance." The pigeon completed its mission, and the British sailors were rescued.

In 1956, with the advent of electronic communication devices, the Army no longer kept pigeons as emergency backups to telephones and telegraphs and sold the last of its homing pigeons. The history of the homing pigeon came full circle, so that today the birds once again are used mostly in pigeon racing, in Europe and the United States. The Swiss, though, still keep several thousand homing pigeons as a backup in case modern communications systems fail.

How does a homing pigeon find its way? Strong instinct tells it to return home from wherever it's set free, but patient training begun before the bird is a year old helps to hone this instinct. First, the trainer keeps the pigeon cooped for several weeks to establish the coop as the home base. Then the trainer places the bird on the roof of the coop so that it learns to recognize the structure from the air. Soon after, the trainer teaches the pigeon to enter the coop through a trapdoor, often by rewarding it with food. This is an important step, because the bird isn't considered to have completed a race until it has entered that door and had its identifying leg band removed.

A homer develops its ability to find its way back to the loft much as a young child first learns to navigate inside his home, then around his yard, and finally familiar routes, like the way to and from the grocery store. Flight training is done in all kinds of weather. The trainer first releases the pigeon a mile away from the coop for two or three consecutive days, then from two miles away for several days in a row. He gradually increases the distance, until at the end of about a year the bird can return home from a release site seventy miles away. After about three years of repeated practice, the pigeon is able to fly at an average speed of fifty miles per hour from a distance of five hundred to six hundred miles to its home loft. Two- to three-year-old birds are the fastest, and nesting birds are the most dependable because their instinct to return to their young is so strong.

For centuries, men speculated about how a homer found its way home without miscalculating the direction. Greyhounds follow a mechanical rabbit that leads them around and around a track. Thoroughbred horses respond to the jockeys who ride them. But homers complete their course with no lure to lead them and no commands to follow. Do they use the Sun? Do they recognize landmarks? Do they respond to Earth's magnetic field? As it turns out, homers navigate much as sea captains do; they use all three methods in whatever combination is necessary to fly swiftly and directly to their goal, a process that scientists don't completely understand but that serves the pigeons well.

Using the Sun as a compass, a homer makes adjustments for the time of day and how that hour is represented by the position of the Sun. In other words, the bird has an internal clock that tells it where the Sun should be at any given hour, then it adjusts its route home according to the change in the Sun's position during the day.

On an overcast day, the bird engages a backup navigational system. Although scientists are still trying to determine which organs are used, they do know that homing pigeons (and some other birds) have four cells in the brain that contain magnetite, a compound formed of iron and oxygen. Magnetite provides the pigeon with a built-in detector that's sensitive to Earth's magnetic field. Because Earth is a giant magnet, a compass needle always points to magnetic north. And the pigeon's built-in compass needle is no different. By being able to determine which way is north, the pigeon can fly toward any of the points on a compass; it takes a bearing and flies home, even through fog and rain.

As the pigeon approaches its home loft, visual recognition takes over. The bird no longer has to rely on the position of the Sun or Earth's magnetic field, so it uses landmarks. All those early weeks of training finally pay off when the homer recognizes the roof of its own coop and enters that trapdoor, to win a race or to save a life.

Notable wildlife
  Rock Dove, *Columba livia*

DISCOVERY

1. The Law of Magnetism. People may not have magnetite in their brains, but they do have the brains to build a magnet. Here's a simple one to put together.
  ITEMS NEEDED
    sewing needle (not nickel-plated)
    shallow glass bowl
    water
  PROCEDURE
  1. Place about one-half inch of water in the bowl.
  2. Holding the needle horizontally and as close to the water as possible, carefully place it on the surface of the water. (If you don't set it down just right, the needle will sink to the bottom of the water. You may need to try several times before getting the needle to float.)
  3. Once it's floating, the needle will turn toward north. Sewing needles are made of steel, which in turn contains iron. No matter which way you turn the bowl, the needle will act as a compass needle and turn too, always toward magnetic north.
  Note: This experiment won't work if you use a plastic bowl. Can you figure out why?

2. How's Your Sense of Direction? Some of us seem to have maps in our heads; others need specific directions to get to an unfamiliar place. Since the important thing is to reach your destination, how you do it isn't an issue. But it's fun to practice, to develop an instinct the way pigeons do.
  ITEM NEEDED
    blindfold
  PROCEDURE
  1. Ask your parents to take you for a ride to a nearby but unfamiliar spot in your town while you're blindfolded. Time the ride.
  2. After they stop the car, remove the blindfold.

3. Direct the way home. Tell whoever is driving to turn right or left or to continue straight ahead—whatever feels right.

4. How long does it take you to sight a familiar landmark? How long does it take you to find your way home?

3. Learn Your Landmarks. Pigeons use landmarks to help them find their way home. You do, too. You just may not be aware of it. To prove this fact, draw an aerial-view map from memory.

ITEMS NEEDED

paper   crayons
pencil   ruler

PROCEDURE

1. Start your map by drawing the streets in your neighborhood. Label them.

2. Next, draw any major landmarks, such as a pond or park. Label them.

3. Draw your house next.

4. Finally, fill in neighboring houses and stores, trees, mailboxes, and fire hydrants.

5. Did you find it difficult to draw something from the top view rather than the front view?

Egg Rolls

Put all your eggs in one basket—and WATCH THAT BASKET.
—Mark Twain

ON A NARROW LEDGE ON A SHEER CLIFF, THOUSANDS OF NOISY BIRDS ARE jostling for perching room. The wind blows hard and the surf pounds the jagged rocks below. A very dangerous place to lay an egg and raise a chick, right?

Wrong. It's the best spot in the world for a black-and-white seabird known as the Common Murre. A rocky coastal cliff along the northern Atlantic or Pacific Ocean is safe from cats and human egg collectors, and the communal lifestyle suits the birds just fine. Common Murres nest in such tightly packed colonies that the eggs can't roll very far, and if they do roll, the eggs are conical instead of round, so they roll in circles, with the pointed end inward, rather than straight off the cliff.

When the eggs hatch, the chicks are almost as safe as they were in the eggs. The large number of adult birds provides an impenetrable barrier between the chicks and predatory gulls that are on the outlook for a stray baby. If a chick should happen to wander away from its parents and tumble over the rocky ledge, it has a good chance of safely landing on another ledge below.

These birds are quick to care for each other's eggs and chicks; in fact, when one adult bird leaves the nest to feed at sea, another bird quickly moves in to fill the space and protect the egg or chick. But that doesn't mean that murre parents expect indefinite baby-sitting for their young. Both parents in a mated pair of Common Murres can pick out and retrieve an egg and chick that's gotten away from them. The color of the eggs ranges from dirty white to deep turquoise marked with red, brown, or black spots and splotches. Each egg is unique, and parent murres easily recognize their own. When the eggs have hatched, the parents recognize each hatchling by its voice.

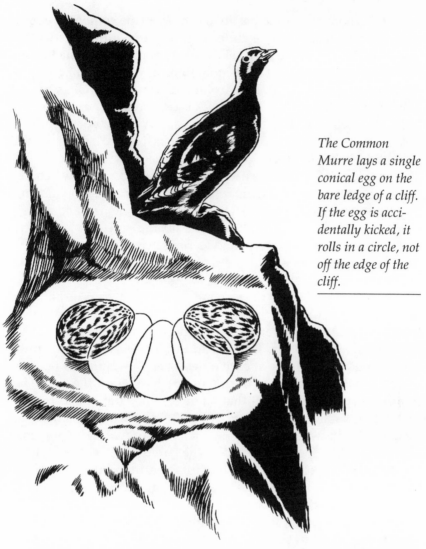

The Common Murre lays a single conical egg on the bare ledge of a cliff. If the egg is accidentally kicked, it rolls in a circle, not off the edge of the cliff.

For the Common Murre, laying one egg a year on a bare cliff is a successful nesting method. Most murre eggs hatch, and most murre chicks grow to adulthood. Another cliff-nesting bird, however, the California Condor, has been less successful in laying and incubating eggs and rearing young.

In the early 1980s, ornithologists began to observe California Condors at their nest sites to learn more about their nesting habits. This information would be valuable for setting up captive-breeding programs to reestablish the species. California Condors lay only one egg every two years, because their chicks take that long to reach adulthood. Over the past two centuries, the combined effects of habitat destruction, egg collectors, hunters' guns, pesticides, lead poisoning, and the birds' slow rate of reproduction had taken the species to the brink of extinction. Ironically, the number of eggs a species lays seems to indicate its life expectancy as well as its rate of maturation. The longer the species is expected to live and reproduce, the fewer eggs it has to lay each year. When left undisturbed, California Condors live for several decades. Nature's system once worked well, but now each condor egg is precious.

Day after day, scientists used powerful telescopes to watch the remaining thirty condors, anxiously hoping to see some nesting activity. In the winter of 1981–82, the female of one pair laid an egg in a nest tucked into a shallow cave on the side of a cliff. The researchers began their vigil—and learned that sometimes even the parents that are supposed to guard the egg can become a danger, as the following account shows.

At first the behavior of the condor parents was typical. Each took its turn incubating the egg. So far, so good. But the peaceful schedule soon was shattered as the condor couple started to quarrel over brooding rights. The two adult birds began their dispute by pecking halfheartedly at each other. Then the argument became more violent, and they began shoving each other off the nest. The fighting became so severe that the egg, now unnoticed by the squabbling parents, was pushed out of the nest to settle on the bare rock of the cliff, where it was easy pickings for marauding ravens. There was still hope for the egg—if the parent birds noticed where it was. But no such luck. As the adults continued their shoving-match, they knocked the egg over the edge of the cliff, where it smashed on the rocks below.

In the late 1980s, the few remaining wild California Condors were rounded up to be used in captive-breeding programs. Since early 1992, several zoo-hatched condors have been released into the wild. The program has proved successful, and environmentalists hope that hundreds of these magnificent birds eventually will soar above the rocky cliffs of the West.

Whether laid and incubated on bare rock or, as with most birds, in a soft, cuplike nest, all eggs have basically the same structure. The outer hard part, the shell, is composed of two main layers of calcium carbonate. The shell contains pores through which the developing embryo absorbs oxygen and releases carbon dioxide.

Just inside the shell lie two very thin, white membranes, or

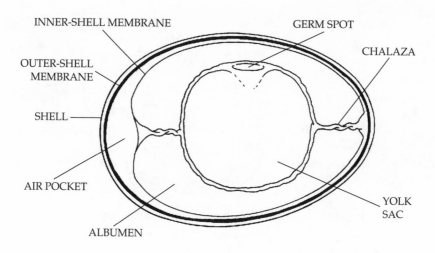

INNER-SHELL MEMBRANE   GERM SPOT

OUTER-SHELL
MEMBRANE

CHALAZA

SHELL

AIR POCKET

YOLK
SAC

ALBUMEN

skins. These membranes are very close to each other except at the blunt end of the egg, where an air pocket separates them. This air pocket acts like a reserve tank of oxygen for the developing embryo.

The albumen is what we call the egg white; it's composed of three very thin layers surrounded by a thicker one. The albumen is the main source of nourishment for about the first two thirds of the developing embryo's life and also holds water needed by the growing chick.

Inside the albumen, the yolk floats in a yolk sac suspended by two twisted, ropelike structures called chalazas. The chalazas anchor the yolk and help protect it from being crushed against the inside of the shell when the egg is jostled. A pinhead-size germ spot on the yolk eventually develops into the embryo. The nutrient-rich yolk feeds the embryo during its final stages of development.

The size of the egg has very little influence on the length of incubation, as two extremes in the bird family show. The pea-size egg of the Bee Hummingbird, the smallest bird in the world, weighs less than two-hundredths of an ounce and hatches in about fifteen days; the three-pound ostrich egg takes about forty-two days—not even three times as long. A chicken egg takes about twenty-one days, and a murre egg about thirty-three. Interestingly, a condor egg takes as long as an ostrich egg to hatch.

When the chick is ready to emerge, it uses its egg tooth, a sharp prominence on its beak, to chip its way out. Some chicks are blind, featherless, and defenseless when they first hatch; these are called altricial birds. Other chicks are feathered and feeding on their own almost from the moment they hatch; these are precocial birds. The

The egg tooth that the chick uses to break out of its shell will later drop off. Its only function is fulfilled during hatching.

chicks of most species develop rapidly, no matter how independent they are when they first peck through the eggshell. So within three weeks of emerging, the once helpless nestling of the Bee Hummingbird is fully feathered and ready to leave the nest; it can gather nectar and fly forward and backward as well as any other hummingbird. And within one month of hatching, the once defenseless Ostrich chick can run at the adult's speed of forty miles per hour. Chickens are on their own as soon as their feathers are dry. And murres are ready to take to sea within a month of hatching.

And condors? Condors don't even leave the nest until they're five months old, can't fly until they're seven months old, and still depend on their parents to feed them well into their second year.

Notable wildlife
Common Murre, *Uria aalge*
California Condor, *Gymnogyps californianus*
Bee Hummingbird, *Mellisuga helenae*
Ostrich, *Struthio camelus*

DISCOVERY

1. Rolling Eggs. The pear shape of a murre egg allows it to roll in a circle if it's pushed. The oval shape of a chicken egg does the same thing, although in a larger circle. Roll an egg and see how this works.

ITEMS NEEDED
uncooked egg in shell

PROCEDURE
1. Roll the uncooked egg on the floor. Does it circle back or roll in a straight line?

2. The Structure of an Egg. Raymond Loewy, the industrial designer who streamlined commercial packaging, named the two most perfectly designed containers ever made. One was the old Coca-Cola bottle. The other was—and always has been—the egg.

ITEMS NEEDED

uncooked egg in shell

vinegar

cup or jar

PROCEDURE

1. Run your fingers over the surface of a chicken egg. Feel the depressions in its surface? The developing embryo breathes through pores located in those depressions.

2. Submerge the egg in vinegar.

3. Check the egg after an hour. Watch the bubbles form in the vinegar as air is released from inside the shell.

4. Keep the egg in the vinegar overnight. The shell will gradually disappear, because vinegar is a weak acid that dissolves the calcium carbonate in the shell.

5. The next morning, rinse off the egg. The rubbery membrane layer will be exposed, and you'll be able to feel the yolk gently rolling inside.

6. Put the egg into a cup or jar, then place it, uncovered, in the refrigerator.

7. Check it daily for several days. You'll notice that the egg shrivels, because it's losing water rapidly.

8. When the egg feels as if it's lost all the liquid inside, open the membranous covering. What's there?

Variation: For a quick view of the inside of an egg, carefully cut a large hole in the side of a chicken egg and take a look at the yolk floating in the albumen. Look for the chalaza, too. IMPORTANT: Adult supervision is needed for cutting the eggshell.

3. Eggshell Planter. The minerals in an eggshell can provide needed nutrients for plants, so the next time you scramble eggs, use the shells to make a natural planter.

ITEMS NEEDED

eggshell	craft glue
one-inch-diameter	soil
plastic curtain ring	small plant

PROCEDURE

1. Break the shell in as straight a line as possible, removing the top quarter.

2. Glue the curtain ring to the bottom of the eggshell to form a stable base. Let it dry overnight.

3. Put soil in the shell to a depth of about one inch.

4. Place the plant in the shell.

5. Fill in around plant roots with soil.

6. Water the plant.

4. Play Roll the Murre Egg. Remember Mark Twain's advice and try to keep all your eggs, whether or not they're in a basket.

ITEMS NEEDED

large piece of paper

crayons or markers

plastic eggs

PROCEDURE

1. Using the illustration as a guide, draw a target on a large piece of paper. The center of the target is worth one hundred points; the outermost circle is worth ten.

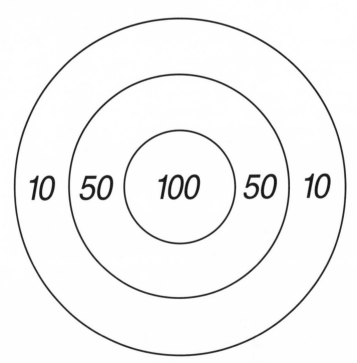

2. Lay the target on a hard surface.

3. Players take turns rolling a plastic egg toward the center of the target. (Why won't the egg roll straight?) The number on the ring on which the egg stops is the score.

4. Add the scores after each turn. The player with the highest score after a dozen turns is the Scrambled Egg.

HERE'S A SIMPLER VERSION OF THIS GAME:

1. Sit across a table from your opponent.

2. Roll six or more plastic eggs, as quickly as you can, toward the opposite side of the table. Your opponent gets five points for each egg that he stops from going over the edge.

3. Now it's your turn to save the eggs.

4. The player with the higher score after five turns is the winner.

5. Have an Egg-and-Spoon Race. Chris Riggio of San Francisco, California, holds the North American record for egg-and-spoon racing. On October 7, 1979, he ran 26 miles, 395 yards in 4 hours, 9 minutes, 45 seconds while carrying a spoon with a fresh egg on it. See how far and fast you can go under the same conditions.

ITEMS NEEDED

dessert spoon	stopwatch
fresh egg	pedometer

PROCEDURE

1. Balance the egg on the spoon and start running.

2. Use the pedometer to measure the distance you run and the stopwatch to time your run.

Several people can participate at the same time, or teams can compete against each other in a relay race.

By the way, it takes one hour and forty-five minutes to boil an Ostrich egg. How long does it take to boil a chicken egg?

Happy Trails

*A man's interest in a single bluebird is worth more than
a complete but dry list of the fauna and flora of a town.*
—Henry David Thoreau

WHEN EUROPEAN SETTLERS FIRST ARRIVED IN NORTH AMERICA, THEY named many New World plants and animals after similar species in the Old World. As a result, one of America's favorite birds lived under a false identity for a while. Because of its rusty breast, the Eastern Bluebird was originally called the Blue Robin after the red-breasted European Robin, even though the bluebird is only distantly related to the European bird. New World naturalists eventually sorted out the nomenclature, and today the bluebirds are in a genus of their own.

Bluebirds are among the most peace-loving birds in the world. They rarely squabble, even over territories. Whereas most birds aggressively defend themselves and their hunting and breeding grounds, the attitude of bluebirds seems to be "the more the merrier." Bluebirds nest within sight of each other, and flocks of them share living space and domestic chores. During the breeding season, bluebird parents may raise several broods. After the first brood fledges and is on its own, these older siblings help the parents care for their younger brothers and sisters.

In winter, bluebirds have a unique and economical method of roosting that allows them to survive the bitterly cold nights of the northern areas of their winter range. Several bluebirds enter the same cavity for the night, settling in on top of each other to take advantage of the shared body warmth. It takes a special kind of tolerance to put up with that much togetherness!

But the peaceful nature of the "bluebird of happiness" has a serious drawback. Although it once inhabited virtually every open field and meadow of North America, the Eastern Bluebird isn't as

Sixteen bluebirds were counted in this cavity. By sharing their warmth, the birds are able to survive cold winters.

common as it once was. In fact, it isn't unusual to meet someone who has never seen one.

Ironically, those same European homesteaders who found such joy in the Blue Robin of their adopted land also imported two species from Europe that threatened the existence of the native bluebirds. Given the pestilence that these two species have become in North America, it's difficult to believe that they hadn't been a great nuisance in Europe as well and that European immigrants weren't relieved to have left them behind. But there's no accounting for whim, and the House Sparrow and the European Starling were brought to the New World.

In 1851 eight pairs of House Sparrows were released in Brooklyn, New York, to introduce a touch of the Old World to North America. They adapted—and reproduced—quickly. About forty years later, in 1890, a fan of Shakespeare released eighty European Starlings in New York City's Central Park as the first of what was intended to be the introduction of all the bird species mentioned in the bard's works. Although the plan was never completed, forty more starlings were released a year later. They, too, made themselves at home. In fact, within eleven years, the starlings had extended their range throughout New York State, New Jersey, and Connecticut. By 1917 ornithologists were apprehensive about the impact that the starlings would have on native birds.

Eastern Bluebirds nest in cavities in trees and fenceposts, and they eat insects, seeds, and berries. House Sparrows and European Starlings also nest in cavities in trees and eat insects, seeds, and berries. And therein lies the problem. The more aggressive sparrows and starlings quickly expanded their ranges to cover the lower forty-eight states and most of Canada, evicting the bluebirds and threatening their food supply.

At the same time, land developers uprooted dead trees, pruned hollow limbs, and cleared meadows and fields, eliminating the traditional natural nesting places of bluebirds. Eventually, even wooden fences were becoming scarce, being replaced by more durable metal or concrete substitutes.

House Sparrows and European Starlings were up to the challenge of thriving in the face of progress. The sparrows turned to porch rafters, holes in walls, billboard braces, eaves, stoplights, and any other cavity in which to build their nests of grasses and weeds. The starling was equally adaptable, adding hollows in cliffs to the sparrow's list of sites. One starling was even found nesting on the rocky shore of an uninhabited island off the coast of Maine.

But the bluebirds couldn't adapt. By the 1930s, they were rare in much of their former range, and from the 1930s to the 1970s, the number of Eastern Bluebirds declined by 90 percent. If thousands of U.S. and Canadian bluebird lovers hadn't taken immediate steps to reestablish the bluebird's domain, we could very well have lost one of our gentlest and most attractive native species.

As early as 1934, Dr. T. E. Musselman set out twenty-five nest boxes to entice bluebirds to return to the fields and meadows of Adams County, Illinois. The success of the houses in an area where bluebirds were already scarce encouraged Dr. Musselman to increase his project to more than one hundred nest boxes along one hundred miles of country roads. Hence, the bluebird trail was born.

A bluebird trail is a succession of nest boxes spaced at least a hundred yards (91.4 m) apart along a road, trail, or other convenient means of access. The nest boxes are constantly monitored to get rid of the ever-present starlings and sparrows that try to nest in them. Consequently, the number of nest boxes on a single trail is limited only by the number of individuals who can routinely check the boxes for usurpers.

Encouraged by Dr. Musselman's success, other bluebird lovers quickly laid out bluebird trails throughout the species' range, for research had indicated that only an organized effort could save the birds. A typical bluebird trail has twenty to thirty nest boxes, but trails with hundreds of bluebird houses aren't uncommon. The longest known trail is actually a network of trails and side trails in Manitoba and Saskatchewan that covers about twenty-five hundred miles (1,563 km) and houses more than five thousand bluebirds every year.

As people monitored the nest boxes, they learned just how vulnerable bluebirds are, especially to House Sparrows. Whereas a European Starling will only attempt to drive away nesting bluebirds, a House Sparrow will enter the nest box, use hammering blows on the head to kill the brooding bluebird, and then build its own nest right on top of the dead bird.

In addition to being one of the most beautiful of our native species, the Eastern Bluebird is also among the most beneficial. Studies show that a bluebird's diet consists almost exclusively of crop-damaging insects such as grasshoppers, beetles, and caterpillars. (In fall, winter, and early spring, when there's a shortage of these insects, bluebirds supplement their diets with native berries and other fruit.) As a result, the loss of the Eastern Bluebird would represent more than the loss of a beautiful, gentle, native species of bird. It would also mean the loss of one of Nature's best pest controls.

Notable wildlife

Eastern Bluebird, *Sialia sialis*
[European] Robin, *Erithacus rubecula*
House Sparrow, *Passer domesticus*
European Starling, *Sturnus vulgaris*

DISCOVERY

1. Bleach-Bottle Birdhouse. You can do your part for bluebird con-
servation by building several of these inexpensive nest boxes. Refer
to the diagram often, and keep in mind that the side with the handle is the *back* of the bottle. IMPORTANT: Adult supervision is
needed for this activity.

ITEMS NEEDED

one-gallon heavy plastic
  bottle with cap
dishwashing detergent
ruler
felt-tip pen
hacksaw
drill with quarter-inch bit

white exterior latex or
  aluminum paint
paintbrush
heavy wire, such as
  coat-hanger wire
wire cutters
pliers

PROCEDURE

1. Wash out bottle thoroughly with detergent and rinse well.
Let it dry.

2. On the front of the bottle, measure six inches from the bottom, and from that point, draw a circle *exactly* one and a half inches
in diameter. A hole this size is large enough for bluebirds to enter
but too small for starlings.

3. With the hacksaw, cut out the hole, being very careful to stay
on the line.

4. Cut a one-by-one-half-inch ventilation hole in the underside
of the handle.

5. Drill four three-eighths-inch holes equally spaced in the bottom of the jug for drainage.

6. Drill two holes two inches apart at the lower back of the jug.

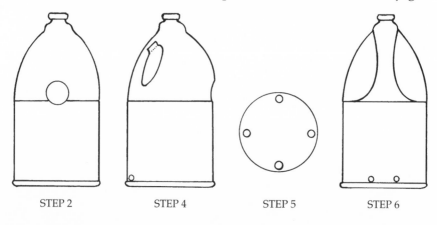

STEP 2   STEP 4   STEP 5   STEP 6

7. Paint the outside of the jug, including the cap, with three coats of paint to reflect sunlight and thereby prevent overheating.

8. Use the wire and pliers to attach the jug to a fencepost, utility post, or galvanized metal pole.

9. Check the jug for eggs and nestlings by unscrewing the cap and peeking inside. Be sure to replace the cap when you're done.

10. When the babies have flown, remove the jug from the post and clean it out. Bend a hook into the end of an eighteen-inch length of wire coat hanger, and fish out the nesting material.

11. Remount the jug. You may get a second brood of bluebirds in the same year if you do this soon after the first brood has fledged.

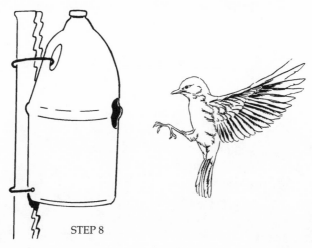

STEP 8

2. Play Bluebird Hide-and-Seek. Remember how bluebirds pile up to keep warm? Well, here's a game that will cause a major pile-up.

PROCEDURE

1. Select someone to be It. This person must find a place to hide that's big enough to hold all the players.

2. Everyone but It counts to twenty while It hides.

3. Everyone begins to look for It. Anyone who finds It quietly joins him or her in hiding.

4. The last player to find the hiding place becomes It the next time.

Nightlights

At the door on summer evenings
Sat the little Hiawatha;
. . . Saw the fire-fly, Wah-wah-taysee,
Flitting through the dusk of evening,
With the twinkle of its candle
Lighting up the brakes and bushes,
And he sang the song of children,
Sang the song Nokomis taught him:
"Wah-wah-taysee, little fire-fly,
Little, flitting, white-fire insect,
Little dancing, white-fire creature,
Light me with your little candle,
Ere upon my bed I lay me,
Ere in sleep I close my eyelids!"
　　　　—Henry Wadsworth Longfellow
　　　　　The Song of Hiawatha

MOST CHILDREN HAVE CAUGHT FIREFLIES IN A JAR AND WATCHED THEM twinkle. Fireflies are invisible during the hot summer days, but as the day cools into evening, they light their lamps and appear everywhere as tiny flashes of light.

Longfellow's reference to fireflies reflects the American Indian's respect for the natural world. Other cultures are not content with just showing reverence for fireflies; they use them for illumination and decoration.

In Japan, for example, fireflies are in demand in summer, when people put them in small cages to illuminate gardens and restaurants. And an inch-long neotropical species of firefly, *Pyrophorus noctilucus*, has such a powerful glow that at one time natives of South America and the West Indies used them as we use lightbulbs or lanterns. They put several of the glowing beetles, called *cucuyo*, in perforated gourds. Then they suspended the gourds from the

Several fireflies in a perforated gourd supplied light for natives of South America and the West Indies.

ceilings of their huts or carried them on nocturnal hunting expeditions. Sometimes the hunters even tied the *cucuyo* to their toes to light their paths. Young girls of these tribes also used the shining creatures as adornment, wrapping them in netting to weave them into their hair or attach them to their clothing.

Pyrophorus has even served the U.S. Army. In

Fireflies are used as living gems in some tropical countries.

1898, when Cuba was fighting for independence from Spain, President William McKinley sent troops to the island to protect the American citizens there. Dr. William Crawford, an Army medical officer, was called upon to tend wounded soldiers. One night, while he was performing surgery, his lamp went out. Dr. Crawford finished the operation by the light of bottles full of *cucuyos*.

Fireflies aren't flies at all; they're Lampyridae, lamp-lighting beetles. Although tropical species may be large, the North American species are about a half-inch long and are brown or black with pale markings. Females have small eyes and are usually wingless. They live in leaf litter, under bark, and in other moist places. Males, on the other hand, have large eyes to help them see well as they fly in the dark on well-developed wings. Firefly larvae also live in damp places, where they feed on snails, slugs, earthworms, and the larvae of other insects. The adults of many firefly species don't eat, but those that do live primarily on nectar and pollen.

Most insects depend on scent to track down a mate, but the firefly is an exception: It relies on sight. Using its species-specific signal, the male advertises for a mate. First he flashes. Then (he hopes!) a female responds with a weaker flash. The flashes are coded messages that must be precisely timed for communication to take place. The patterns of the flashes are so diagnostic that beetle specialists can identify firefly species by counting the frequency of the flashes and the length of time between them. For example, the male of one North American species flashes once every 5.8 seconds; the female gives her answering flash exactly 2.1 seconds after each of the male's. If she flashes too soon or not soon enough, she goes mateless. The males of another species were observed to flash 3 to 5 times a second, with the rate depending on the air temperature. At fifty-five degrees Fahrenheit (13 degrees C), the males produced 3.1 flashes per second, but when the temperature increased, so did the rate of flashes. Fireflies that live east of the Rocky Mountains fly and flash after dark, but species living west of the Rockies fly during daylight hours and don't flash.

Sometimes fireflies use their signals for a purpose other than courting: they use them to lure in a meal instead of a mate. Predatory females use the answering signal of another species to entice an unsuspecting male. The males usually approach cautiously, but if the female imitates his species' code well enough, he may be fooled into joining her in what he expects to be marital bliss, only to end up as a gastronomic delight.

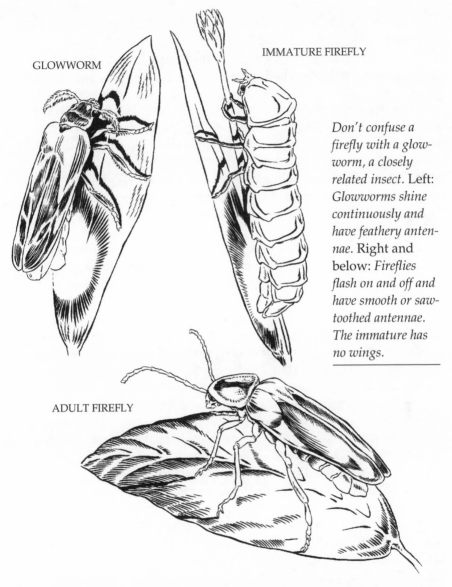

GLOWWORM

IMMATURE FIREFLY

Don't confuse a firefly with a glow-worm, a closely related insect. Left: *Glowworms shine continuously and have feathery antennae.* Right and below: *Fireflies flash on and off and have smooth or saw-toothed antennae. The immature has no wings.*

ADULT FIREFLY

The males of one species in Thailand seem to believe that there's safety in numbers. Instead of flitting and flashing individually, they gather in the trees along a river and signal in unison. Flashing at the rate of 120 times a minute, they all turn their lights on and off at the same time. Fireflies in South America carry the synchronized flashing one step farther. One group of fireflies flashes together in one rhythm on one side of a river, while another group flashes together in another rhythm on the other side of the same river. The effect is the same as if someone had strung the trees with tiny lights and then kept flipping them on and off.

Fireflies use a combination of chemicals and oxygen to produce their light. The light, which glows as a pastel green, yellow, or white, depending on the species, is 98 percent efficient, so it releases almost no heat. One or two abdominal segments of the firefly contain special cells called photocytes. Each photocyte contains the pigment luciferin and the enzyme luciferase, and each photocyte is connected to a tiny air tube. When the firefly wants to signal, it opens the air tubes to allow oxygen into the photocytes. When the oxygen combines with the luciferin and luciferase, light is produced. Then the light bounces off a layer of reflecting cells to shine through an area of transparent skin. When the firefly isn't flashing, the light-producing segments appear ivory colored. Fireflies begin to let their lights shine early, as faintly glowing eggs. And frogs and toads sometimes eat so many fireflies that their bodies glow with flashing lights.

To date, scientists have been unable to reproduce the firefly's efficient light, but they have discovered some unusual uses for it in medicine and ecology. For example, luciferin and luciferase light up in the presence of certain enzymes found in all living cells. As a result, the luciferin-luciferase flash test can be used to test blood stored for transfusions. Healthy blood cells light up in the presence of the two chemicals; diseased cells do not. The flash test can also reveal bacterial diseases in people and pollutants in air and water. In addition, the bodies of fireflies taste awful to most insect eaters, other than toads and frogs, and make many of them extremely ill. Thus it's being considered as a natural repellent for nuisances such as gypsy moths in trees, mice in basements, pigeons on roofs, and sharks in shallow water. Researchers recently discovered that this same "poison" stimulates heartbeats in humans, so it may someday be used to treat certain cardiovascular diseases.

DISCOVERY

1. Get Familiar with Fireflies. Like Hiawatha, you can enjoy just watching fireflies dance and flash. But you can easily learn more about how these little creatures make their lights shine.

PROCEDURE

1. Fireflies aren't hard to catch, so scoop some up off the grass.
2. While holding them cupped in your hands, look closely at

their abdomens. Watch their lights blink. Do you see how the skin over the illuminating segments retains an ivory afterglow between flashes?

3. Count the number of seconds between flashes.

2. Firefly Communication. See if you can talk to the fireflies in your neighborhood.

ITEMS NEEDED

flashlight

watch with second hand

PROCEDURE

1. A female of our most common North American species responds to the male 2.1 seconds after he flashes. Shine your flashlight once every 2 seconds to imitate her signal.

2. How long does it take to lure a male to your flash?

3. How many males can you attract in ten minutes?

3. Firefly Code. Communicate with your friend using only firefly-type signals. This is a group activity; the more, the merrier!

ITEMS NEEDED

one flashlight per player   pen or pencil

one scrap of paper   stopwatch (optional)

per player

PROCEDURE

1. Choose a Firefly Captain to develop the flashing codes. This person must sit out this time but can participate later.

2. The Firefly Captain creates two flashing codes, showing the number of flashes and the number of seconds between them by using a dot to represent each flash and a dash to represent each second. To flash by code, switch the flashlight on and off once for each flash, and count the seconds between the flashes in the traditional way: one thousand one, one thousand two, one thousand three, and so on. Here are two examples:

Code A: flash-flash . . . count three seconds (one thousand one, one thousand two, one thousand three) . . . flash . . . count three seconds. Repeat.

Code B: flash . . . count six seconds . . . flash . . . count two seconds. Repeat.

3. Write one code on half the slips and the other code on the other half. Then mix up the slips of paper and hand them out.

4. The object of the game is to see which team can come

together first. Designate spots where each team is to meet. Each participant must flash his or her light using the code on the paper and must find anyone else whose flash matches his or her own. Because firefly females must answer males in a specific amount of time, you may want to use a stopwatch to time the game. At the end of five minutes, the team with the most members wins.

You can expand this game by creating additional firefly codes, and you can play with any number of people. The number of teams and codes is up to you.

4. Firefly Lantern. Do as the people of the West Indies once did and light up your life with fireflies. IMPORTANT: Adult supervision is needed for this project.

ITEMS NEEDED FOR A

unwaxed gourd (available in fall)	hacksaw with thin blade long-handled metal spoon
detergent	twenty-four-inch length
plastic pot scrubber	of cheesecloth

ITEMS NEEDED FOR B

pencil	protective goggles
craft knife	vise
hacksaw with thin blade, or electric saw	wire
	wire cutters
drill with eighth-inch bit	

Note: You may want purchase a cured gourd or grow your own for this project. Gourds sold for ornamental use are often waxed, which makes them unsuitable for craft projects; however, you may be able to find unwaxed gourds at a local produce stand.

PROCEDURE A

1. Soak the gourd in warm, soapy water for an hour to soften the outer skin.

2. Thoroughly scrub the gourd with the pot scrubber to remove the softened skin.

3. Cut the top off the gourd about one-third of the way down.

4. Remove the seeds with the spoon. (Dry and save the seeds to plant in spring.)

5. Soak both pieces of the gourd for another hour to soften the pulp inside, then scrape it out with the spoon.

6. Tie the two pieces of the gourd in a cheesecloth bag in the manner of a hobo's pack, and hang in a cool, airy place to dry. A

garage is ideal. Drying will take from three to six months, depending on the size of the gourd.

Note: The mold that sometimes grows on the outer surface during the three-to-six-month curing process may stain the gourd. If the discoloration bothers you, you can toast the gourd to make the color uniform. Lightly coat the gourd with vegetable oil, then toast it in a conventional oven heated to 300 degrees. *Turn off the oven before putting the gourd inside.* You can repeat the process several times.

When the gourd is dry, you can make the lantern. Because gourd sizes and shapes vary and because precision isn't necessary here, the directions are somewhat general.

PROCEDURE B

1. Draw pencil lines to mark the rectangles for the "doorway" of the lantern.

2. Score the lines with the craft knife.

3. Use the hacksaw to cut out the rectangular pieces.

4. Mark holes around the top and bottom of the gourd and along two sides of the rectangles, lining up the holes as best you can. Mark two holes on one side of each rectangle. Finally, mark two holes at the top of the gourd.

5. Drill the marked holes.

6. Mark and drill holes throughout the gourd. You can create a design or simply place them at random.

7. Wire the pieces together. The holes along one side of each rectangle are used for hinges; the two corresponding holes will become part of the latch. Thread wire through the two holes at the top to make a hanger.

8. Put fireflies inside the completed lantern, and take the lantern into a dark room.

9. See if you can read by the fireflies' light. Can you imagine doing delicate surgery by their light?

10. See if their light seems to shine brighter in a smaller space, like a closet.

11. When their light begins to dim, let the fireflies go. What happens? (The light of fireflies dims when the insects are caged; by letting them go, you give them a chance to "recharge" and shine for another night.)

Alternative: Use a one-quart jar to hold your fireflies. Be sure to punch some air holes in the lid of the jar before you put the fireflies inside.

Nature's Plow

It may be doubted whether there are many other animals which have played so important a part in the history of the world as have these lowly organized creatures.
—Charles Darwin

CHARLES DARWIN SPENT FORTY-TWO YEARS OF HIS LIFE STUDYING EARTH-worms in England before publishing *Formation of Vegetable Mould through the Action of Earthworms.* In this work, Darwin calculated the amount of earth churned up each year by an acre of earth-worms to prove the creatures' value for building soil. He also noted another valuable service that worms provide: They preserve arche-ological artifacts. If the ruins of ancient cities had been left exposed for hundreds of years to the corrosive elements in air and water, they would have eroded with time. But as worms burrowed their way under and around centuries-old cisterns, pottery, columns, walls, and even the prehistoric megaliths of Stonehenge, they buried them and saved them for modern study.

Sound impossible? Consider a few facts. Darwin found that earthworms process more than fifty tons of earth and organic mat-ter every year. Several years later, researchers determined that worms working in clay turn over only eleven tons of topsoil per acre per year but in good soil churn up almost twenty-five tons. Each worm eats its own weight in leaves, grass, and soil every day. If you consider that an acre of garden soil supports at least one mil-lion earthworms, then it's easier to understand how they produce twenty-five to fifty tons of organic fertilizer a year and cultivate the soil better than three gardeners each working eight hours a day. Although it may take centuries for fallen leaves, twigs, and other plant material to disintegrate and mix with earth to produce an inch of topsoil, earthworms do the job in only a decade.

One by one, each earthworm does its part. It digs several tunnels to use as storage places for bits of dead leaves and pieces of root and as escape routes from centipedes, slugs, shrews, moles, birds, frogs, and toads. As the worm burrows, it eats dirt and acts as a living compost bin. The worm's passages loosen the soil and allow air to penetrate the deep underground layers; this prevents roots from decaying in what could otherwise be soggy conditions. The worm digests carbon, nitrogen, and other minerals and expels them in a form called casts. The casts become part of the soil and serve as natural fertilizer to give seeds and young plants a nutritional boost. All that tunneling and churning also keeps the soil from becoming hard and dry; because of the worm's activity, the soil stays loose and easily absorbs rain.

But what about the worm itself? What gives it the ability to work so hard and perform so many functions? Even though earthworms are completely harmless, most of us avoid touching them because they're squishy and squirmy and slimy and slippery. But those very characteristics make the earthworm one of Nature's most streamlined creatures.

The earthworm is squishy and squirmy because it has no bones or legs. To move forward, the creature lengthens the front part of its body and pushes through the soil. Then it pulls up the rear part to "catch up" with the front. The earthworm is slimy and slippery because its tough skin secretes two kinds of mucus. One helps the creepy critter slide easily through the soil and protects it from bacterial infections; the other has a foul odor that repels enemies. As the worm moves, it leaves behind some of that mucus, which hardens and cements the tunnel walls. Four pairs of tiny bristles called setae on all but the first few and last few segments give the earthworm traction.

Earthworms have no lungs or gills to take in oxygen and expel carbon dioxide; they breathe through their skin. The skin must stay moist to do its job, so during the day worms stay underground, burrowing in the warm, damp earth and taking oxygen from tiny air spaces between grains of soil. Worms emerge during daylight hours only in a heavy rain, when water fills the air spaces in their burrows and threatens to drown them. Earthworms stranded on pavement when the sky clears dehydrate rapidly and die. After sunset, these night crawlers venture above ground to feed.

The earthworm has no eyes or ears, yet it's able to perceive minor changes in its environment. Light receptors in the skin are concentrated at the head and tail; other receptors scattered along the

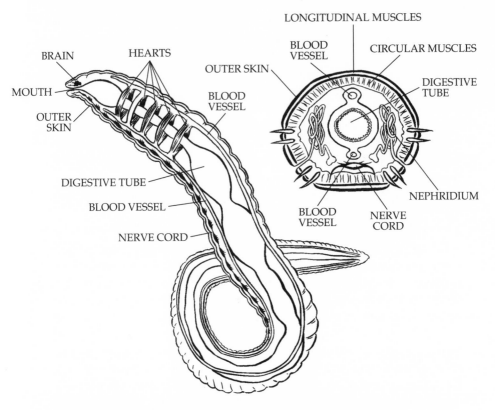

*The earthworm is an excellent example of economy of design. An inner tube,
called the coelom, contains the creature's simple two-lobed brain, five hearts,
and intestine. At the end of the intestine is the nephridium, the organ that
acts like the human kidney to filter waste products. The outer tube consists
of two kinds of muscles covered by reddish brown skin. Longitudinal muscles
allow the worm to become shorter and thicker, and circular muscles give it
the ability to become longer and thinner. A nerve cord runs along the full
length of the underside of the body, between the inner and outer tubes.*

body are sensitive to changes in temperature, touch, soil chemicals,
and sound vibrations. Even when feeding during the relative safety
of the night, the earthworm keeps the tail end of its body anchored
in the soil as it stretches over the surface to feed. At the slightest hint
of danger, the worm retreats into the protection of its burrow so
quickly that it's been described as "an animated rubber band."

In spring, summer, and early fall, earthworms burrow close to
the surface of the earth. When the weather gets cold, however, they

dig deeper: from four to fifty-eight inches, depending on the climate. There they curl up into a large, tight ball with hundreds of other earthworms to hibernate below the freeze line. In hot, dry climates, worms estivate, sleeping away the hottest time of the year at a depth of as much as seven feet.

The earthworm is a hermaphrodite—an animal that is both male and female—but two worms must exchange sperm to cross-fertilize their eggs. About four days after mating occurs, a sticky, saddlelike cocoon forms about midway along each worm's body. The mature eggs are fertilized in the cocoon, which contains a milky-white substance to nourish them. Then the worm contracts its muscles to push the cocoon forward and over its head. Finally, the cocoon hardens, its ends close, and the worm buries it in moist soil.

Four weeks later, one to eight tiny earthworms emerge. They resemble bits of pink string and are miniatures of their parents. The body is formed of ringlike segments, but the earthworm doesn't grow additional rings as it gets older; the segments simply increase in size until the worm matures in about six months.

The adult worm will probably belong to one of the two most common earthworm families in North America: the red worms and the gray worms. These grow to an average length of seven inches—much smaller than world's longest earthworm, the twelve-foot giant of Australia. This giant worm, which makes a gurgling sound as it burrows in the soil, is food for the duck-billed platypus. Can you imagine a robin large enough to pull that earthworm out of the ground?

One of the most frequently asked questions about earthworms is whether they can survive if cut in two. The answer is yes and no. Worms have amazing regenerative powers, an ability shared by many simple creatures. It you cut off its head, it will probably grow a new head. And if you cut off its tail, it will probably replace that. But if you cut the worm in half, it more than likely will starve to death before its new head is complete. Moral? Don't cut up earthworms. The research has been done, and there's no sense in purposely hurting any living thing.

Without earthworms, our soil could support only a small percentage of the plant life that it does with earthworms. So the next time you dig up a worm or find one stranded on a sidewalk, put it back in the earth. The flowers you love to smell and the food you love to eat depend on that little guy.

Notable wildlife

Gray earthworms, *Allolobophora* spp.
Red earthworms, *Lumbricus* spp.

DISCOVERY

1. Earthworms in Their Environment. As we study things first-hand, we respect them more for the services they perform. See for yourself how the earthworm supports plant life.

ITEMS NEEDED

trowel	cornmeal
one-quart jar (may be larger)	soil from garden or field
sand	black paper
purchased potting soil	tape

Note: Earthworm activities should be attempted only in spring and summer, when the worms are near the surface of the ground.

PROCEDURE

1. Prepare the jar as shown in the illustration. Sprinkle water on the surface.

2. Dig up two or three earthworms, or wait until a rainfall and pick up earthworms from the surface of the ground. For more of a challenge, collect your worms on a warm summer night by using a flashlight to catch two or three worms feeding above ground. *Never pull on an earthworm.* Although earthworms have some ability to regenerate lost parts, you should do everything you can to avoid hurting them. Therefore, when digging, dig deeply into the soil so that you can get under worms to collect them.

3. Put your worms in the jar. Wrap the black paper around

POTTING SOIL

SAND

GARDEN OR FIELD SOIL

CORNMEAL

As they burrow, the worms in the jar mix the sand, soil, and cornmeal. In the wild, they mix soil and decaying plant and animal matter in the same way.

the outside of the jar and tape it together to form a sleeve. Worms prefer darkness, so you'll have to provide it for them.

4. Check on them daily by removing the sleeve. How long does it take them to reach the bottom of the jar? Do they return to the top? Do they stir up the soil, sand, and cornmeal as they burrow? Replace the sleeve after each observation.

4. Put a piece of lettuce in the jar at night. Use a flashlight to watch your worms feeding and note how long it takes until the light causes them to retract into the soil.

5. When you have finished studying the worms, put them back outside. But if you want to learn more about worms, go on to the next activity before releasing them.

2. Worm Watching Up Close. Once you get to know an earthworm well, you may never say "yuck" again.

ITEMS NEEDED

earthworm	vanilla
damp paper towel	small flashlight
cotton ball	

PROCEDURE

1. Put the worm on a damp paper towel and observe the way the worm crawls. Can you see the setae? Hold the worm to feel the setae, and use a magnifying glass for a closer look. If you don't like to hold the worm, set it on a piece of paper and put your ear to the paper to hear the scratching sound that the setae make.

2. Gently touch the worm. The surface of its body may feel icky to you, but that coating of mucus helps the worm move through the ground and keeps the skin moist so that it can breathe.

3. Shine a flashlight on the worm. Does it try to get away from the brightness?

4. Put some vanilla on a cotton ball and hold it near—but not touching—the worm. How does it react? Try again with rubbing alcohol. *Do not touch the worm with the cotton ball.* If you do, you may damage its skin.

5. Put your worm back outside. It's happiest, and does the most good, in its natural environment.

Tap-Dancing Turtles

My friend, you are not graceful—not at all;
Your gait's between a stagger and a sprawl.

Nor are you beautiful: your head's a snake's
To look at, and I do not doubt it aches.

As to your feet, they'd make an angel weep.
'Tis true you take them in whene'er you sleep.

No, you're not pretty, but you have, I own,
A certain firmness—mostly your backbone.

—Ambat Delaso, *To My Pet Tortoise*

LAND TURTLES, LIKE THE POET'S PET, ARE AWKWARD AND CHUNKY. THEY plod clumsily through the woods, feeding on mushrooms, berries, leaves, grubs, and worms. They have no teeth, but the edges of their jaws are exceptionally sharp. Because they're cold-blooded and don't need a great deal of fuel, turtles eat very little. The animal's hit-or-miss approach to finding food sometimes leaves it hungry, but fortunately this slow-moving creature can survive without food for months.

Delaso doesn't indicate what kind of turtle he had. It may very well have been a Wood Turtle, a popular pet and what experts say is the friendliest and most outgoing of all turtle species. The Wood Turtle is also considered the most intelligent. Most land turtles eat whatever they come across in their wanderings. But when food doesn't turn up, the Wood Turtle stomps its feet—not because it's throwing a tantrum, but because it's calling for room service.

First the Wood Turtle selects a damp or muddy spot, such as the bank of a creek or the forest floor. Then it stomps at a rhythm of about one stomp per second. Each stomp grows more and more

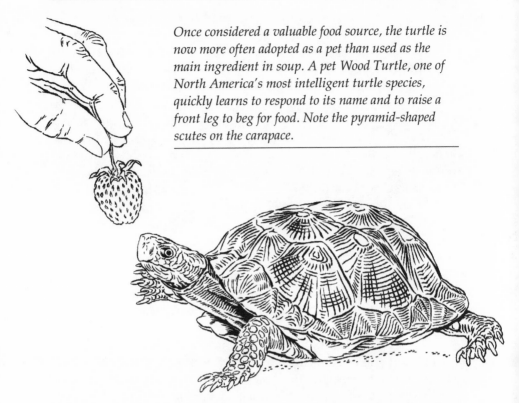

Once considered a valuable food source, the turtle is now more often adopted as a pet than used as the main ingredient in soup. A pet Wood Turtle, one of North America's most intelligent turtle species, quickly learns to respond to its name and to raise a front leg to beg for food. Note the pyramid-shaped scutes on the carapace.

forceful. Using first one foot for a series of stomps, then the other, the hopeful Wood Turtle stomps for thirty minutes to two hours. Earthworms are disturbed by the vibration and travel to the surface of the soil, emerging only inches from the turtle's feet, where the turtle snaps them up.

A naturalist studying the stomping behavior of Wood Turtles tapped on the soil, duplicating the rhythm and force of the turtle's legs. He brought four worms to the surface in fifteen seconds! No one knows why worms respond to a variety of vibrations, but they do. They can be attracted by children jumping on a lawn, a power mower left in one spot with its engine running, and the scurrying of a robin's feet. One theory is that the vibrations sound like moles, other worm eaters, moving through the ground. Another is that the vibrations mimic the rhythm of raindrops, leading the worms to surface to avoid drowning in their tunnels. Whatever the case, the worms respond and the turtles eat.

While the turtle is first developing in the egg, its ribs and backbone are like that of any other land vertebrate. Gradually, bony plates, or scutes, begin to grow over and fuse with the vertebrae of the backbone and down the ribs to form the carapace, or upper shell. The scutes are usually gray, green, brown, spotted, or mottled to blend in with mud, riverbeds, and dead leaves. The lower shell, called the plastron, protects the turtle's belly. The plastron is joined to the carapace only on the sides of the body. The turtle pokes its legs, head, and tail out through openings at the front and rear of the shell. These openings also give the turtle room to breathe. When the turtle inflates its lungs, its shell opens slightly, and it can move its legs in and out. But because the ribs are fused to the shell, the turtle can't completely expand its lungs without additional power, so muscles near each leg contract to create more space in the body cavity for the lungs to fill with air. When the muscles relax, the lungs deflate. If a turtle eats too much, its fat body prevents it from completely closing its shell. When a predator threatens a turtle, it pulls its head, legs, and tail into its shell. Some species, like the box turtles, lock themselves in. They're able to close their shells so tightly that even a knife blade can't fit between the upper and lower shells.

The seven-inch-long Wood Turtle roams the woods, fields, and swamps of the northeastern and midwestern United States and parts of southern Canada. It has a wide, brown shell and red-orange markings on its neck and legs. Its tail is almost as long as its carapace, and its scutes are pyramid shaped, giving it the descriptive species name *insculpta,* or sculptured. Although Wood Turtles usually travel alone, they congregate to hibernate during the coldest months of the year in old muskrat holes or in the muddy bottoms of creeks and ponds. They breathe underwater through an opening under the tail called the cloaca.

Notable wildlife
    Wood Turtle, *Clemmys insculpta*
    Box turtles, *Terrapene* species

DISCOVERY

1. Do the Wood-Turtle Tap. Worm charming is a competitive event in Great Britain, where in 1980 Tom Shufflebotham coaxed 511 worms out of a plot of ground measuring 9.24 by 9.24 feet in the allotted time of thirty minutes. Mr. Shufflebotham vibrated a garden fork in the soil to attract his worms and attain the world record, but to be a true researcher, you need to duplicate the method used by Wood Turtles, then record the data.

ITEMS NEEDED
    watch or stopwatch
    paper
    pen or pencil
PROCEDURE

1. Lie down on the damp ground.

2. Tap twice with your index finger, then twice with your middle finger. Repeat this for five minutes. Record the number of worms you brought to the surface and the time it took to do so.

3. Tap four times with one finger and four times with the other for five minutes. What happens?

Remember, the Wood Turtle taps for at least thirty minutes, so to get results you may have to be extra patient. Use a chart like the one below to record your data.

Date: _____, 19_____

Time: _____

Weather Conditions : _____

Rhythm of Taps*: ____/____ Length of Time Tapped: _____ minutes

Number of Worms: _____

*Record the number of taps with each finger. For example, if you tap twice with one finger, then twice with the other, record the rhythm as 2/2.

2. Make a Walnut-Shell Wood Turtle. Make one or more of these turtles to use in a woodland scene.

ITEMS NEEDED
    one walnut shell half
    one popcorn kernel
    unshelled almond
    four dried lima beans
    dark brown and red craft paint
    yellow construction paper
    dark brown or black felt-tip marker
    craft glue
    scissors
PROCEDURE

1. Trace around the walnut shell on the construction paper.

2. Referring to the diagram, glue the almond onto the pointed end of the walnut shell for the turtle's head; glue the four lima beans along the sides of the shell but not under it for the legs; and

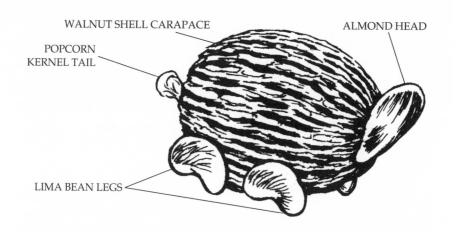

WALNUT SHELL CARAPACE
ALMOND HEAD
POPCORN
KERNEL TAIL
LIMA BEAN LEGS

glue the popcorn kernel at the rounded end of the shell for the tail. Hold the tail in place while the glue sets. Let the glue dry overnight.

3. Cut out the construction paper pattern. This is the undershell, or plastron, for your turtle. Referring to the illustration, use the felt-tip pen to draw the markings of the plastron on the paper. Set the paper plastron aside.

4. Paint the walnut shell turtle with brown paint. Let it dry.

5. Paint red markings on the turtle's legs and neck. Let dry.

6. Glue the construction paper plastron to the bottom of the shell. Your Wood Turtle is now complete.

7. Collect moss, sticks, stones, pieces of bark, and dried flowers and arrange them in a bowl or box. You can use a small mirror surrounded by moss as a pond. Add the turtle.

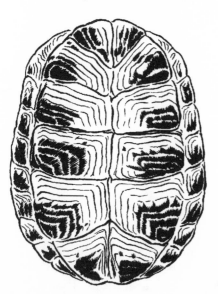

Alternative: Eliminate the plastron, and put a marble under the walnut shell to make a turtle that "walks." You can make several rolling turtles, then hold turtle races by pushing them down a slanting board.

With its bright yellow and dark brown markings, the plastron, or lower shell, of the Wood Turtle is distinctive.

Treasure Hunters

Once, far back in the high Sierra, they stole my snow-goggles, the lid of my teapot, and my aneroid barometer; and one stormy night, when encamped under a prostrate cedar, I was awakened by a gritting sound on the granite, and by the light of my fire I discovered a handsome Neotoma *beside me, dragging away my ice hatchet, pulling with might and main by the buckskin string on the handle.*
—John Muir

WOULD YOU TRADE YOUR BREAKFAST FOR A PIECE OF ALUMINUM FOIL OR your lunch for a brass button? A woodrat would. And would you build your house of sticks, stones, tin cups, hair combs, and reading glasses? A woodrat would.

Sometimes, when returning to its nest with a piece of food, a woodrat comes across something more interesting, say a button or a gum-wrapper. The little creature rarely goes more than a few feet without carrying something in its mouth, and it won't hesitate to drop food to pick up a newfound treasure, especially a shiny one. The woodrat often makes its exchange in a cabin or at a campsite, leaving whatever it was originally carrying in trade for whatever it picks up. As a result, the nest of this packrat, or trade-rat, contains whatever it can get its little white paws on, including feathers, nails, keys, false teeth, shells, silverware, and bottle caps, as well as sticks and stones and animal bones.

Several species of woodrats range throughout North America. These harmless, nocturnal rodents aren't related to true rats, the non-native Black Rats and Norway Rats. Woodrats are oversized woodmice, about eight inches long, with large ears, bright eyes, soft buff-colored coats, white bellies and feet, and furry tails. They're native to North America, and their diet consists primarily

A woodrat is about the size of a guinea pig, seven to nine inches long, excluding the tail. Note the hairy tail of this Desert Woodrat. This is one feature that distinguishes woodrats from Black Rats and Norway Rats.

of seeds, nuts, fruits, roots, mushrooms, and vegetation, with a few insects thrown in for animal protein.

All woodrats store food. Nuts and seeds keep well, and grass dries into nutritious hay. The Bushy-tailed Woodrat goes one step further: It cuts twigs, lays them on a ledge to cure in the Sun, then deposits them in its pantry. In many cases, the food is stored in a pile of sticks and debris separate from the nest. Because they store far more than they can ever eat, and because many generations of woodrats use the same nest, the amount of unused food steadily accumulates, giving scientists information about the plant life that grew in the area decades earlier.

Woodrats are versatile, building their nests out of available materials. Species that live in mountains build their rubbish-heap nests on rock ledges, whereas woodrats of the woods and open meadows build nests of sticks on the ground or in trees. For a small creature, the woodrat builds an unusually large nest, one that's generally two to four feet (61 to 122 cm) in diameter at the base and almost as high. Some nests are tepee-shaped; others are just piles of debris. Two species, the Mexican Woodrat and the Bushy-tailed Woodrat, don't build nests at all but simply scatter sticks and rubbish among the crevices in rocks and cliffs and under logs or tree roots.

Woodrats that live in the Southwest take special precautions to protect themselves from predators. Living in open country with little natural cover, the woodrat can't conceal its nest, but it has a unique way of defending it. The Southern Plains Woodrat and the White-throated Woodrat build their nests in cactus plants, using sticks, bones, and cactus spikes as building material. As a final defense against the swift little Kit Fox, which hunts them, they cover the nest with pieces of the desert's prickliest cacti, the chollas, building a barricade of cholla stems in front of the entrance. They have no trouble running over thousands of needlelike spines, even though their feet are soft and unpadded, and they carry the needle-covered cholla stems in their mouths without puncturing their lips or tongues.

Southwestern woodrats use cactus spines in their nests. The little creatures are small enough to scramble easily over and around the long, sharp cactus spines without being hurt, although larger, predatory animals are not so fortunate. A coyote that charges after a woodrat and begins to dig it out of its well-defended nest quickly learns a painful lesson.

Notable wildlife
Black Rat, *Rattus rattus*
Norway Rat, *Rattus norvegicus*
Bushy-tailed Woodrat, *Neotoma cinerea*
Mexican Woodrat, *Neotoma mexicana*
Southern Plains Woodrat, *Neotoma micropus*
White-throated Woodrat, *Neotoma albigula*
Kit Fox, *Vulpes macrotis*

DISCOVERY

1. Be a Woodrat. Woodrats are always busy, and they often exchange things and move them to new places. Sometimes they move their entire nests. Pick a place and go into the trading business.

ITEMS NEEDED

penny	stick of gum
marble	nut
piece of hard candy	other small objects

PROCEDURE

1. Choose a spot, such as under a rock, in a hollow tree, or at the base of a tree root, and leave something small there.

2. Let a friend, a sister, or a brother "discover" the "treasure," claim it, and leave something else in its place.

3. Do this every day for a week. How imaginative can you be about what you leave?

2. Become a Collector. Start a collection of whatever strikes your fancy, such as buttons, rocks, state spoons, or stamps with flowers on them. Searching for items to add to your collection is as much fun as finding them!

Don't Get Rattled

*I have the same objection to killing a snake that I have
to killing any other animal, yet the most humane
man that I know never omits to kill one.*
—Henry David Thoreau

YOUR PALMS ARE SWEATY, YOUR MOUTH IS DRY, AND YOUR BLOOD RUNS
cold. You've just heard the buzzing of a rattlesnake. Where is it?

You spot the snake. A Western Diamondback. Coiled and ready
to strike.

Don't panic!

You know that although most rattlers would rather turn tail
and retreat, the Western Diamondback is exceptionally short-tem-
pered. And bite for bite the Western Diamondback produces
enough venom to kill nine men. If it feels cornered, watch out!

Maybe you can back away slowly from the cold-blooded reptile. Maybe.

After several heart-stopping moments, the snake crawls away,
because even though it is aggressive compared to other snakes, this
pariah of the desert is one of the most timid creatures on Earth.

Rattlesnakes live only in the New World, where about thirty
species range from southern Canada to northern Argentina and
Uruguay. Rattlers generally seek only mammals and birds as prey,
because reptiles and amphibians are resistant to their venom and
are difficult to subdue. In fact, because of their own immunity to
the rattlers' poison, whipsnakes, indigo snakes, and kingsnakes
prey on rattlesnakes. Snakes usually are immune to the venom of
other snakes of their own species. It is ironic then, or perhaps
poetic justice, that rattlesnakes not only can kill others of their own
species, but also can accidentally commit suicide if they strike in
defense and hit themselves instead.

Like all snakes, rattlers are deaf. They're able to detect the
nearby movement of many predators by picking up vibrations

from the ground, but they aren't able to hear a trumpet blast just a few feet away. In addition, their eyesight is poor, although they can distinguish between light and shadow.

In the Southwest, there's a legend that a prairie dog, a Burrowing Owl, and a rattlesnake can happily coexist in the prairie dog's burrow. What really happens is that the prairie dog digs the burrow and the Burrowing Owl moves in if the prairie dog abandons it. If a rattlesnake moves in, whatever is living there—animal or bird—hastily moves out. The snake enters the burrow only to get a meal.

To hunt and capture prey without using sight and sound, the rattlesnake uses special organs to pick up the scent and heat of warm-blooded animals. To smell, it flicks its forked tongue in and out of its mouth, picking up particles from the air and the ground. Then it inserts the tips of its tongue into two small cavities in the front part of the roof of its mouth. These cavities together are called Jacobson's organ. By taking repeated readings of the chemical contents of its surroundings, the rattler can "sniff out" prey.

Because rattlers rely so much on their sense of smell, campers can use mothballs to repel them. The snakes detest the smell, so a few moth crystals in a backpack and two or three mothballs placed in tent corners keep the reptiles away.

In addition to scent, the rattlesnake also uses built-in heat-detecting devices to find food. A rattler is a pit viper. These snakes have a deep dent between the eye and the nostril on each side of the head. Each pit is made up of two chambers separated by a thin membrane, or skin. A heat-sensitive nerve connects the pit to the brain. The heat-sensing pits help the snake locate and capture the small, warm-blooded mammals and birds it eats.

The rattlesnake swallows its food whole, so once it has captured its prey, it immobilizes it to keep it from struggling free. This is when the venom is put into use. The venom is produced in glands located above the fangs. When the rattlesnake punctures its victim's skin, the venom is pumped through the hollow fangs and into the wound. The venom of other poisonous snakes, such as cobras, affects the nervous system of the prey and causes paralysis, breathing difficulties, and eventually heart failure and death. The venom of rattlesnakes, however, attacks the tissues and destroys blood vessels, causing victims to die of internal bleeding.

Rattlesnakes lay their rubbery eggs in early spring. The newborn rattlers emerge about five months later, fully fanged and able to hunt and kill as well as a full-grown snake. Consequently, when a female

The rattlesnake's fangs fold back when its mouth is closed. When the mouth is open, the fangs protrude. Note the large shaded organ; this is the internal poison duct.

snake lays her eggs, her job is done. She doesn't need to stay around to care for her well-equipped offspring.

Rattlesnakes are born with a buttonlike piece of dry, hard skin called a birth rattle. A rattle is added each time the snake sheds its skin, or molts. The first molt takes place when the snake is ten to fourteen days old. The adult rattlesnake molts two to four times a year, depending on the food supply. If food is plentiful, it grows more quickly, outgrows its old skin faster, and molts more often than if food is scarce.

Because the rattles are loosely attached, segments can wear off or be lost to a predator that grabs a snake by the tail. To determine the age of a rattlesnake, a herpetologist (a scientist who studies snakes) first looks for the distinctive button at the end of the tail. If the button is still attached, then the rattler has lost no segments and its age can be estimated by assuming that every three segments represent about one year of age. If the button is missing, however, it's difficult to determine how old the snake is, although the fact that the rattles become larger as the snake grows older does provide some clue to its age.

The rattles vibrate in a wave that starts at the base of the tail and ends at the tip, and the buzzing sound gets louder as the wave moves outward. Each complete wave is called a cycle. The speed of the vibrations has been clocked at almost one hundred cycles per second when the temperature was 104 degrees Farenheit (40 degrees C) down to about twenty-one cycles per second at 50 degrees Farenheit (10 degrees C).

Contrary to common belief, rattlesnakes don't always rattle

when threatened. In fact, they rarely do. A study conducted in Arizona revealed rattlesnakes rattle before striking only 4 percent of the time. Other studies showed that rattlesnakes rattle when out in the open but remain silent when hidden under a log or bush. In the latter case, the animal relies on silence for protection. By the way, other types of snakes, such as cottonmouths, copperheads, and a number of nonpoisonous species, also vibrate their tails when in danger, even though they have no noise-making rattles. Sometimes the charade pays off; if a trembling tail brushes against leaves or grass, it mimics the sound of a rattlesnake.

A rattlesnake doesn't rattle to warn prey when it's about to strike; to do so would be counterproductive. The rattlesnake rattles so that it doesn't have to strike. Every time the rattlesnake bites, it uses up some of the venom stored in the poison glands. If it strikes at a bison or elk in an attempt to protect itself, it would use up precious venom. Then, with little poison left, it would have to wait several weeks for the glands to produce and store another supply of venom. So in some circumstances, venom is more important than food to the reptile. Although it can live several months without eating, having little or no venom leaves it defenseless against its natural enemies.

In spite of its deadly venom and warning signals, a rattlesnake's life isn't easy. The Peccary and Greater Roadrunner, both of southwestern deserts and brushlands, prey on rattlers. The Peccary's thick layer of fat forms a barrier between the wild pig's skin and its bloodstream, so a bite from a rattlesnake does no damage. The roadrunner teases the rattlesnake into striking, then pecks it on the head to kill it. Throughout North America, hawks and eagles also prey on rattlesnakes. To capture one safely, they make several mock attacks on a rattlesnake until it uncoils. Then these birds of prey grasp the rattler behind its head with one talon and in the middle of the body with the other to capture it without becoming the victim of its poisonous fangs. And if a flock of Wild Turkeys finds a defenseless rattler, the cocks kill the snake by striking it with their beaks and wings.

Even people eat rattlesnake meat, which is reputed to taste like chicken. At the Rattlesnake Round-up, held on January 30 in Whigham, Georgia, experts demonstrate how to catch and cook the snakes. If the event were held in Kansas, the date would have to be changed from time to time, because it's illegal to eat snakes on Sundays in the Sunflower State.

People often wonder whether rattlesnakes can climb trees. Well, they can and they can't. The great naturalist John James Audubon certainly believed that he saw a rattler chase a squirrel up a tree, race after it through the branches, then finally leap on it when it jumped to the ground. Audubon did in fact see a snake do this. But he almost surely observed a Black Rat Snake, a species that at a glance might resemble a dark rattlesnake. And although it has no rattles, the rat snake vibrates its tail; if the tail strikes dry leaves, the noise sounds very much like that of a rattler.

Rattlesnakes are heavy and bulky. They certainly can't move quickly enough to pursue a speedy squirrel, but they occasionally do plod up a rough-barked tree to plunder a woodpecker's hole or robin's nest or to get out of reach of flooding water, especially if the tree is growing at an angle. Rattlesnakes usually go no higher than ten or twelve feet in search of prey, however. A rattlesnake is not going to drop into the bowl of potato salad if you picnic under a tree!

Notable wildlife
Western Diamondback, *Crotalus atrox*
Black Rat Snake, *Elaphe obsoleta obsoleta*
Peccary (Javelina), *Pecari angulatus*
Greater Roadrunner, *Geococcyx californianus*

DISCOVERY

1. Spiral Serpent. The Eastern Diamondback (*Crotalus adamanteus*) of the southeastern United States has the distinction of being the heaviest venomous snake in the world. According to Guinness, one seven-foot, nine-inch specimen weighed in at thirty-four pounds. But you can make an almost weightless diamondback—and it won't bite, either!

ITEMS NEEDED

sheet of paper, eight and a half by ten inches	crayons or markers
	large-eyed sewing needle
pencil	button or carpet thread
scissors	thumbtack

PROCEDURE
1. Trace the diagram of the snake onto the paper.
2. Color the spirals in a diamondback rattler pattern.
3. Cut out the spiral, carefully following the lines.

Using this four-inch pattern as a guide, enlarge it so that its outside diameter is eight inches.

4. Thread the needle with a twelve-inch length of thread, and make a knot at one end.

5. Push the needle up under the head and pull the thread through so that the knot remains on the underside.

6. Use a pencil and spool to balance your snake. Roll the spool between your palms to make the snake spin. Alternative: Suspend your snake from the ceiling, and watch it spin with the breeze.

The finished serpent.

2. Diamondback Dart-Away. There's nothing a hungry roadrunner likes better than a big, juicy rattlesnake. Take turns being the Roadrunner and the Rattlesnake in this game.

ITEMS NEEDED

blindfolds	stones
newspaper	stopwatch
tin can	

PROCEDURE

1. Form a circle about twenty feet in diameter with ten or more players.

2. Blindfold two players.

3. Give one blindfolded player, the Roadrunner, a rolled-up newspaper. Give the other, the Rattler, the can with the stones in it. Place these two players on opposite sides within the circle. It's the job of the other players to keep the two opponents inside the circle.

4. When the Roadrunner yells, "Rattle," the Rattler shakes the can. The Roadrunner tries to catch the Rattler by following the sound, and the Rattler tries to avoid being caught by the Roadrunner. The Rattler continues to shake the rattle as long as the Roadrunner tells him to do so.

5. When the Roadrunner smacks the Rattler with the newspaper, the two opponents change roles.

6. The Roadrunner who swats the Rattler in the shorter amount of time challenges a new Rattler.

3. Make Some Rattles. The sounds of the rattles differ among the different species of rattlesnakes, although the largest snakes generally have the loudest rattles. How many different types of rattles can you produce?

ITEMS NEEDED

plastic bottles of all sizes, with lids

round cardboard boxes of all sizes, with lids

metal spice cans, with tops

coins, nuts, macaroni, stones, buttons, screws, bells, and
    other small, hard objects

tape recorder (optional)

PROCEDURE

1. Put different numbers and combinations of objects in different containers. What kinds of sounds do you get when you put screws in tin spice cans? Macaroni in cardboard boxes? Coins in plastic bottles? Is the sound louder when you put in more objects?

2. Optional: Tape record the different combinations. Write down what you used to produce each of a dozen sounds, then see if a friend can identify them when you play them back. Have your friend do the same experiment with you.

4. Make a Rattlesnake Tail. Each time a rattlesnake molts, it grows another rattle. Mark special events in your life by adding to your own rattlesnake tail.

ITEMS NEEDED
    long piece of yarn, string, or ribbon
    large wooden bead
    smaller wooden beads

PROCEDURE

1. Tie the large bead, the "birth rattle," at the end of the string

2. Each time you have a birthday, get an A on your report card, master a piano piece, or reach some other goal or milestone, add a bead. You may want to color code the beads so that one color stands for each type of accomplishment.

3. Tie a loop in the top of your string and hang it from a wall, or drape it across a dresser or bookcase.

Taking Root

The first instinct of the stem . . . [is] the instinct of
seeking light, as of the root to seek darkness—what
words can speak the wonder of it?
—John Ruskin

WE TEND TO NOTICE ONLY THE OBVIOUS. TAKE A TREE, FOR EXAMPLE. IN spring we enjoy the scent of its flowers. In summer we sit in the shade of its leaves. In fall we gather its fruit and marvel at its fiery foliage. And in winter we admire the stark symmetry of its branches. The truth is, though, that without its roots—the parts we don't see—that tree wouldn't be standing at all.

Roots hold a tree firmly in the ground. They absorb water and minerals from the soil. And they carry that nutrient-filled water to other parts of the tree. Roots also store surplus food through fall and winter so that in spring the tree will have a jump-start on another year's growth.

Trees have one of two types of root systems. Some species send down an initial strong, straight taproot. As the tree matures, the taproot continues to serve as the primary root, and smaller, lateral roots grow outward from it. An old hickory may have a taproot that reaches down as far as one hundred feet.

In other species, the root system is fibrous; many lateral roots extend in all directions directly from the base of the trunk. As a result, the roots of a 165-foot maple may reach only 8 feet deep but spread out to cover an underground area with a diameter equal to the height of the tree.

Each type of root system has an advantage over the other. A tree with a deep taproot can withstand strong winds because it is so well anchored. A tree with a fibrous system, on the other hand, is better able to survive droughts, because its shallow roots absorb the small amount of water that penetrates only the top layers of soil.

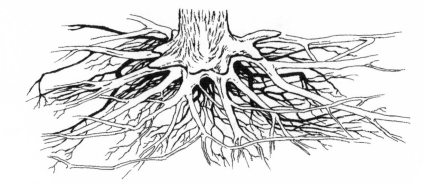

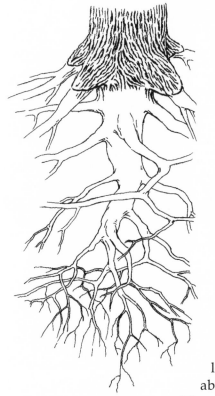

Roots anchor the tree and absorb nutrient-filled water from the soil. Some trees grow lateral roots that stabilize and feed the tree (above). *Other trees send down an initial taproot as the sole support of the tree throughout its life* (left).

Growing from the lateral roots are smaller feeder roots. Feeder roots tend to grow more abundantly in the area where rain drips from the tree. Many feeder roots grow well beyond this drip line, though, for they actually search for water, maneuvering around clay, rocks, and other roots in their quest for moisture. When the feeder roots find water, they soak it up through millions of tiny, sometimes microscopic, root hairs. Each smooth, white hair is only one-two-thousandth to one-third of an inch long, but it wiggles around in the soil, absorbing moisture all along its length. The water, which carries the mineral nutrients that the tree needs to stay healthy, moves into the feeder roots, upward through the trunk, and outward through the branches to the leaves.

Each feeder root ends in a root cap made of tough cells that are continually being sloughed off and replaced as the root moves through the soil. Lengthwise growth of the root takes place just

By absorbing several gallons of water a day, the millions of root hairs provide the tree with most of the water it needs. New root hairs grow as old ones shrivel and die, and when water is abundant they wear out and are replaced very quickly.

behind the cap, where cells rapidly multiply and force the root cap forward.

Tree roots, as they plumb the ground for food and minerals, enable the existence of the complex structures that we call trees, structures that are often more than one hundred feet tall. Shallow or deep, roots are needed to anchor and maintain every tree in the forest.

Not all roots grow com-
pletely underground. The
Baldcypress, for example,
which grows in flooded
swamps and along stream-
banks in much of the eastern
United States, sends special-
ized root growths in the form
of hollow knees from the sub-
merged roots up through the
surface of the water to collect
oxygen. This tall, cone-pro-
ducing, needle-bearing tree
isn't an evergreen; it's a
deciduous conifer that drops
its needles in winter.

DISCOVERY

1. How Roots Work. This simple procedure will allow you to watch roots in action.

ITEMS NEEDED

plastic sandwich bag with zip top
paper towel
two or three dried beans
red or blue food coloring or ink
jar lid about two inches in diameter

PROCEDURE

1. Wet the paper towel, then put it and the beans in the sandwich bag. Make sure that the beans are lying on top of the paper towel. Seal the bag.

2. Put the sealed bag in a dark place to sprout. In the absence of light, the sprouted roots will be white.

3. When the roots are about an inch long, mix the food coloring or ink with water to make a medium shade of red or blue. Pour the mixture into the jar lid.

4. Lean the sprouted beans against the inside edge of the lid with their roots dipped into the colored water. What happens?

2. Counting Roots. An ambitious researcher counted the roots and estimated the number of root hairs of a rye plant. The 13,815,762 roots had a combined length of 387 miles and were covered with about 14 billion root hairs. You, too, can be a researcher.

ITEMS NEEDED

carrot or radish with roots and root hairs (one straight from
the garden is best)
tweezers

PROCEDURE

1. Use the tweezers to pluck each root as you count.

2. Record the number, using the standard ꓕꓕꓕꓕ method.

3. Don't give up!

If a three-foot rye plant has more than 13 million roots and 14 billion root hairs, how many of each do you think a hundred-foot tree has?

Branching Out

The spring snows begin to melt, leaving soft, wonder-
ful-smelling bare patches about the Maple trunks in
the sugar bush. . . . A nippy frost at night freezes
little blobs of ice at the ends of the Maple twigs. A
prodigal sun melts them and warms the bare
branches. "Sap's runnin'!" The mysterious signal is
sounded and the annual miracle is on. . . .
—Thomas E. Ripley

IT WOULD BE DIFFICULT TO FIND ANYONE IN NORTH AMERICA WHO doesn't enjoy pancakes topped with maple syrup. Real maple syrup, that is, not the artificially flavored sugar water bottled commercially. Green plants are the only living things that manufacture their own food, and the sap of the Sugar Maple is stocked with nutrients ready to give the tree a boost in spring.

Sap is a product of the tree's inner bark. Recently, the outer bark of the spindly Pacific Yew, a tree that loggers once burned as waste, has become so valuable that the yew can't be left unguarded. The evergreen's bark contains taxol, a substance effective in the treatment of several types of cancer. It takes roughly sixty pounds of dry bark to make enough taxol to treat one person for one year, and each tree produces about fifteen pounds of bark worth $2 to $10 a pound. At those prices, poachers must be kept from stripping the bark from the relatively rare yew to sell to pharmaceutical companies.

There's nothing new about using tree bark as a source of medicine. For example, a tea made from the inner bark of certain oaks is said to stop vomiting; when gargled, it's reputed to soothe a sore throat. The bark of eucalyptus trees has been used to lower fevers and to alleviate the symptoms of bronchitis, asthma, and other respiratory troubles. And a paste made of the ash of juniper bark and water seems to soothe itching and promote the healing of skin sores.

The bark of several species of cinchona, or quinine tree, a South American evergreen, was once an important source of quinine, used to treat malaria patients. Because quinine's side effects include nausea, skin rash, and permanent damage to vision and hearing, new drugs have replaced it as a treatment for malaria. However, the cinchona still gives us quinidine, a derivative of quinine used to regulate heartbeats in cardiac patients.

In North America, we rely on many bark products from other parts of the world. The outer bark of the Cinnamon Tree of India, Sri Lanka, and other tropical areas is ground into a powder that we use to flavor apple pie. When peeled and allowed to curl as it dries, the bark becomes the cinnamon sticks that spice up our hot apple cider. The exceptionally thick outer bark of the Cork Oak, a tree that grows in Spain, Portugal, and Africa, is used to make bottle stoppers, insulation, gaskets, floor coverings, tires, and shotgun cartridges.

It's obvious that we depend on the inner and outer bark of several kinds of trees for medicines, flavorings, and other products, but what do these two layers do for the tree? Let's start from the outside in and take a look.

The outer bark's primary function is to protect its inner, working layers from wind, sunlight, freezing temperatures, parasitic plants, wood-boring insects, disease, and to a certain degree, fire. A tree grows from the inside out, and its bark must accommodate its increasing girth. The bark of a young tree, or sapling, is smooth. In some species, such as beeches and birches, the bark stretches easily and remains smooth as the sapling matures. In other species, the bark cracks and dries out as the tree grows, giving oaks, ashes, pines, and most other trees their rough outer covering. The pattern and texture of bark is so varied and distinctive that trees bare of leaves in winter can still be identified.

Just inside the outer bark is the inner bark, or phloem. The cambium, only one cell thick, lies just under the phloem. Although the cambium is the thinnest layer of the trunk and branches, it's also the most important one, for it's the life-giving part of the tree, the growth layer that makes new inner bark and wood. Beavers rely on the nourishment of the cambium when they eat bark to supplement their water-lily diet.

When the green cells of the cambium divide, the outermost cells become the phloem and the innermost become the xylem. The phloem and xylem cells each form a system of pipelines running up and down the branches and trunk. The phloem pipelines carry food manufactured by the leaves down to the roots; the xylem pipelines carry minerals and water, in the form of sap, from the roots up to the leaves. The system is so efficient that food manufactured by all leaves is carried to all roots, and sap is carried from all parts of the roots to all upper parts of the tree. As a result, even if there is less water in one area of the ground than another, the

xylem cells carry equal amounts of sap to all upper parts of the tree. And if one side of the tree gets more sunshine than the other, the phloem cells still take equal amounts of food to all lower parts of the tree.

In a young tree, almost all of the trunk is sapwood, the layer of xylem that transports growth-promoting sap. As the young tree grows, though, the xylem cells of the sapwood eventually become inactive and form the tree's heartwood, the dead wood that fills up with hardened gum and resin and gives the tree a strong, rigid central core. New xylem cells in the sapwood continue to carry sap to the leaves, but as old xylem cells die, they form additional layers of wood, what we use as lumber.

You can read a tree's life story by looking at the annual rings. Each year's growth shows as a distinct ring, and each ring consists of two concentric circles: an inner, lighter circle that shows the rapid spring growth, and an outer, darker circle that represents the slower summer growth. The tree develops wider rings in years when there is plenty of moisture and narrower ones in times of drought. During a year when an insect attack, disease, or late freeze causes the tree to lose its leaves, the corresponding ring will be narrow. Scars from physical damage also

New shoots are smoother and lighter than older ones, which darken and roughen with age. At the base of the new shoot is a bud scale scar, a mark that shows where the previous year's growth ended. The distance between scars represents the annual growth of the branch.

show in the rings. Narrower rings near the center of the trunk indicate that the sapling was shaded by older, taller trees. As the young tree grows taller each year, however, it generally develops wider rings.

The trunk and branches grow thicker as the tree increases in girth from the inside outward, but how does the tree get taller? Each winter a bud develops at the end of each branch and at the tip of the trunk. These aren't leaf buds; they're terminal buds so small that you may need a magnifying glass to see them. Each terminal bud contains a green stem called a shoot and is surrounded by a layer of tiny hairs that insulates the new growth from cold. The buds and the hairs are protected by scales. Some buds have only one enveloping scale, others have two scales that close tightly, and still others have several overlapping scales. There may also be an additional outer coating of small hairs. The scales hold the minute bundle together until warm weather causes the buds to swell. Then the new shoot emerges. As the shoots grow, the tree gets taller and its branches get longer.

Notable wildlife
Sugar Maple, *Acer saccharum*
Pacific Yew, *Taxus brevifolia*

DISCOVERY

1. Measure Tree Growth. Some parents keep track of their children's growth by having them stand against the wall at six-month intervals and marking each new height. It's easier to measure a tree, because each year's growth is clearly marked by Nature.

ITEMS NEEDED
    ruler
    pencil
    paper
PROCEDURE
1. Use the ruler to measure the distance between the bud scale scar and the tip of new growth of twelve branches on the same tree.

2. Is the distance the same for all the branches?

3. If the distance varies, add the different measurements together and divide by twelve to calculate the average growth.

4. Measure the growth of several different kinds of trees in the same way. Do some species grow faster than others?

2. Make a Cork Reindeer. Who says you can't find new uses for old things? Use cork bottle stoppers to make a reindeer.

IMPORTANT: Adult supervision is needed for this activity.

ITEMS NEEDED

    four wooden matches

    cork about two inches long

    cork about one and one half inches long

    three small twigs

    glue

    scissors or craft needle

    black felt-tip pen, small movable eyes, small black beads, or
        black glass-headed straight pins (optional)

    wire cutter

PROCEDURE

1. Using the point of one blade of the scissors or the craft needle, make a hole on each side of the smaller cork for the twig antlers. Use the illustration as a placement guide.

2. Put a drop of glue in each hole. Then push the twigs into the holes. This is the reindeer's head. Let the glue dry for several hours.

3. Again using the illustration as a guide, make a hole in the underside of the head.

4. Make holes in the larger cork, the reindeer's body, for the four legs, the tail, and the neck. Pay close attention to the illustration for their placement.

5. Light the four matches and immediately blow them out. The black tips are the reindeer's hooves. Put a drop of glue in each of the leg holes and insert the matches. Let the glue dry for several hours.

By following the directions, you can make one reindeer or a whole herd of them.

6. From the remaining twig, cut a piece one-fourth inch long and one an inch long. Use the longer piece for the neck and the shorter one for the tail. Glue these pieces in place when the glue holding the antlers and legs in place has thoroughly dried.

7. If you want your reindeer to have eyes, you have several choices. You can glue the two movable eyes or black beads to the head, draw the eyes on with a felt-tip pen, or cut the shaft of two glass-headed pins to about one-quarter inch long and push them into the cork head.

3. Make a Trunk Rubbing. If you're lucky enough to find a smoothly cut trunk, you can record its history.

ITEMS NEEDED

large sheet of white paper
soft pencil (number one or number two)
thumbtacks

PROCEDURE

1. Lay the paper across the cut top of the trunk.

2. Secure the paper to the trunk with thumbtacks.

3. Gently rub the pencil over the paper. The pattern formed by the rings of the trunk will be transferred to the paper.

4. Count the rings to determine the tree's age. Do you see any scars? If you do, what do you think made them?

4. Make Bark Rubbings. Each tree species' bark texture and pattern are as distinctive as the shape of its leaves. Take these rubbings in summer so that you can recognize the trees all year round.

ITEMS NEEDED

several sheets of typing paper
soft pencil (number one or number two)
thumbtacks

PROCEDURE

1. Tack a sheet of paper to each of several kinds of trees.

2. Make a rubbing of each type of bark by gently rubbing the side of the pencil lead over the paper.

3. Label each rubbing according to the general type of tree, such as maple, oak, or sassafras.

4. In winter, see if you can identify other leafless trees by matching your bark rubbings to the tree trunks.

5. Make a Trunk Planter. What once supported a tree will again serve to support plant life. IMPORTANT: Adult supervision is needed for this activity.

ITEMS NEEDED

section of tree trunk from a fallen tree; cut ten to twelve
inches high and eight to nine inches in diameter

chisel   pothos plant
potting soil   clay saucer

PROCEDURE

1. Using the chisel, hollow out the trunk section to make an opening about eight inches deep and six inches wide.

2. Fill the space with soil to a depth of five inches. Position the pothos, then fill the remaining space with soil to within one inch of the top.

3. Set the trunk planter in the clay saucer, and water the soil thoroughly.

4. Put the plant where it can get indirect light. Water the soil whenever the surface feels dry to the touch.

Alternative: Set an already potted plant in the chiseled-out hollow.

Green Blood

A generation of men is like a generation of leaves: the wind scatters some leaves upon the ground, while others the burgeoning wood brings forth—and the season of spring comes on. So of men one generation springs forth and another ceases.
—Homer

IN 1912 SCIENTISTS CRACKED THE CHLOROPHYLL CODE TO REVEAL THAT one molecule of the green substance is composed of 137 atoms. One atom is magnesium; the remaining 136 are nitrogen, carbon, and oxygen. In itself, that combination of atoms wasn't startling—until it was seen in the light of another compound. If that lone atom of magnesium were replaced with an atom of iron, the molecule of chlorophyll would become a molecule of hemoglobin, the red pigment in blood. The formulas of chlorophyll and hemoglobin are so much alike that scientists nicknamed their new discovery "green blood."

For hundreds of years, farmers and botanists knew that every green plant—be it a potato vine, a cornstalk, or an apple tree—needed water and sunlight to grow and to produce fruit. But they didn't know how the plant used the water and light. Then in 1818 two French chemists isolated chlorophyll and began to unlock the secret life of the plant.

When the seed of a tree sprouts, it sends a tiny, two-leaved shoot through the surface of the soil. Through a process called photosynthesis, those two small leaves of that seedling immediately begin to manufacture food. First the roots absorb water and minerals from the soil, which combine to produce sap. Then the pipeline of xylem cells carries the nourishing sap up through the seedling's stem and out to the leaves.

In the leaves, the chlorophyll absorbs sunlight, which in turn

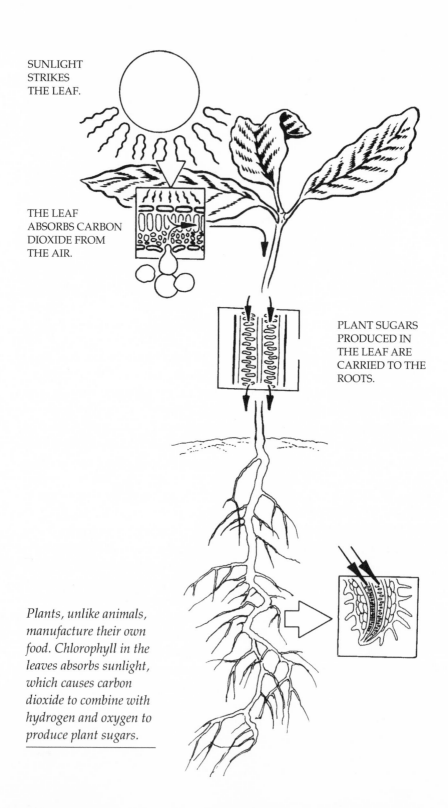

SUNLIGHT
STRIKES
THE LEAF.

THE LEAF
ABSORBS CARBON
DIOXIDE FROM
THE AIR.

PLANT SUGARS
PRODUCED IN
THE LEAF ARE
CARRIED TO THE
ROOTS.

Plants, unlike animals, manufacture their own food. Chlorophyll in the leaves absorbs sunlight, which causes carbon dioxide to combine with hydrogen and oxygen to produce plant sugars.

causes carbon dioxide from the air and oxygen and hydrogen from the sap to combine, producing a sugar called glucose. The glucose then combines with nitrogen, sulfur, and phosphorus, also contained in the sap, to produce starch, fat, protein, and vitamins. These essential nutrients are carried back down to the roots by way of the descending pipeline of phloem cells to be used as food or to make new cells. This continues throughout the plant's life, so in an adult tree, water and minerals travel all the way up the trunk, through the branches, and out to the leaves, and the nutrients manufactured in the leaves travel all the way back through the branches, down the trunk, and into the roots.

Leaves take in the carbon dioxide from the air through thousands of tiny pores called stomata. Each pore consists of two kidney-shaped cells lying side by side with an opening between them. The stomata, which open in the morning and close at night, are found on both the top and the underside of the leaf, but they're present in greater numbers on the underside. A square inch of the underside of an apple leaf may hold 250,000 of the tiny pores.

Trees—in fact, all green plants—use some water in making food, but they release most of it. Just as we exhale invisible moisture when we breathe out, trees release the water into the air in an invisible process called transpiration. Deciduous trees such as oaks, maples, sumacs, aspens, and other broad-leaved species that drop their leaves in winter transpire more than do narrow-leaved evergreens. In general, evergreens retain more moisture to protect their slender needles from the drying heat of the Sun in summer and to sustain them through winter. (Evergreens do shed their leaves, but not all the leaves drop at once.)

A large oak tree may drink an amazing three hundred gallons of water each day, but it uses only a quart to sustain itself. The rest escapes as vapor through the stomata in its leaves, cooling the surrounding air. As a result, the air temperature is lower in a forest than in open country. Even the air among the stalks in a cornfield is cooler than the air along the edges of the same field, for each corn plant transpires about fifty gallons of water during its growth.

When the air is so humid that it can't absorb all the water that the trees transpire, the water collects in droplets along the edges of the leaves. This isn't dew but water released though special guttation valves at the ends of the veins; and it isn't vapor, as in transpiration, but the more concentrated liquid form of moisture.

If one small plant transpires this much, it's easy to see how the leaves in an acre of trees may transpire more than twenty-five hundred gallons of water a day. Put a glass over a plant and see this for yourself.

The leaves of trees and other green plants continue to manufacture food as long as there's sufficient sunlight and moisture to do so. Although trees growing near streetlights usually keep their leaves later into autumn, most trees don't have the benefit of an artificial source of daylight, so as sunlight decreases, leaves stop functioning, the chlorophyll gradually disappears, and fall colors burst into glory.

In the leaves, the chlorophyll is contained in the chloroplasts. In addition to chlorophyll, the chloroplasts hold minute amounts of xanthophyll, a yellow pigment, and carotene, a red-orange pigment. As the green pigment of chlorophyll diminishes, different proportions of xanthophyll and carotene, depending on the species of tree, produce varying shades of yellow, gold, orange, and red. Thus the diminishing amount of sunlight triggers the colors of autumn.

But a different process takes place to produce some of the other colors. A chemical change in the unused glucose trapped in the leaves at the end of each growing season causes the production of the pigments for reds, rusts, maroons, and purples. These pigments, called anthocyanins, aren't present in the leaves during summer; they're formed when the leaves are exposed to bright sunlight during the day and cool temperatures at night. Unlike xanthophyll and carotene, anthocyanins aren't contained in the chloroplasts but instead are manufactured in the upper cell layer of the leaf and can be dissolved in water.

The leaves of trees that contain a lot of tannin, or tannic acid, such as hickories, chestnuts, walnuts, and some oaks are brown in fall, not brightly colored. Most trees produce some tannin as a protection against hungry insects. The acid not only causes the insects discomfort but also prevents the digestion of the leaf protein. After a tannin attack, the insect suffers from indigestion and lack of nourishment, so it moves on to another tree.

Eventually, a separation layer of cells grows at the point where the leaf is attached to the branch, forming a barrier between the leaf and the sap-supplying branch. The leaf dies, and it falls to the ground with the next gust of wind.

DISCOVERY

1. The Function of Stomata. Trees breathe through the stomata in their leaves just as people breathe through the pores in their skin. See what happens when the stomata are clogged.

ITEMS NEEDED
   small houseplant
   petroleum jelly

PROCEDURE

1. Coat all the leaves on the plant with petroleum jelly. Be sure to cover the top and underside of each leaf.

2. Water and feed the plant as usual.

3. What eventually happens to the plant? It has suffocated, just as you would if your skin were painted with something that sealed all the pores.

2. Observe Guttation. Out in the open, water vapor evaporates into the air. But in a sealed situation, the air soon becomes saturated and water collects along the edges of leaves.

ITEMS NEEDED
   plastic sandwich bags
   twist-ties or pieces of string

PROCEDURE

1. Tie plastic sandwich bags over several leaves on a tree.

2. Check the bags an hour later. What has happened?

Variation: Put a drinking glass or jar over an entire houseplant, making sure the rim of the glass or jar meets the surface of the soil to seal off outside air.

3. Extracting Chlorophyll. You can easily remove the green pigment from a healthy leaf by following the steps below.

IMPORTANT: Adult supervision is needed for this activity.

ITEMS NEEDED

juice glass   rubbing alcohol
jar twice as wide as the   teakettle or small pan
   glass but only about   water
   an inch taller   green leaf

PROCEDURE

1. Boil enough water to fill the jar.

2. Put the leaf in the jar, then pour boiling water over it.

3. Let the leaf soak for about thirty minutes to break down the walls of the chloroplasts.

4. Take the leaf out of the water and put it in the juice glass, then pour in enough rubbing alcohol to cover the leaf. Pour most of the hot water out of the jar.

5. Put the juice glass into the jar with the remaining hot water. Add more hot water to bring the water level to just below the rim of the glass. Then wait about an hour.

6. At the end of the hour, the leaf will be pale green to white, depending on the type, and the alcohol will be green with chlorophyll. Try leaves from different kinds of trees. Do some release more pigment than others?

4. Monogram a Tree. Observe how sunlight influences pigment production in leaves.

ITEMS NEEDED

tree that has red leaves in fall, such as maple or oak
nontransparent tape, such as black electrical tape or masking
   tape

PROCEDURE

1. In spring or summer, when the leaves are green, use the tape to form the initial of your first name on six leaves on the tree.

2. Wait two weeks. Remove the tape from three of the leaves. What do you see?

3. Wait until the other three leaves change color before removing the tape. What happened?

Following the Leader

The leader is a stimulus, but he is also a response.
—Eduard C. Lindeman

SCIENTISTS STUDYING TENT CATERPILLARS OBSERVED AN UNUSUAL EVENT. A colony of hungry caterpillars was devouring the leaves of a tree. Suddenly the caterpillars all stopped chewing and hurried back to their tent. Sensitive instruments monitoring atmospheric conditions soon revealed the reason for the caterpillars' strange behavior: Within half an hour of their return to the nest, a cold front passed through the feeding area. If the caterpillars hadn't anticipated the severe drop in temperature, the whole colony probably would have died.

In midsummer, female Eastern Tent Caterpillar Moths lay shiny masses of brown eggs on the twigs of trees and shrubs, especially cherry trees, apple trees, and other members of the rose family. When the quarter-inch-long caterpillars begin hatching the following spring, usually in late May or June, each immediately begins to eat, moving its strong-toothed jaws from side to side as it defoliates the tree or bush in which it lives. Within two weeks, the caterpillar is more than an inch long. It has a yellow stripe down the center of its back and dark blue dots along each side, and its body is covered with black spines. The spines contain an irritant that repels most would-be bird predators.

Eastern Tent Caterpillars are truly happy campers. Three hundred to four hundred of these hairy larvae live communally in a silken tentlike web attached to a fork in a tree or shrub. The tent is their haven. Woven in layers, it collects the heat of the Sun on clear days, slows heat loss during cool weather, lessens moisture loss in dry weather, and sheds water when it rains. Until the caterpillar is fully grown, it stays in the shelter of the tent on cold, rainy days and during the nights but spends sunny days eating and eating and eating.

As if to make up for the fact that the adult moth eats nothing during its short life, the larval caterpillar takes the time to strip each leaf to the veins before going on to the next one. As it travels along a branch in its constant search for food, each caterpillar lays down a silken strand. Then, when it's ready to return to the tent, it simply follows the path home. Even when there are several nests in one tree, a caterpillar seldom loses the way back to its nest.

In each caterpillar colony there are very active members as well as very sluggish ones. The active members seem more alert to possible danger and take the responsibility of prodding the others into action. If a colony has a disproportionate number of inactive members, the lack of response to the stimulus of oncoming rain, wind, and cold often results in the death of the whole colony. A healthy colony needs several alert leaders to get the rest of the group moving quickly to the protection of the tent.

In a successful nest, after feeding for about six weeks, each caterpillar has grown so much that it has molted its skin several times. It also has accumulated enough stored food to nourish it through the pupal stage in its self-made cocoon. To produce a cocoon, the caterpillar uses a tube called a spinneret on its lower lip. Two glands in its mouth secrete a sticky liquid through the spinneret. The liquid strand hardens into a strong, yellow thread

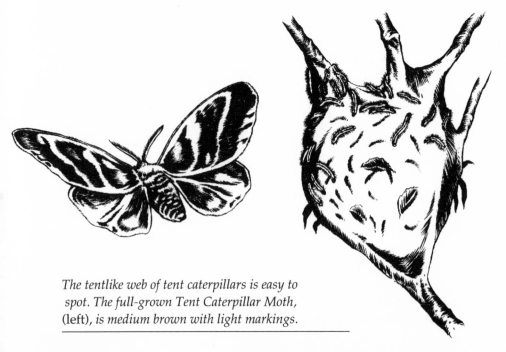

The tentlike web of tent caterpillars is easy to spot. The full-grown Tent Caterpillar Moth, (left), is medium brown with light markings.

when exposed to air. When the caterpillar is ready to form a cocoon, it wraps two leaves around its body. Then, as the liquid silk oozes from the spinneret, the caterpillar moves its head from side to side, sewing the edges of the leaves together into a cozy, green sleeping bag.

While in the cocoon, the pupa is neither caterpillar nor moth; it's a creature experiencing a complete transformation. Weather conditions dictate how long it will take to complete the metamorphosis from larva to adult. As a result, cool weather delays the process.

Although most moths and butterflies remain in the pupal stage all winter, the adult Eastern Tent Caterpillar Moth emerges only two to three weeks after the caterpillar has spun its cocoon. The crawling, brightly colored, voracious caterpillar has become a fasting, buff-colored, winged adult. The caterpillar's sole mission was to eat, grow, spin a cocoon, and transform itself into a moth; the moth's only purpose is to reproduce. After mating, the female moth finds a suitable tree on which to lay her eggs, and then she dies.

In some years, tent caterpillars pose a severe threat to trees and shrubs. The Yellow-billed Cuckoo once represented an important control for the caterpillars. But the cuckoo is now a threatened species because of habitat destruction in its wintering grounds. Northern Cardinals and other insect-eating birds just don't provide the same balance for the caterpillar population that the cuckoo did. And left unchecked, one caterpillar colony can easily strip a tree of its foliage, and then move on to the next. Sometimes they find another wild tree. But often they invade gardens to munch on rose bushes.

Nature does have one other built-in control besides birds, however. Once in a while, caterpillars run out of food, and only a few from each colony survive to form cocoons. When this happens, the population the following year is smaller. As a result, heavy infestations of tent caterpillars occur in cycles. When the population of healthy caterpillars outgrows the amount of available food, the species experiences a "crash." Caterpillars die, and trees and shrubs are given a chance to recover.

Notable wildlife

Eastern Tent Caterpillar Moth, *Malacosoma americanum*
Yellow-billed Cuckoo, *Coccyzus americanus*
Northern Cardinal, *Cardinalis cardinalis*

DISCOVERY

1. Raise Your Own Caterpillars. No one completely understands how metamorphosis takes place, but you can still observe the results of this mysterious process by raising your own caterpillars. Several species of tent caterpillars range throughout North America, and their nests are easy to spot. Follow these directions to prepare one jar for each pair of caterpillars that you intend to collect.

ITEMS NEEDED

one-quart jar	rubber band
dirt or peat	label
cheesecloth or paper towel	

PROCEDURE

1. Put about two inches of moist dirt or peat in the jar.

2. Carefully collect two caterpillars by clipping off the twig or twigs on which they are crawling. Don't touch the caterpillars. Remember, the stiff hairs on their bodies contain a substance that keeps away most birds—*and* irritates human skin. Put the caterpillars, twigs and all, into the jar.

3. Cover the top of the jar with a piece of cheesecloth or paper towel held by a rubber band.

4. Record on a label the date and time you collected the caterpillars, the type of tree or other plant on which you found them, the dates of molt, and the dates the caterpillars formed cocoons. Put the label on the outside of the jar.

5. Put the jar in a safe place away from sunlight; too much heat inside the jar may kill the caterpillars.

6. Sprinkle water on the dirt or peat every day to keep the leaves from drying out. Provide new leaves for food as necessary, and replace wilted uneaten leaves with fresh ones.

7. Watch for changes in behavior. When a caterpillar stops eating, it's probably getting ready to molt or to spin its cocoon. If it molts, observe whether it eats its cast-off skin.

8. When the moths emerge, write the date on the label, take the covering off the jar, and set the jar outside to let them escape. Don't touch the moths; they're delicate, and it's easy to injure them.

One year, we collected two caterpillars on May 23. Caterpillar A began its cocoon at the bottom of a twig on May 30; Caterpillar B began to form its cocoon high on a twig on May 31. Both took two days to complete the task. The conditions inside the jar were warm and dry, and Caterpillar B emerged as a moth on June 16. Caterpillar A never emerged.

The following year, we collected two more caterpillars. These two attached their bare cocoons, unwrapped in leaves, to the rim of the jar. Both were kept in the same warm, dry atmosphere, and both emerged as moths about two weeks later.

Do you think that the location of the cocoon determines whether the creature completes metamorphosis? Or do you think that because of natural law, only 75 percent of all caterpillars become moths? If so, how would this help the environment? How would you try to prove what percentage of all tent caterpillars become moths?

2. Christmas Ball Wrap. Create a Christmas ornament in much the same way as a caterpillar makes its cocoon.

ITEMS NEEDED

paper clip	embroidery thread or yarn
wire cutters	in two or more colors
craft glue	Styrofoam ball two inches
	in diameter

PROCEDURE

1. Cut the paper clip so that you have a curved loop with two one-inch prongs.

2. Put a drop of glue on the end of each prong, and insert them one-half inch deep into the Styrofoam ball. Let dry overnight.

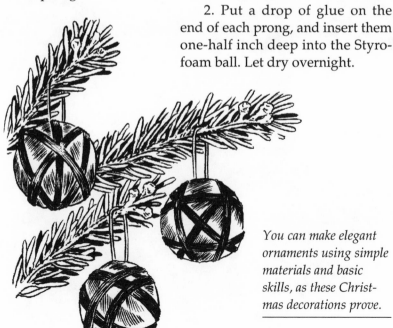

You can make elegant ornaments using simple materials and basic skills, as these Christmas decorations prove.

3. Use one color of the thread or yarn as the base color. Wrap the ball until it's covered, gluing down the ends.

4. Use the other color or colors to create a pattern. The illustration will give you some ideas.

5. Hang the ornament from your Christmas tree, or make several to give as gifts.

3. Follow the String. A tent caterpillar lays a trail to find its way home. You can do the same with a ball of string.

ITEMS NEEDED

ball of string

PROCEDURE

1. Tie one end of the string to something firm, like a doorknob or chair leg.

2. As you unroll the string, wrap it around heavy furniture—not the floor lamps, please!—and outside around trees and fenceposts. Use the whole ball if you want to. Crossing over already laid string is okay.

3. Give the end of the string to a friend and let him or her follow the string's path. Make sure that your friend winds the string back into a ball.

4. Now change places, so that your friend lays the string and you follow the path.

National Champion Trees

*. . . the species of large trees are much more numerous
in North America than in Europe: in the United
States there are more than one hundred forty species
that exceed thirty feet in height; in France there are
but thirty that attain that size.*
    —F. Andrew Michaux

MEASURE YOUR WAIST; THIS IS MEASUREMENT 1. MEASURE YOUR HEIGHT;
this is Measurement 2. Now, take the following two measurements
of your head: starting from your eyebrows, measure back over the
top of your head to the base of your skull; starting from the middle
of one ear, measure up and over the top of your head to the middle
of the other ear. Add these two figures together, and divide the
sum by two to get the average; this is Measurement 3. Now add
Measurements 1, 2, and 3 together. What does the total mean?
When it comes to measuring people, the figures have no meaning.
But when it comes to measuring trees, they're all-important.

American Forests (formerly the American Forestry Association)
maintains a register of champion trees. Each tree represents the
largest of its species, the honor given when the sum of three measurements, converted to points, is greater for that tree than for any
other of its kind. To find a tree's total points, American Forests uses
the following formula:

$$\begin{array}{ccccc} \text{trunk} & & & \text{average} & \\ \text{circumference} & + & \text{height} & + & \text{crown spread} & = & \text{total points} \\ \text{(in inches)} & & \text{(in feet)} & & \text{(in feet)} \end{array}$$

The trees of the West Coast have the most impressive measurements. For example, at this writing a Coast Redwood near the
Northern California coast is 363 feet tall, boasts a girth at chest
height of 638 inches, and has a crown spread of 62 feet, for a total
score of 1,017. Another record holder is the 2,500-year-old Giant

Sequoia named General Sherman, which is 275 feet tall, 998 inches around, and 107 feet across the crown, giving it a total score of 1,300. (Incidentally, it weighs 1,400 tons.) Although this tree is more than 7 feet shorter than the Coast Redwood winner, its trunk circumference is greater, and its overall score makes it the champion not only for its species and for the West Coast and North America, but also for the world. Over the centuries, General Sherman has survived lightning strikes, heavy snowfalls, earthquakes, fire, and damage from insects and fungi. Other West Coast winners include a 329-foot-tall Coast Douglas-fir in Oregon with a total score of 782 and a Sitka Spruce in Washington that is only 191 feet tall but measures a chubby 707 inches around its waist, giving it 922 total points.

Eastern trees also have their champions. Tied for the record as the largest Eastern White Pine in the United States are two Michigan trees. One is 201 feet tall, measures 186 inches in circumference, and has a crown spread of 52 feet, with a total score of 400; the vital statistics of the other are 181–202–64, with a total score of 399. (Trees with scores that fall within five points of each other are designated as co-champions.) Other champion trees of the East include an American Beech with a score of 371; a Paper Birch, the species from which American Indians made canoes, with 326; and a Common Baldcypress in Louisiana, with 748. Incidentally, more than two hundred species have had no nominees.

Obviously, some species grow taller and wider than others, and scores among the more than 750 champions vary greatly. Short champs include the Lotebush and Guajillo, both Texas specimens, with scores of 30 and 36; the Big Sagebrush in Washington, with 38; the Common Juniper in Michigan, with 37; the Bottlebrush Buckeye in North Carolina, with 39; and the Poison Sumac in New York, with 54.

A tree has three main parts: the roots, the trunk and branches, and the leaves. Together, the branches and leaves form the crown. To make a champion tree, all of these parts must efficiently fulfill their roles in the presence of adequate sunshine, rainfall, and nutrients. Although each of these roles has been explored in detail in earlier chapters, here's a quick review. The roots absorb water and nutrients from the ground and transport them through tiny pipelines up the trunk and through the branches to the leaves. The leaves use energy from the Sun to convert carbon dioxide and

The trunk and the branches together give a tree its height, width, and shape, making some trees national champions. The trunk of a needle-leaved tree, such as the pine, larch, fir, spruce, juniper, or cedar, grows straight upward. Branches grow out from the side of the trunk. The longer lateral branches near the base of the trunk give the tree its conical shape. The trunk of a broad-leaved tree, such as the elm, oak, or maple, divides near the base into large, spreading branches, which give the tree its general form. Smaller lateral branches form the rounded crown.

water into sugars that fuel cell formation in the trunk, branches, and roots. As the cells divide under the bark of the trunk and branches, those parts grow thicker. A tree grows taller as its branches grow longer. Every year, a bud forms at the end of the trunk and each branch. Each bud develops into a shoot that lengthens and thickens as it grows, adding to the tree's mass.

The West Coast champions, the Coast Redwoods and the Giant Sequoias, grow to astounding dimensions because they live where rainfall is plentiful even in winter and where fog provides moisture during the hot summer months. As an added benefit, the needles of these evergreens, or narrow-leaved trees, lose little moisture through transpiration, or evaporation, because so little of their surface area is exposed to wind and sun. They are designed to be champions.

Because trees continue to grow as long as they live, champions are often dethroned. Of the 754 trees recognized as champions in 1990, 116 lost their titles in 1992. Even though tree growth is often responsible for the change in champions, sometimes different trees take the title when previously overlooked specimens are discovered.

CHAMPION TREES

State	Tree	Circumference in inches at 4½ feet	Height in feet	Crown spread in feet
Alabama	*Longleaf Pine*	**94**	**105**	**42**
Alaska	*Sitka Spruce* (WA)	707	191	96
Arizona	*Yellow Paloverde*	[112]	[48]	[66]
Arkansas	*Shortleaf Pine* (MS)	133	138	75
California	*Coast Redwood*	**638**	**363**	**62**
Colorado	*Blue Spruce* (UT)	186	122	36
Connecticut	*White Oak* (MD)	37	79	102
Delaware	*American Holly* (AL/VA)	119/135	74/55	205/203
Florida	***Sabal (Cabbage) Palmetto*/(GA)**	**45/70**	**90/62**	**139**/140
Georgia	*Live Oak* (LA)	439	55	132
Hawaii	*Kukui*	No national champion reported for this species		
Idaho	*Western White Pine* (CA)	394	151	52
Illinois	*White Oak* (MD)	374	79	102
Indiana	*Tuliptree* (Yellow Poplar) (VA)	374	146	125
Iowa	*Oak species*			
Kansas	*Plains Cottonwood* (CO)	432	105	93
Kentucky	*Tuliptree* (Yellow Poplar) (VA)	374	146	125
Louisiana	***Common Baldcypress***	**644**	**83**	**85**
Maine	*Eastern White Pine* (MI)	186/202	201/181	52/64
Maryland	***White Oak***	**374**	**79**	**102**
Massachusetts	*American Elm* (KS)	312	100	91
Michigan	***Eastern White Pine***	**186/202**	**201/181**	**52/64**
Minnesota	*Red Pine* (MI)	123	154	96
Mississippi	***Southern Magnolia***	**243**	**122**	**63**
Missouri	*Flowering Dogwood* (VA)	110	33	42

State	Tree	Circumference in inches at 4½ feet	Height in feet	Crown spread in feet
Montana	*Ponderosa Pine* (CA)	287	223	68
Nebraska	*American Elm* (KS)	312	100	91
Nevada	***Single-leaf Pinyon***	**139**	**53**	**66**
New Hampshire	*Paper Birch* (ME)	217	93	65
New Jersey	*Northern Red Oak* (NY)	370	66	89
New Mexico	***Two-leaf Pinyon***	**213**	**69**	**52**
New York	*Sugar Maple* (CT)	269	93	80
North Carolina	*Pine species*			
North Dakota	*American Elm* (KS)	312	100	91
Ohio	*Ohio Buckeye* (KY)	146	144	32
Oklahoma	*Eastern Redbud* (TN/VA)	120/108	36/39	27/42
Oregon	***Coast Douglas-fir***	**438**	**329**	**60**
Pennsylvania	*Eastern Hemlock* (WV)	224	123	68
Rhode Island	*Red Maple* (MI)	222	179	120
South Carolina	*Sabal (Cabbage) Palmetto* (FL/GA)	45/70	90/62	14/30
South Dakota	***Black Hills Spruce***	**89/97**	**93/89**	**25/36**
Tennessee	*Tuliptree* (Yellow Poplar) (VA)	374	146	125
Texas	*Pecan* (TN)	231	143	115
Utah	***Blue Spruce***	**186**	**122**	**36**
Vermont	*Sugar Maple (CT)*	269	93	80
Virginia	***Flowering Dogwood***	**110**	**33**	**42**
Washington	***Western Hemlock***	**370/316/291**	**241/202/227**	**67/47/49**
West Virginia	*Sugar Maple* (CT)	269	93	80
Wisconsin	*Sugar Maple* (CT)	269	93	80
Wyoming	*Plains Cottonwood* (CO)	432	105	93

Each state has chosen a common tree to represent it, and each state tree except Hawaii's has a national champion somewhere in the United States. The champ usually is growing somewhere other than its home state, however, as you can see from the table. The information for national champions growing in their home states is in **bold** type; the locations of champion trees growing in states other than their home states are noted by state abbreviations in parenthesis. In some cases, when the total scores are within five points of each other, two or more trees share first place; these co-champions are indicated by slashes separating their measurements.

For more information on champion trees, write to National Register of Big Trees, P.O. Box 2000, Washington, DC 20013.

Notable wildlife

   Coast Redwood, *Sequoia sempervirens*
   Giant Sequoia, *Sequoia dendron giganteum*
   Coast Douglas-fir, *Pseudotsuga menziesii*
   Sitka Spruce, *Picea sitchensis*
   Eastern White Pine, *Pinus strobus*
   American Beech, *Fagus grandifolia*
   Paper Birch, *Betula papyrifera*
   Common Baldcypress, *Taxodium distichum*
   Guajillo, *Acacia berlandieri*
   Big Sagebrush, *Artemisia tridentata*
   Common Juniper, *Juniperus communis*
   Bottlebrush Buckeye, *Aesculus parviflora*
   Poison-Sumac, *Toxicodendron vernix*

DISCOVERY

1. Measure a State Tree. Find your state tree in the table. Then locate one of these trees near your home, take measurements, and compare them with those of the national champion for that species. For example, if you live in Colorado, measure a Blue Spruce and compare its size to the champion Blue Spruce, which grows in the neighboring state of Utah. Have fun!

   ITEMS NEEDED
      tape measure or string
      yardstick

   PROCEDURE FOR MEASURING THE TRUCK CIRCUMFERENCE

   1. Use a tape measure to measure the trunk circumference at a point four and a half feet above the base of the tree. Use a string if the tape measure isn't long enough.

   PROCEDURE FOR MEASURING THE HEIGHT OF A TREE

   1. Hold your arm straight out in front of you. Have a partner measure the distance from your eye to the end of your arm. This is Measurement A.

   2. Using the sketch as a guide, grasp a yardstick so that thirty inches extend from the top of your fist to the end of the yardstick. This is Measurement B, or thirty inches.

   3. Back away from the tree while holding the yardstick as described in Step 2. Make sure that you are staying on ground that is approximately level with the tree's base. Stop when the stick

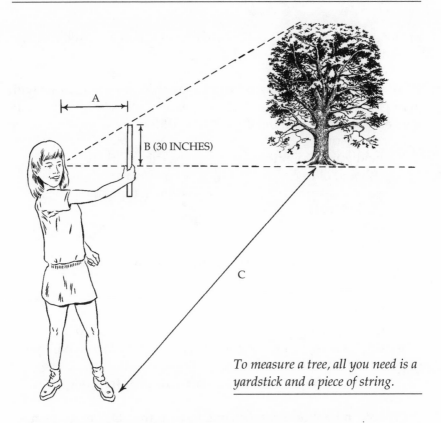

To measure a tree, all you need is a yardstick and a piece of string.

above your hand appears to be the same length as the tree. You should be sighting over your hand to the base of the tree and, without moving anything but your eye, sighting over the top of the stick to the top of the tree.

4. Measure the distance from your feet to the base of the tree. This is Measurement C.

5. Using the formula $\dfrac{A}{B} = \dfrac{C}{D}$, compute D.

Measurement D, in feet, is the tree's height.

Note: If you hold the yardstick at the point that corresponds to your arm length, then the distance from the tree will equal the tree's height.

PROCEDURE FOR MEASURING THE AVERAGE CROWN SPREAD

1. Mark the outline of the crown on the ground by pushing sticks into the soil directly under the outer tips of the branches.

2. Measure the distance between the two sticks that are farthest apart and the two that are closest together. Add the two measure-

ments together and divide by two to calculate the average crown spread.

2. Adopt a Tree. Watching a tree change through the seasons will help you understand the effects of weather and seasons and will tell you how important that tree is to wildlife.

ITEMS NEEDED

field guide (identification
　　book) of trees
paper
posterboard

pencils, markers,
　　and crayons
camera (optional)

PROCEDURE

1. Pick a tree.

2. Watch for and record early signs of spring, such as leaf buds.

3. Note the kinds of flowers and seeds it produces.

4. Collect a leaf, flower, and seed. Mount them on posterboard, and write down descriptions.

5. Using a field guide, identify the species of your tree; be sure to consider where it's growing as well as what it looks like in making your identification.

6. Draw or photograph four pictures of your tree, one for each season.

7. List any wildlife you observe in your tree. Do any birds nest in your tree? Do insects feed on it?

Butterflies on the Move

What is food for one, is to others bitter poison.
—Lucretius

ONE OCTOBER DAY IN RHODE ISLAND, A KINDERGARTEN TEACHER FOUND two Monarch Butterfly caterpillars feeding on milkweed plants. The caterpillars had hatched too late in the season to develop before winter, and they would undoubtedly freeze to death. The teacher picked enough leaves to feed them for several days and took them to her schoolroom, where they ate and ate and ate. Soon the caterpillars spun chrysalises (the plural of chrysalis, the case in which the metamorphosis to butterfly takes place).

A few weeks later, two full-grown butterflies emerged. But the Monarch migrates south for the winter, and it was long past time for the last flight. The two butterflies would never survive if released in the frigid November air. They had been rescued from freezing to death as caterpillars; now they faced the same fate as butterflies.

The teacher had a idea. She made a tiny cage and put the two Monarchs inside. Then she took the precious parcel to the United Airlines counter at the airport and asked to speak to the customer service supervisor. The supervisor listened carefully while the teacher told him that she needed to purchase tickets for the two butterflies. Without hesitation, the supervisor arranged for the Monarchs to be flown south free of charge. Those two butterflies flew south as no other Monarchs ever had—in the cockpit of a United Airlines jet. When released, they flitted into the warm air, never knowing how close they had come to not completing their normal migration cycle.

To understand that migration cycle, we must first look at the breeding practices of the Monarch. The Monarchs' breeding range extends from southern Canada southward throughout most of the United States, but the butterflies winter in the Caribbean, Mexico, and southern California. As the breeding season approaches, they become restless at their wintering grounds with the urge to move northward to mate and lay eggs.

To be alluring to females, the male Monarch resorts to a tactic well known to humans: He uses "cologne." He has a patch of scent-producing scales called androconia on each of his hind wings. To activate the scent, he uses a hairlike wand that extends from the last segment of his abdomen to rub the androconia. This "scratch and sniff" method releases the enticing aroma and attracts the female, which "smells" it through special receptors in her antennae.

The butterflies mate along their northward route, and the female begins to lay eggs. As she flies northward, she lays up to

A fully fattened adult Monarch weighs less than half a gram. It would take sixty-five or seventy of them to weigh as much as an ounce. Yet that delicate Monarch endures the long trip from eastern Canada to Mexico and partway back again.

five hundred eggs within a seven- to nine-day period. She is careful to choose large patches of milkweed so that her offspring will have plenty to eat when they hatch. Once she has finished her egg laying, she lives out her remaining twenty to thirty days feeding on nectar.

As soon as they hatch, the caterpillars begin to eat. They grow quickly, molting several times as they mature. Then they enter the resting, or pupal, stage called the chrysalis. When the adult butterflies emerge from the chrysalis, they mate, then continue northward. This cycle repeats itself as many as four times before summer begins to wane and shortened daylight hours signal that it's time to fly south for the winter.

Each adult Monarch of all but the final generation of the breeding season survives for only four to five weeks. But that final brood of butterflies has a very different agenda. As the brisk days of autumn approach, these butterflies begin to gorge themselves on nectar, storing fat for the long journey south. In September and October, while most butterflies are facing the death that comes with the onset of winter, all of the remaining Monarchs in North America are gathering in great swarms to begin the long flight to the wintering grounds.

Consider the hordes of Monarchs that winter in Mexico. By the time the Monarchs reach Texas, the horde is made up of so many butterflies that it takes hours for them to pass overhead. The butterflies flit and glide along on the breeze in an endless powerful motion that belies their frailty. It's difficult to believe that any one of the butterflies passing overhead already may have flown a thousand miles (1,600 km) or more and may still have a thousand miles more to go. If the breezes are favorable, the butterflies sometimes conserve energy by continuing through the night. In fact, by using high-altitude wind currents at elevations from fifteen hundred to seven thousand feet (450 to 2,135 m) to carry them southward, and by eating along the way, the Monarchs arrive in Mexico fatter than when they began their flight southward.

More than one hundred million Monarchs make the two-month trip to Mexico each year. How do they know where to go? The knowledge isn't passed on from generation to generation, for the parents of these migrating Monarchs died on their return trip to their northern ranges. And they have no memory of a previous migration, as these butterflies have never flown south before. In fact, these Monarchs are four generations removed from the butter-

Map of Monarch migration routes. A tagged female Monarch released near Brighton, Canada, on September 6, 1986, was recaptured on a mountain near Angangueo, Mexico—more than twenty-one hundred miles away, measured in a straight line. The actual distance that the butterfly traveled could be double that distance.

flies that knew the location of the wintering area in the Mexican mountains. How do they find that precise spot? This phenomenon is one of Nature's most mysterious events. Scientists have been studying Monarch behavior for decades, and they still have no clue as to how the Monarchs are able to perform a feat unparalleled in the natural world.

The Monarch Butterfly has another feature that sets it apart from other butterflies. Because of the very specific diet it follows from caterpillar to butterfly, the Monarch ranks among the most "protected" creatures on Earth. Monarch caterpillars feed exclu-

A bird tries to eat a Monarch only once. Studies with captive birds show that after a single distasteful experience, even the hungriest bird can't be induced to eat another one. Curiously, one dedicated researcher who sampled Monarchs reported that they have the flavor of dry toast.

sively on the leaves of milkweeds and nightshades. The plants of both families contain milky, foul-tasting, toxic juices. As the caterpillars ingest the juices, the poisonous properties of the plants accumulate in their bodies throughout the different stages of their development to adult Monarchs.

The adult Monarch feeds on the nectar of other plants, not milkweeds and nightshades. By doing this, it adds toxic alkaloids extracted from these other plants to its internal arsenal of poisons. Thus, the Monarch uses two completely different chemical protections at different stages of its life.

Notable wildlife

Monarch, *Danaus plexippus*
Milkweeds, *Asclepias* spp.
Nightshades, *Solanum* spp.

DISCOVERY

1. Monarch Butterfly Tree. When the Monarchs finally reach Mexico, they hang in trees, looking like thousands of ornaments on a Christmas tree. Make your own version of this display.

ITEMS NEEDED

paper   craft glue
pencil   bare branch
tape   flowerpot
scissors   soil
crayons or markers

PROCEDURE

1. Fill the flowerpot with soil, and "plant" the branch.

2. Trace the Monarch pattern.

3. Tape the pattern to a window.

4. Tape a sheet of paper over the pattern, and use the pencil to lightly trace the Monarch as many times as you want. Be sure to transfer all lines onto both sides.

5. Color the Monarchs on both sides using the color key. The wings of Monarchs are essentially the same colors on the upper side and the underside, although the underside is paler.

6. Cut out the Monarchs.

7. Use a dab of glue to attach the butterflies to the branch. The more Monarchs, the better!

UPPER SIDE AND UNDER-SIDE DARK BROWN OR BLACK

UPPER SIDE RUSTY ORANGE, UNDERSIDE PALE YELLOW

DOTS: WHITE AND PALE YELLOW

Trace this illustration and color it as indicated to make your own Monarch tree. Color the body black. Color the wings as indicated.

Five Useful Wild Plants

What is a weed? A plant whose virtues have not yet been discovered.
    —Ralph Waldo Emerson

WHERE DO YOU GET YOUR VEGETABLES? FROM THE PLANTS GROWING IN your lawn or along roadsides, or in cellophane-wrapped packages in grocery stores? What about medicine? Do you pluck headache cures and cough drops from a field? Or do you buy synthetic remedies packaged in colorfully labeled boxes and bottles and sold in pharmacies? Although you may accept the idea that wild plants are valuable as food and medicine, like most people you probably don't put that idea into practice. Maybe you should think about changing your habits and consider the many things wild plants have to offer.

Take the dandelion, for instance. Its genus name, *Taraxacum*, means "remedy for disorders." Every part of the plant—leaves, stems, flowers, and roots—can be used for food or medicine. The dandelion was one of the original bitter herbs of Passover, and its use as a remedy for kidney and stomach disorders dates back to the ancient Egyptians.

Dandelions grow only in nitrogen-poor soil, so their presence is the sign of a poorly maintained lawn. The deep taproot of the dandelion is difficult to destroy, and its fluff-propelled seeds are easily scattered by the wind. As a result, the dandelion is the most widely distributed of all the medicinal herbs. It is also the most widely used. Tea brewed from the leaves helps alleviate indigestion, gives the body a vitamin boost, acts as a diuretic, and helps lower abnormally high blood pressure.

The bane of manicured-lawn lovers today, the dandelion was an important plant for the Europeans who brought it to the New World. Using the food stored in its taproot, the dandelion plant stays green well into winter and blooms with the first warm spring sunshine. Pioneers boiled the greens to render a spring tonic; a dose of the vitamins and minerals that the plant provided really did make people feel better after a winter-long lack of fresh greens. They boiled the older, less tender leaves before eating them as a cooked vegetable, and they used the young leaves raw in salads. Early settlers also brewed a coffeelike drink from the roasted roots, made wine from the flowers, and chewed the vitamin-rich stems as we chew gum. The food value of dandelions was rediscovered during the Depression years, when the leaves once again became a staple leafy vegetable in the absence of spinach and other greens.

What early-American settlers knew only by experience has now been proved scientifically. Analysis shows that dandelion leaves are rich in vitamin A, vitamin C, and the B vitamins. In fact, ounce for ounce, dandelion greens contain 50 percent more vitamin C than tomatoes, double the protein of eggplant, and twice the fiber of asparagus. In addition, their iron content equals that of spinach, and their potassium content exceeds that of bananas. Not bad for a weed.

The common name for the persistent yellow flowers that dot spring lawns is dandelion, which comes from the French dent de lion, *meaning "lion's tooth." The long, slender leaves of the plant are, in fact, deeply serrated. This hardy wildflower is an important source of nectar for bees. Songbirds eat the seeds. Even bears take advantage of its nutritional value.*

Goldenrod is another maligned wild plant that deserves a better reputation. For years, the plant's beautiful yellow, plumelike flowers were blamed for causing runny noses and itchy eyes in allergic people. At one point, government-sponsored studies proposed that all species of goldenrod be eradicated. Further research revealed, however, that only 1 percent of the pollen drifting on late-summer breezes came from goldenrod plants. To the surprise of goldenrod haters, the primary cause of hay fever was the pollen from ragweed, a rather inconspicuous plant that shares its growing area and blooming season with the more prominent goldenrod. And ironically, today goldenrod is processed as a treatment for hay fever.

Pioneers to the New World appreciated the more than one hundred varieties of native goldenrods. A literal gold mine in Colonial times, all species of goldenrod were considered such useful herbs that shiploads were sent back to England, where the dried leaves were sold to make medicine.

The genus name of the goldenrod, *Solidago,* refers to the ability of the plant to make a person well, or "solid." A tea made from the fresh or dried leaves and flowers of goldenrod is reputed to be a treatment for kidney ailments; American Indians used the brew to break down stones in the urinary tract.

Then there are cattails. They can certainly be a nuisance, for they sometimes choke irrigation ditches, rice fields, reservoirs, and other watery areas. But they are also so useful as a food source that the late Euell Gibbons, the expert on edible wild plants, called them the "supermarket of the swamps." Here are just a few of the things you can do with cattails.

Peel the shoots to expose the tender white cores; then eat them raw or cooked like asparagus. Eat the immature green flower spikes as you do corn on the cob, by boiling them and serving them with butter. Scrape the outside bud material from the spike and mix it with bread crumbs, beaten egg, and milk; then bake the mixture as a casserole. Mix equal parts of the yellow pollen and wheat flour to make a protein-rich flour. Finally, boil or bake the starchy core at the base of each sprout, and serve it with salt and butter.

Although not so versatile as the cattail, Common Milkweed also can be prepared and eaten in several ways. The shoots can be boiled and eaten like asparagus, the leaves steamed like spinach, the unopened flower buds cooked like broccoli, and the young pods prepared like okra. The roots of Common Milkweed can also be boiled and eaten. A tonic made from the plant is reported to function as a diuretic, alleviate asthma symptoms, and help expel gallstones. Cooking destroys the mild toxicity and bitter flavor of the juice in the Common Milkweed's stems and leaves.

Horehound, a common plant in waste places along the Pacific Coast, isn't a serious pest. On the contrary, this white, woolly member of the mint family contains a substance called marrubin, an expectorant and appetite stimulant. The liquid made from boiling is made into cough drops, and honey made from the flowers can be used as a cough suppressant. In addition, horehound can be used to expel worms, relieve sore-throat pain, and treat diseases of the respiratory tract.

Notable wildlife
   Common Dandelion, *Taraxacum officinale*
   Goldenrod, *Solidago* spp.
   Common Cattail, *Typha latifolia*
   Narrow-leaved Cattail, *Typha augustifolia*
   Common Milkweed, *Asclepsias syriaca*
   Horehound, *Marrubium vulgare*

DISCOVERY

1. Dandelion Salad. Bears and other wild animals depend on the nutrition in dandelions to keep them healthy. You can, too.
   ITEMS NEEDED
      dandelion leaves
      lettuce (optional)
      salad dressing (optional)
   PROCEDURE
   1. Check with your parents to make certain that no chemical weed killers have been used on your lawn. If not, gather some young dandelion leaves when the plants first appear in spring.
   2. Wash the leaves and remove tough stems.
   3. You can mix the tender leaves with lettuce or eat them alone with your favorite salad dressing or cook them in a covered pan until they are just tender, boiling them in the smallest amount of water possible. The water left on the leaves after washing them is usually enough for cooking.

2. Roots for Lunch. The roots of many plants have always been important foods for people. For example, in the 1600s French explorer Samuel de Champlain noted that the Algonquins, Iroquois, and Hurons survived famines by eating roots. Two hundred years later another explorer, Meriwether Lewis, and his party lived through the winter of 1805 by eating wapatoo, a root that grows in marshes and near water. You too can make a meal entirely of taproots and tubers.

ITEMS NEEDED

potatoes, yams, carrots, beets, turnips, radishes, and onions

PROCEDURE

1. Peel the potatoes and cook in boiling salted water for about twenty minutes.

2. Scrub the beets, then cut the tops off. Brush them with oil, and bake them in a 350-degree oven until tender (one hour or longer). Peel, slice, and season with butter, salt, and pepper.

3. Scrub the yams. Bake in a 375-degree oven until soft (fifty minutes or longer). Eat as you would a baked potato, with butter, salt, and pepper.

4. Eat the turnips, radishes, and onions raw. Peel the turnips and onions, and cut the tops and roots off the radishes before cutting them into thin slices.

3. Root Crops. Grow some nutrition by following these directions.

ITEMS NEEDED FOR A	ITEMS NEEDED FOR B
carrot	large sweet potato,
beet	about five inches long
two shallow dishes	three toothpicks
	one-quart jar

PROCEDURE A (TO GROW FERNLIKE PLANTS)

1. Cut about two inches off the tops of the carrot and the beet. Be careful to keep the leaves intact.

2. Place the carrot top in one dish and the beet top in the other.

3. Add about a half inch of water to each dish, and put the dishes in a sunny spot.

4. Change the water daily to keep it fresh.

5. When roots appear, plant the carrot and beet in sandy soil with only the fernlike leaves showing.

6. Set the pot in a sunny window, and keep the soil moist at all times.

Grow a vinelike plant from a sweet potato. Roots always grow downward, and leaves always grow upward.

PROCEDURE B (TO GROW VINELIKE PLANTS)

1. Insert the three toothpicks in the sweet potato about one-third of the way from one end. (It doesn't matter which way is up; smaller roots grow from all parts of the sweet potato, which is actually a taproot.) The toothpicks should form a triangular support for the sweet potato.

2. Rest the toothpicks on the edge of the jar.

3. Fill the jar about halfway with water.

4. Change the water daily to keep it fresh.

5. Put the jar in a sunny window, and watch the vine grow.

An Underground Monarchy

The ant finds kingdoms in a foot of ground.
—Stephen Vincent Benet

IF YOU EVER SEE A NUPTIAL FLIGHT OF ANTS, YOU'LL NEVER FORGET IT. Thousands of ants swarm over the ground and lift into the air on unfamiliar wings. This is the only time in their lives when they can fly. Some unknown signal has told them that the time is right to crown new queens and to establish new colonies. As ants of the same species from several colonies meet in the air, the males mate with the females.

When the marriage ceremony is over, each female has been fertilized for life. She drops to the ground and rubs her body against a stone or blade of grass to get rid of her now useless wings. She is now a queen, and she must find a suitable place to set up a new nest, where she'll spend the ten to fifteen years of her life doing nothing but laying eggs. Nestbound, she will lay a million eggs every few years. The fate of the males is no better. Having fulfilled their role, they remain above ground to die.

Although thousands of queens are fertilized during one marriage flight, only a few survive to establish colonies; probably no more than one in a thousand lives long enough to lay eggs. Birds, frogs, toads, mice, lizards, and other predators take advantage of having so many ants in one place at one time as they snatch thousands of ants from the ground and the air. Many of the queens that do escape and begin to nest are killed later by flooding, cold, drought, fungal diseases, or starvation before they can raise the first generation of eggs. In most species of ants, only one queen is present in a colony; if she dies, the colony also dies. In other species, more than one colony may live together peacefully under the rule of multiple queens; naturally, having more than one queen increases the chances of the colony's survival.

When the urge to establish new colonies hits, ants take wing for the only time in their life.

The queen herself must care for the first generation of eggs and larvae. Now that she has escaped floods, fungus, and foes, she must survive without food until the new ants emerge. She relies on stored body fat to stay alive and to give her the energy to lay and tend the eggs and to care for her newborns.

The first generation of ants consists of wingless, nonfertile females, or workers. They are weak and undersized because they have been nourished only with the queen's saliva, yet within a few days of hatching they begin to serve the colony by finding food for the famished queen.

Workers groom themselves, each other, and the queen. The bodies of ants are covered with hair, and to stay healthy, they must keep it clean by combing it with short, stiff hairs on their legs. Softer leg hairs serve as a brush. These soft hairs are hollow and exude a lubricant that causes dust particles to stick together so that they can be easily combed and brushed out. Workers also use their tongues and mandibles, or jaws, as cleaning tools. The physical contact that takes place when ants care for each other helps to bond the members of the community into a unit.

But the strongest sense of community spirit is the colony's distinctive odor, or pheromone. The queen uses her sticky saliva to daub the eggs and workers with the scent that literally keeps her colony together, a scent that belongs to no other ant colony, even another one of the same species. The workers carry on this practice with subsequent generations. Their licking does more than reinforce the queen's scent, because their saliva also provides the developing eggs with the nourishment and stimulation needed for growth. A fungicide in the saliva prevents the growth of mildew on the eggs as they lie in their dark, damp nurseries. And the saliva helps the eggs stick to each other, making it easy for the workers to carry groups of them to lower chambers when predators or floods threaten.

Most ant eggs are shaped like tiny grains of rice. Each egg has a yolk covered by a thin outer shell. The temperature of the air regulates the speed at which the eggs mature. They grow quickly in warm weather and slowly in cool, so it may take days, weeks, or months before the larvae emerge. To speed up the development of the eggs, workers tote them above ground on warm, dry days, carrying them back into the safety of the nest at night.

As the egg grows, its thin shell stretches and becomes almost transparent. The larva that eventually hatches has no eyes and is shaped like a prickly little worm with large, pincerlike jaws. The hairs that cover the bodies of the larvae enable them to cling together in clusters that the workers can readily transport from chamber to chamber and from above ground to below. The hairs also prevent the larvae from resting on the damp earth, which would encourage the growth of fungus. The workers lick the larvae to keep them moist and feed them regurgitated liquid food or fresh insects until they enter the pupal stage.

The developing larva sheds its skin several times before entering the pupal stage. Then, as a pupa, it waits quietly while its body completes the transformation from egg to adult. The pupae of some ants spin silk cocoons; others change from larva to adult without benefit of a protective covering.

When the young ant, called a callow, is ready to emerge, workers help it out of its pupal skin. If the pupa is in a cocoon, workers cut the cocoon open from top to bottom to release the weak, pale callow. In a few hours, the callow is able to walk. And in a few days, the callow has darkened and has become strong enough to drag a dead insect fifty times its own weight to the nest. It is ready to spend the five years of its life serving the colony. In a division of labor that is in some species based on size and in others on age, some workers feed and care for the queen, and others tend the eggs and larvae, gather and store food, clean and repair the nest, and defend the colony. Each ant has its task, and each ant is important.

In four or five years, the colony is strong enough to divide. Male ants hatch from unfertilized eggs and inhabit the nest for the few weeks of their lives. They don't eat or work; they just wait for the time to fertilize the new queens. Then one day the ants in the colony become restless, like nervous brides and grooms. The work-

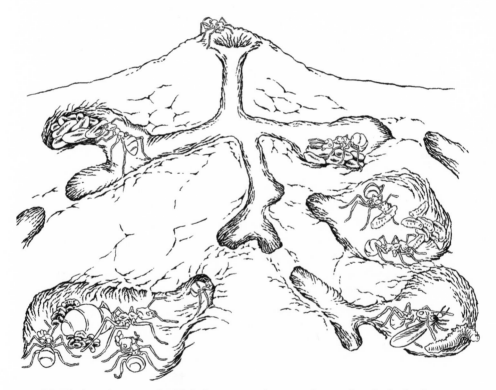

North American ants build their nests underground or under the bark of a tree. Long tunnels connect several chambers that have special purposes, including separate nurseries for eggs and larvae, food storage areas, garbage dumps, and cemeteries.

ers keep them from the nuptials, however, until one day, triggered by a motivation that so far remains undiscovered, they finally allow the wedding to take place.

An ant colony is a matriarchy. The queen establishes the colony. Her descendants maintain it. In this well-organized society, each member is valuable and necessary. From the moment of birth, every member of an ant colony does a specific job that contributes to the operation of the entire ant community. If it didn't, the colony would die.

Notable wildlife

Ant, Family Formicidae

DISCOVERY

1. Ant Antics. It may look like ants scurry around aimlessly, but give them a task to complete, and see what happens.

ITEMS NEEDED

anthill

cookie crumbs

sugar cubes

PROCEDURE

1. Find an ant colony under a rock, in your garden, or under leaves in the woods.

2. Scatter cookie crumbs on the surface of the nest. How long does it take the ants to find them? How do they carry them to store them in the nest?

3. Put a sugar cube about six inches from the entrance to the colony. How long does it take the ants to find it? (They use their sense of smell to find food.) What do the ants do with such a large object? Put another sugar cube twelve inches away from the nest. What happens? What do the workers do when you put out two sugar cubes at the same time?

2. Be a Worker Ant. Make yourself useful—and surprise your family at the same time.

ITEMS NEEDED

paper

jar

pen or pencil

PROCEDURE

1. Cut a sheet of paper into several pieces, each about two by three inches.

2. Write a task that contributes to the welfare of your family on each piece. Some suggestions for daily chores are washing dishes, drying dishes, preparing breakfast, making all beds, and feeding the cat. Weekly tasks might include vacuuming, dusting, scrubbing toilets, washing the car, and watering plants.

3. Fold the pieces of paper and drop them in the jar.

4. Each Monday morning, pull out a piece of paper. Do the chore described on that piece as often as needed for a full week.

5. Repeat the process every Monday until you have used up all the pieces.

3. Ant Colony. Adopt an ant colony and watch how the ants work.

ITEMS NEEDED

> one yard white cloth, purchased or cut from an old sheet
> pointed trowel
> tweezers
> one-quart jar or larger
> two small jars with lids (poke holes in lids)
> small sponge
> cheesecloth
> dark paper or cloth large enough to cover large jar
> photographer's red bulb (optional)

PROCEDURE

1. Find an anthill or look for a colony under a rock or leaves. Spread the white cloth nearby.

2. With the trowel, remove the top layer of soil and put it on the cloth. The soil will contain worker ants, which will be easy to see on the white background. Because ants bite when defending their nest (remember those pincers that are present from birth?), use the tweezers to carefully lift twenty to thirty ants into one small jar.

3. Collect about the same number of eggs, larvae, and pupae from their special chambers; place them in the other small jar. These are very small, so just collect some of all the little white things you see.

4. Follow the tunnels with the tip of the trowel, exposing them as you look for the queen. She's much larger than the workers and won't be scurrying around. Put her in the jar with the eggs, larvae, and pupae.

5. Fill the large jar to within two inches of the top with dirt from the anthill. Dump the ants from the two small jars into the larger one. The ants you've collected will establish a colony in the jar, and the colony may live for several generations.

6. Feed the ants bits of nuts, meat, and crackers; sweet cereals; pieces of fruit; and dead insects. Ants aren't finicky eaters, but be sure to offer them a variety of foods to keep them healthy. Dampen the sponge, and put a drop of honey on it. Remove uneaten and unstored food each day so that it doesn't decay, ferment, or mildew.

7. Ants prefer darkness, so cover the jar when you aren't observing them. To keep them visible even in the dark, hang the photographer's red bulb nearby.

8. When you no longer want to observe your ants at work, release the colony in a shady spot by carefully dumping out the dirt and ants. They'll soon establish a colony in their new location.

The Ways of the Ant

None preaches better than the ant, and she says nothing.
—Benjamin Franklin

IN THE 1930S, AN AMERICAN FREIGHTER DOCKED AT MOBILE, ALABAMA, with a few ants as stowaways. These pioneer Red Fire Ants quickly reproduced and marched steadily north, east, and west at an average rate of twelve miles a year. They now occupy 250 million acres in eleven southern states.

The Red Fire Ant is native to Brazil, where invasions of the insect cause whole villages to be deserted. It's related to the Black Fire Ant of North America. Whereas the black ant goes unnoticed, however, its red cousin has become such a serious problem in North America that $6 million is spent every year trying to control the recent immigrant.

Red Fire Ants bite and sting at the same time. Working as a team, several ants crawl on their victim; going up a pant leg is a favorite tactic. Then, on the release of a chemical signal given by one ant, all attack at the same time. Each ant bites to stabilize itself; then it stings, injecting the victim with a toxin that raises pustules in people who are mildly allergic but causes more serious reactions, such as difficulty breathing or even death, in others.

In Brazil, the Red Fire Ant has several natural enemies. It has none in North America. Ecologists have learned through experience that importing natural controls from other countries brings its own problems. Yet, environmentally safe pesticides are useless against these fire ants. Not only do the poisons dissipate too quickly, but they kill native ant species, as well as the invaders. Pesticides that disrupt the metamorphosis of the fire ant from larva to adult show some promise, but they can't be used near water, because they also kill water organisms. Targeting the egg-laying queens would be the logical solution, but a colony may have as many as five hundred queens, all busily laying millions of eggs.

Fortunately, not all ants of North America are vicious. The several species of leafcutting ants, for example, are not only peaceful but also fun to watch. These ants have large heads to accommodate the powerful jaws they use as hedge clippers to trim pieces from leaves and flowers. But they don't eat the vegetation. Instead, they chew the pieces into a soggy mash and carry it back to the nest, where they store it in special chambers. In the dampness and darkness, it provides an excellent growing medium for fungus, which they do eat.

Harvester ants are restricted to the warm, dry, sandy soil of the U.S. Southwest, Florida, and Kansas. Workers use their pincerlike jaws to pick up seeds from the ground or to cut them from wild grasses and weeds. Then they carry the seeds back to the mound-shaped nest. Some species of harvester ants feed bits of the hulls, or outer coverings, to the larvae. The hulls contain lipids, fats the larvae need to develop into adult ants. Other types of harvester ants eat the inner starchy meat of the seeds and discard the hulls. If the seeds get damp, worker ants carry them, one by one, to the surface to lay them in the Sun to dry. Seeds that sprout are left to grow to provide more seeds.

Leafcutting ants are not uncommon and often can be seen walking along in single file, each ant carrying its piece of vegetation held high off the ground. Because they look as though they're shading themselves from the Sun, leafcutting ants are also called parasol ants.

The practices of harvester ants help wildflower seeds germinate. The ants often collect the seeds of bloodroots, spring beauties, trilliums, and violets. Sometimes whole seeds are buried along with discarded hulls and the bodies of dead ants. Experiments indicate that the plants that grow in the ants' accidental garden are larger, are more numerous, and live longer than those from seeds scattered by the breeze, for they are buried below the soil surface in a moist environment instead of landing on top of the soil where animals can eat them and where wind and heat can dry them out before they become rooted. Seeds "planted" by ants also grow better than those sown by humans in the same area, because the combination of materials buried with the seeds provides a rich organic fertilizer.

Whereas some ants, such as leafcutting and harvester ants, are farmers, others work in wood. Carpenter ants chew large holes in dead or decaying trees, and in the woodwork of buildings, to carve out tunnels and rooms. Unlike termites, they don't eat the wood, but their handiwork still can cause a great deal of structural damage to a home. In the wild, carpenter ants are best controlled by the Pileated Woodpecker, a large bird that can strip thirty feet of bark in fifteen minutes to get to the ants. The stomach of one woodpecker was found to contain twenty-six hundred carpenter ants.

Honey ants, the last major group of North American ants, feed on the sweet substance called honeydew secreted by certain insects. Depending on the species, these ants have several ways to guarantee an unending source of honeydew.

Some honey ants keep herds of aphids, which suck plant juices and then secrete honeydew, much as people keep and milk dairy cattle. To get their favorite food, the ants stimulate the secretion of honeydew by stroking the abdomens of the aphids. Just as human ranchers move cattle from pasture to pasture, honey ants move their herds of aphids from plant to plant. Some honey ants even take the aphids into the nest to lay eggs. When the newborn aphids hatch, the worker ants tote them outside to feed on plant juices. In fact, the ants are so attentive to their charges that they even scratch the soil away from the base of a plant to expose its roots. As the aphids deplete the juices in one root, the workers carry them to another one.

Other species of honey ants become dependent on the sweet secretions of tiny Ant-loving Beetles. One of these golden-brown

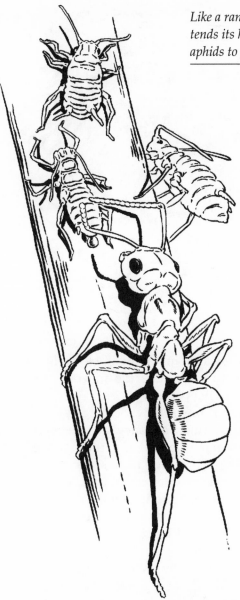

Like a rancher with milk cattle, a honey ant tends its herd of aphids. The ant "milks" the aphids to get the sweet honeydew they produce.

beetles enters the colony with one purpose in mind: to be tended to and fed by the ants. The ants seem to ignore the beetle, until a few of them brush against its body and discover the honeylike substance. These few ants begin to neglect their duties to the colony; in return for the honey, they feed the beetle and groom it, just as they do their own larvae. As the glands on the beetle's body continue to secrete the honeydew, more and more ants hover around the sweet-tasting insect. Eventually, the ants are "hooked." They neglect the eggs and the larvae and ignore the queen. They even feed the colony's eggs and larvae to the beetle, and sometimes to the beetle's larvae, too. The once highly organized society dies, and the well-tended beetle moves on to another ant nest.

A few butterfly larvae, especially those of the hairstreaks and blues, have established a symbiotic relationship with ants. One example is the Karner Blue, a delicate, mauve-winged butterfly with a wingspan of about one inch. The pea green caterpillar of the species feeds on the leaves of lupine, locoweed, and alfalfa. But the short, fat, slug-like larva rarely finishes eating its first leaf before being adopted by

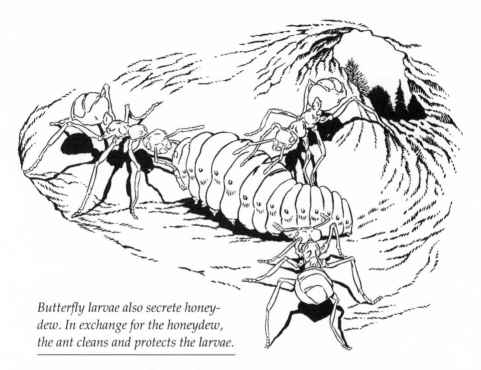

*Butterfly larvae also secrete honey-
dew. In exchange for the honeydew,
the ant cleans and protects the larvae.*

ants. The ants feed on its honeydew and, in payment, clean their
host and defend it from predators. In some cases, the ants take the
larva into their nest, establishing a living pantry.

Some species of honey ants use callows, newly emerged ants,
as living storage containers. In North America, honey ants that perform this unusual activity range from northern Mexico through the
southwestern United States, where they live near scrub oaks.
Workers collect nectar from abnormal growths, called galls, on the
oak trees. They swallow the nectar, then regurgitate it later to feed
it to the ants that serve as honey pots. The honey pots become so
full of honey that they look like small, golden grapes; because of
this shape, they are called rotunds.

After a rotund is stuffed full of honey by the collecting workers, workers boost it to a spot on the ceiling of a special chamber.
When a hungry ant gently nudges the hanging honey pot, the
rotund responds by contracting the muscles of its abdomen to
squeeze out a drop of honey.

The Indians of Mexico and the southwestern United States collect the honey by pressing it out of the rotunds. This ant honey is
reputed to have a sweeter taste than bee honey. In addition, the
crushed bodies of rotunds are placed on wounds as an effective

A single colony may have as many as three hundred rotunds clinging to the ceiling for the rest of their lives, each storing eight times its weight in honey. When food is scarce, workers get their nutrition from the rotunds.

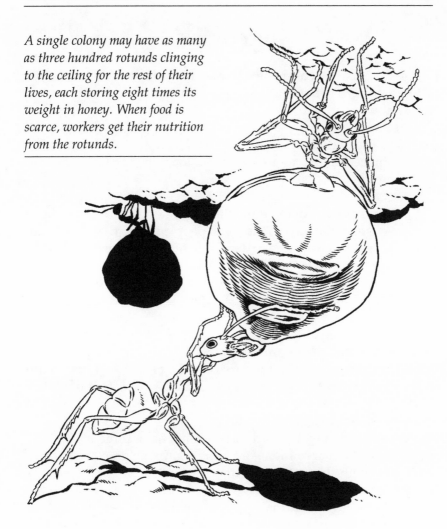

healing agent. Since sugar is a natural antiseptic, there is merit to this practice.

The specialized behaviors of native North American ants can be appreciated. Each type has a niche in the North American ant world, eliminating competition for the same food and habitats.

Notable wildlife
    Ant, Family Formicidae
    Ant-loving Beetle, Family Clavergeridae
    Aphid, Family Aphididae
    Pileated Woodpecker, *Dryocopus pileatus*
    Karner Blue, *Lycaeides melissa samuelis*

DISCOVERY

1. Ant Careers. Try collecting and raising the foods that ants prefer. You don't have to squeeze rotunds for honey, but you do have to grow mold!

ITEMS NEEDED

at least four types of honey	plate
bird seed mix for parakeets	magnifying glass
bread	

PROCEDURE

1. Honey ants. Compare the flavors of honey from four different areas of the world. Just as some people prefer the taste of ant honey to bee honey, you may decide that Canadian bees make better-tasting honey than Argentinean ones.

2. Harvester ants. Scatter some seeds on the ground. Don't cover them. Don't water them. Just let the Sun and rain do their work. Do your seeds sprout and grow?

3. Leafcutting ants. Dampen a slice of bread and put it on a plate. Keep the bread damp. In a few days, fuzzy grayish-green patches should appear on the surface of the bread. That fuzzy stuff is fungus that grew from spores in the air. Use a magnifying glass to get a closer look.

2. Egg Carton Ants. Like all insects, ants have three main body parts: a head, an abdomen, and a thorax. Using an egg carton to make an ant illustrates these distinct segments well.

ITEMS NEEDED

cardboard egg carton	paper punch
scissors	four twelve-inch
black crayons, markers,	black pipe cleaners
or paints	white paper

PROCEDURE

1. Cut the egg carton lengthwise down the middle.

2. Now cut the six-cup piece in half. You should end up with two sections with three cups each.

3. Paint or color the sections black.

4. Punch holes in the middle cup, which represents the thorax, for the legs.

5. Punch two holes in the head for the antennae, as illustrated.

6. Thread three pipe cleaners through the holes for the legs.

7. Cut one pipe cleaner in half.

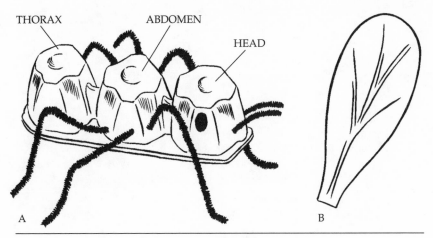

THORAX   ABDOMEN

HEAD

A   B

A. A finished egg carton ant. Notice the three separate parts of the insect's body: head, abdomen, and thorax. B. Pattern for wing. Use for ants taking part in a nuptial flight.

8. Thread the pipe cleaner halves through the antenna holes.

9. If you want to get your ant ready for a nuptial flight, use the pattern to make a pair of wings and glue them into place.

Alternative: Use marshmallows instead of an egg carton. Poke toothpicks into the marshmallows to hold them together, and use toothpicks for the antennae and legs. You can make several of these and take them with you on a picnic. It will probably be the first time in history that ants are welcome at a picnic!

3. Edible Ants-on-a-Log. Entomologists, scientists who study insects, dined on mealworm balls with tomato sauce and spiced crickets at the dinner commemorating the one hundredth anniversary of the New York Entomological Society. Chocolate-covered ants weren't listed on the menu, but they are sold in specialty shops. Try this version of crawly cuisine instead.

ITEMS NEEDED
> banana
> peanut butter
> raisins

PROCEDURE
1. Split the banana.
2. Spread it with peanut butter.
3. Sprinkle on the raisins.
4. Enjoy!

Marshes, Rivers, and Oceans

The Rise and Fall of the Ocean

*It is even said that many ebbings and risings of the
sea always come round with the moon and upon
certain fixed days.*
—Aristotle

IMAGINE A HUGE SEA MONSTER LURKING DEEP IN THE OCEAN. YOU'VE
never seen it, and neither has anyone else, but you know it's there
because of what happens to the shoreline. When the monster
inhales, its mighty breath pulls on the coastal waters and causes
the water level to fall. When it exhales, it blows the water back to
the land, and the water level rises. With such evidence of its power,
you hope and pray that the colossal creature never sneezes!

Based on what we know today, that story sounds silly. But it is
one of the ways that ancient civilizations explained the daily cycle
of the tides. Later, around 77 A.D., the Romans recognized the relationship between the patterns of the tides and the positions of the
Moon and the Sun. For several centuries, in tide tables that date
back to 1213 A.D., scientists and sailors charted this relationship.
But although they observed and recorded the patterns, they still
didn't understand what caused them. It wasn't until 1687 that Sir
Isaac Newton explained the reason for the tides when he proposed
that gravitation was the cause.

Earth's gravity draws everything within its reach to its center.
The same force that pulls a falling apple toward the ground also
pulls the Sun and Moon toward Earth's center. But the Sun and
Moon, with gravities of their own, each exert an opposing force. If
they didn't, they, too, like the apple, would crash to the ground.
This battle of mighty forces keeps us in place and also causes the
four daily tides.

Everything rises and falls with the tides, because the Moon
pulls on Earth's atmosphere, land, buildings, and inhabitants as
well as on its bodies of water. Every time the Moon's pull causes

the oceans to rise ten feet, it also causes the land to rise about six inches. That means that twice a day the Empire State Building—in fact, the entire island of Manhattan—is sometimes as much as twenty inches taller than it is at other times. Of course, a land tide doesn't cause actual inches to be gained or lost—the Empire State Building is always 1,250 feet tall—but it does change how high the building is in relation to sea level.

The word *tide* is from the Anglo-Saxon *tyd*, which means "seasons" in the general sense of time or cycles. The rise and fall of the tides are so regular that we, like the Romans, can easily chart them. Tides change according to a twenty-four-hour-and-fifty-two-minute cycle, so high and low tides are almost an hour later each day. Typically, there are two daily high tides and two daily low tides. Each cycle consists of about six hours and thirteen minutes. The general term for the tidal flow of seawater is tidal current. Specifically, the flow towardthe coast is called the flood tide and the flow away from the coast is called the ebb tide.

An English proverb states that time and tide wait for no man. Tides certainly do keep a regular schedule, as we can see from their daily cycle. Let's start with what's known as high-high tide, when the flood tide comes farthest up on the beach. The water level gradually falls from high-high tide until after about six hours it's at its lowest ebb in the cycle, called low-low tide. About another six hours later, low-high tide occurs; at this point in the cycle, the tide has risen again, but not to the level of high-high tide. After roughly another six hours, the tide is back to a low point, although not so low as the low-low tide; this phase is called the high-low tide. In the final six hours or so, the tide goes back to the original point, high-high tide. So the cycle runs like this: high-high, low-low, low-high, and high-low, then back to high-high to start the cycle again. But instead of describing such a complicated system of daily tides, we generally refer to the phases simply as high tides and low tides.

Besides the daily fluctuations in the tides, there is also a monthly cycle that operates on about a two-week schedule. To understand what happens, you need to understand some astronomy. The Sun is twenty-seven million times larger than the Moon, but the Moon is closer to Earth. As a result, the Moon's pull is stronger than the Sun's. In fact, the Moon's pull usually accounts for 60 percent of the force of the tide, and the Sun's for about 40.

Usually.

During Full and New Moons, Earth, the Moon, and the Sun are in a straight line in the sky. The combined gravitational pull of the Sun and Moon on Earth results in exceptionally high-high tides called spring tides. (In this case, the word *spring* has nothing to do with the season of the year.) During the First Quarter and Third Quarter phases of the Moon, the Sun and Moon are out of alignment and form a triangle with Earth. As a result, the gravitational pulls of the Sun and Moon cancel each other out, causing unusually low-low tides called neap tides.

We can't see the tide-caused changes in solid objects, but we certainly can see them in varying degrees in bodies of water like oceans, large lakes, and major rivers. The amount of water involved and the physical features of the shoreline influence the effects of tides and determine the difference in water level between high and low tides. This difference is called the amplitude. The tide on Lake Superior, the largest of the Great Lakes, is only two inches because that body of water is so expansive. But where bodies of water are narrow, the water reaches farther inland. Thus the Saint Lawrence River has a tide that runs almost 300 miles inland; the relatively wider Hudson River has a tide that extends 150 miles inland. Along ocean shores, the vast amount of incoming water generally has space to stretch out evenly, so it rises only a few feet during high tides. The line of seaweed and other debris that you see along ocean shores marks the limit of the incoming tide.

In bays with narrow openings, the amplitude can be dramatic. The greatest tidal range is found in Nova Scotia, where a four-foot-high wall of seawater rushes from the Bay of Fundy and forcefully bores upstream, against the natural flow of the water, to the Petit-codiac River. The difference between high and low tides there is sometimes more than fifty feet. To take advantage of the hundred billion tons of seawater that move in and out of the bay with each tide change, fishermen hang nets at the high-water mark to collect the fish that the incoming water brings to shore. At low tide, the fishnets look like volleyball nets for giants.

Although tides are powerful, they should not be confused with tidal waves. Tides are a regular movement of ocean currents. Tidal waves, on the other hand, are caused by undersea earthquakes or by hurricanes far out in the open sea. The Japanese word *tsunami*, meaning "storm wave," is a better way to describe the huge wave's destructive powers.

Tides don't destroy life; they sustain it. Around the world, tidal

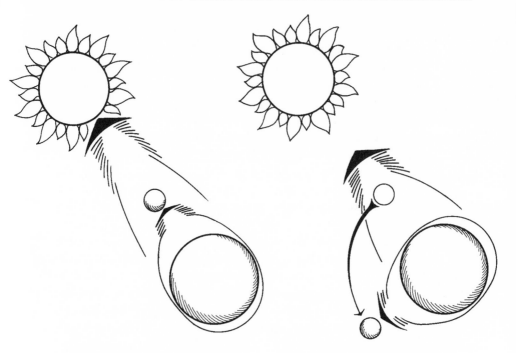

When the Sun, Moon, and Earth are in a straight line, the exceptionally strong gravitational pull causes the extra-high spring tide.

When the Sun and Moon are at right angles to Earth, their opposing gravitational forces cancel each other out, causing the weak neap tide.

pools are divided into the same three general zones—upper, middle, and lower—each of which supports different kinds of plant and animal life. The lichens, algae, and tiny periwinkles of the upper zone have adapted to being dampened only during the highest tides. Barnacles, mussels, and limpets cling to the rocks of the middle zone, where the tide continuously ebbs and flows. And starfish, crabs, sponges, anemones, and fish prowl the lower zone, where they are hardly ever exposed to air.

Tides provide safety for the eggs and young of several marine animals. On the East Coast, for example, the Atlantic Horseshoe Crab relies on the high tides of late spring and early summer to carry it ashore to lay its eggs, and then to push sand over those eggs to protect them from predators and incubate them in the Sun's warmth while they mature. And on the Pacific Coast, thousands of seven-inch-long (17.5-cm-long) California Grunions ride the waves to shore from March to August on the second, third, and fourth nights after each full moon. On the beach, each female buries her tail in the wet sand and expels her eggs, and the males fertilize them. Their spawning mission completed, the fish enter the next wave and ride it back to the safety of open water. In two weeks' time, during the next high tide, hundreds of thousands of glistening little grunions pop out of their eggs, wiggle up through the sand, and ride in the water film to the Pacific.

Tides form a unique habitat for coastal creatures. When the tide recedes, it leaves pools of water among the rocky shorelines. These tidal pools are home for a wide variety of sea animals, including starfish; small fish and shrimp; sand dollars, sea urchins, and sea anemones; sponges; periwinkles, limpets, and other snails; oysters, clams, abalones, mussels, and other bivalves; hermit crabs, lobsters, barnacles, octopuses, and other crustaceans; and an assortment of sea worms. Sea turtles lay their eggs in the tidal pools, and shorebirds find food in them.

Tides also bring in cool water to maintain the proper temperature in the pool, and replenish the microscopic plants and animals to feed the hundreds of creatures that live there. There is evidence that certain types of plant plankton multiply more rapidly during the full moon and when the tide is high. The reason? Evidently, the intensity of polarized light is more favorable at this time than at others.

Notable wildlife
Atlantic Horseshoe Crab, *Limulus polyphemus*
California Grunion, *Leuresthes tenuis*

DISCOVERY

1. Feel the Force of Gravity. You can feel for yourself how two opposing tugs like the gravitational pulls of the Moon and Earth work.

ITEMS NEEDED
length of heavy string, about thirty inches long
metal nut

PROCEDURE
1. Tie the metal nut to one end of the string to act as a weight.

2. While standing outdoors in an open area, swing the weight so that it revolves around and around in a circle. Your hand is Earth and the weight is the Moon.

3. As you swing the weight, try to hold your hand in exactly the same spot. Can you?

*When you swing a weight
like this, what you experience
is equivalent to the tug of the
Moon on the end of an imaginary string. We see evidence
of this pull at the seacoast, in
the form of the tide.*

4. You've discovered that you can't hold your hand still. You can't keep your hand from moving in a small circle, because it's pulled outward by what is known as the centrifugal force of the weight on the end of the rope.

5. Experiment with different weights at the end of the rope, and notice the different effects.

2. Explore a Tidal Pool. The number of plants and animals that live in a tidal pool is amazing. How many things can you find and identify?

ITEMS NEEDED
    canvas shoes
    bucket

PROCEDURE

1. During low tide, look for crabs, starfish, tiny fish, anemones, and other creatures in a tidal pool. To protect yourself from stinging sea animals and sharp stones and shells, be sure to wear canvas shoes. And never pick up a creature in your hands; use the bucket to scoop it up for a closer look.

2. Notice the abundance of algae, an important food source for sea animals.

3. Look carefully at what you find, but leave living creatures where you find them. You may, of course, collect empty shells.

The Well-Balanced Lobster

*"You may not have lived much under the sea—"[said
the Mock Turtle] ("I haven't," said Alice)—"and
perhaps you were never even introduced to a lobster—" (Alice began to say "I once tasted——" but
checked herself hastily and said "No never")....*
　　　　—Lewis Carroll, "The Lobster-Quadrille"
　　　　Alice's Adventures in Wonderland

IF YOU WERE INTRODUCED TO A NORTHERN LOBSTER, YOU WOULD LEARN
that it uses its legs to breathe and its antennae to smell and feel.
You'd also find out that its teeth are in its stomach, its blood is blue,
and the first three of its five pairs of legs end in claws, with huge
pincers on the first pair. This arrangement of form and function
may seem strange to us, but it certainly works well for this aquatic
crustacean.

Let's get to know the Northern Lobster by starting at the front
of its body. Chemical-detecting hairs on the antennae are as much
as a million times more sensitive than our noses and tongues. In
turn, the hairs have more than four hundred kinds of receptors,
each of which is sensitive to a different chemical. Through these
fine-tuned hairs, the lobster interprets molecules in the surrounding water as we use our senses of smell and taste. During the day,
the lobster lives under rocks or in burrows in the sand, but when it
ventures out at night, it rapidly vibrates its antennae to "sniff out"
a crab, a snail, a small fish, a smaller lobster, or even a dead animal
as food. The hairs are also highly sensitive to the movement of
ocean water. So while the lobster is out hunting, its antennae can
pick up the slightest stirring made by the stealthiest movements of
the sneakiest octopus, one of its worst enemies. The signal that an
enemy is nearby tells the lobster to take cover immediately.

When the lobster catches something to eat, it tears apart the
food with its two large front claws. The Northern Lobster develops

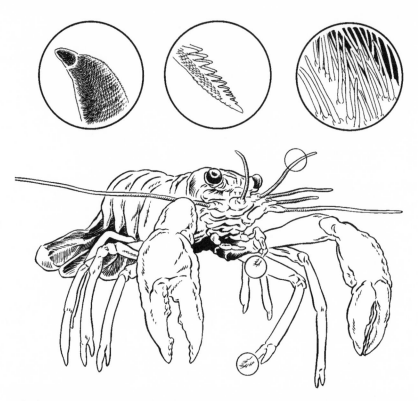

The lobster is really a hairy animal. Hedgehog hairs (top left) on the insides of the pincers at the ends of the walking legs sense minute chemical changes. Serrated hairs (top center) on the lobster's mouthparts and legs give the animal a sense of touch. And fine hairs (top right) on the antennules have more than four hundred types of sensory receptors, each of which picks up a certain chemical.

one front claw larger than the other, the only species to do so. It uses the smaller, serrated cutter claw to grasp its prey and the stronger, heavier crusher to break open clams, mussels, and other hard-shelled ocean creatures.

The Northern Lobster may be either right- or left-handed, depending on which claw develops as the crusher. Nine out of ten people are right-handed, but the lobster's chances of growing up either right-handed or left-handed are pretty much fifty-fifty.

Because many people consider the meat in the Northern Lobster's large crusher to be a delicacy (Alice probably did!), trapping lobsters is a major industry along the Atlantic Coast. In an attempt to increase the lobster's commercial value, biologists have tried to coax the crustaceans to develop two crushers instead of one crusher and a cutter. The scientists first determined that exercising the front claws caused their growth. They found that only six of every twenty-six lobsters raised on smooth-bottomed aquariums developed a crusher, while most of those raised on a bed of broken shells, mud, or even plastic buttons developed one. But if an aquarium-raised lobster had even one chip of shell to grasp and pinch with its dominant claw, that claw was likely to develop into a coveted crusher.

The researchers assumed that if exercising one claw more than the other produced a crusher, then exercising both claws equally would produce two crushers—and twice as much edible meat. So the scientists designed an exercise program for the laboratory lobsters to make sure that each lobster's right claw was exercised as much as its left. In a perverse protest of the scientists' efforts, the exercised lobsters failed to develop even the one normal crusher. When it came to making crushers, it didn't matter how much exercise the claws got—it only mattered that one claw got more of a workout than the other.

Once it has eaten its fill, the lobster stores excess food in its stomach. When the lobster needs nutrition, three toothlike structures in its stomach grind meat and bits of shell into very small pieces. The food particles then pass to digestive glands, where fats, proteins, and carbohydrates are digested and used by the creature's body.

Whereas the foremost pair of the lobster's legs become huge claws, the remaining four pairs are small and are used for walking. Feathery gills attached to the bases of these legs extend into a body cavity called the gill chamber. When the legs move, they act as eight pump handles, forcing water between them and the carapace, or upper shell. Once inside the body, the water flows forward and upward over the gills, which act as our lungs do, extracting oxygen and releasing carbon dioxide.

Lobsters are true blue bloods because their blood is copper based rather than iron based as ours is. In the veins, the color is a very pale blue, but when oxygen from the air mixes with the blood, a chemical reaction darkens the blood to deep blue.

The lobster's life cycle from egg to adult begins in summer. The female, or hen, lays five thousand to one hundred thousand eggs, depending on her age and size, and carries them under the curve of her tail. She lays her first clutch when she's about five years old, then lays subsequent clutches at two-year intervals. The following spring, the male, or cock, fertilizes the eggs, which the hen has been carrying for almost a year. She continues to carry them for another ten to eleven months, until she finally shakes thousands of larvae out of the eggs and into the coastal waters of the Atlantic Ocean.

The translucent newborns are less than a half inch (1.25 cm) long. They rise to the surface of the water to spend their first month of life drifting, and provide an easy source of food for seabirds and fish. Only one out of every thousand little lobsters survives to sink to the ocean floor and grow to maturity.

The lobster continues to grow as long as it lives, and it molts its chitin-and-calcium exoskeleton as it grows. Chitin is a flexible covering related to proteins and is the same material that forms the outer covering of insects. The chitin is hardened by calcium except where it needs to remain flexible, such as in the leg joints. When the creature is ready to cast off its too-small shell, its body releases a chemical that softens the hard covering. Then the lobster expands its muscles, pushes from inside the shell to split it open, and backs out of the old shell. The molting process takes only about fifteen minutes, but the lobster is left unprotected for about six weeks until its new shell calcifies.

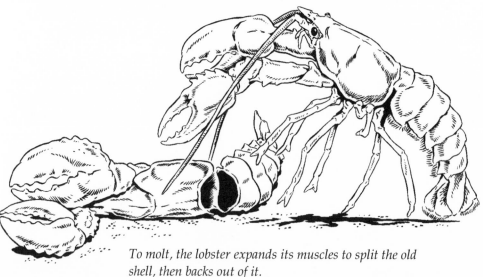

To molt, the lobster expands its muscles to split the old shell, then backs out of it.

Lobsters grow slowly and molt often. A lobster has molted five times by the time it's an inch long. A five-year-old, two-pound, ten-inch lobster may have molted twenty-five times. As the lobster ages, it molts less frequently, so an older individual may molt only once every few years.

The Northern Lobster's outer shell is usually dark green, but one in thirty million lobsters is bright blue, golden yellow, tangerine orange, or white. Color mutations often happen throughout Nature, but in the Northern Lobster's case, brightly colored individuals have another characteristic that makes them different: They grow twice as fast as their drab counterparts. As a result, finding and breeding enough fast-growing, odd-colored lobsters to stock lobster farms may someday give a boost to the lobster industry.

Interestingly, no matter what its original color, when the lobster is boiled its shell turns red. The high temperature of boiling water breaks down the violet pigment astaxanthin into another violet pigment, atacin. The release of atacin gives the cooked lobster's shell its bright red color.

When the lobster loses its old covering, it also temporarily loses its sense of balance. All forms of animal life have an organ that furnishes this sense of equilibrium. Man's sense of balance is located in the three semicircular canals of the inner ear. The position of the fluid in these canals tells your brain which way is up, even when you're upside down. When you move your head, you disturb the liquid in the canals. Sometimes, though, because of disease or other physical problems, these canals get out of order and cause dizziness, even unconsciousness.

The lobster has no ears of any kind. Instead, at the base of each of the lobster's antennules, the shorter of its two pairs of antennae, is a sac called a statocyst. These chitin-lined statocysts are covered with sensory hairs, hairs that are sensitive to touch. Sensory nerves lead from the hairs to the brain. To acquire its sense of which end is up, the lobster scrapes its antennules on the ocean floor to pick up grains of sand. The sand enters the statocyst and becomes attached with mucus to the sensory hairs. When the lobster is turned sideways or upside down, the law of gravity comes into play and the position of the sand grains changes. The lobster knows that it's right side up when the sand grains are once again correctly in place.

In order to prove that lobsters use grains of sand to give them their sense of balance, researchers carefully removed the sand from the statocysts of a lobster and replaced it with bits of iron. When the scientists held a magnet over the lobster's head, the iron bits clung to the top of the statocysts. Since this is where the sand grains would lie if the lobster were on its back, the sensory hairs signaled the brain that the lobster was upside down, the lobster promptly turned over. Then it really was upside down, although the iron bits told a different story. The lobster remained on its back until the researchers took away the magnet and let the creature's own sensory devices function properly.

Notable wildlife
Northern Lobster, *Homarus americanus*

DISCOVERY

1. Lobster Parts. Unlike Alice, you can really get to know a lobster by visiting a city aquarium or a seafood market and identifying some of this arthropod's unusual parts. (Arthropod means "jointed leg.")

PROCEDURE
1. Use the diagram on the next page to help you identify the parts of a lobster.

HEAD
(1) Two pairs of antennae ("feelers"). One pair is very long, but the other pair, located near the eyestalks, is short. All four antennae are used to smell and touch by picking up vibrations made by nearby creatures. In order to keep a constant watch for prey, as well as for enemies, the lobster constantly moves its antennae and its eyestalks.

(2) One pair of eyestalks. At the ends of these stalks are compound eyes, which are made up of hundreds of tiny lenses and are able to note even the slightest motion in the water. The eyes combine hundreds of separate images into one detailed picture, much as we put together the pieces of a jigsaw puzzle.

THORAX
(1) Four pairs of thin, jointed walking legs.
(2) One pair of large legs that end in strong claws. The larger of the two has thick teeth to crush prey, while the smaller has sharp teeth to tear food apart.

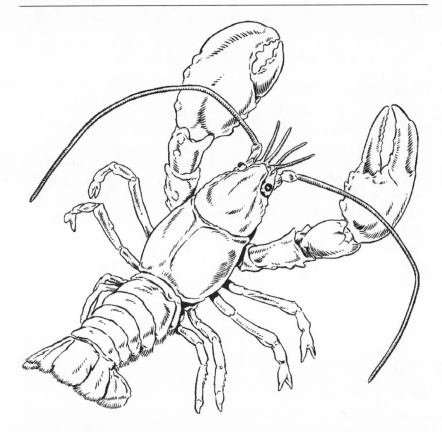

ABDOMEN and TAIL

(1) The fan-shaped tail. When the lobster wants to propel itself backward, it straightens its tail, then suddenly flips it downward.

(2) The feathery swimmerets under the tail. These help the lobster move through the water. In the female, they also hold the eggs until they hatch.

2. Be a Spinning Top. You'll really feel unbalanced when you get through with this!

PROCEDURE

1. Close your eyes and spin around in a circle.

2. Feel dizzy? The fluid in your inner ear is moving against the tiny hairs inside the canals to tell your brain that you're temporarily off balance.

3. Stand still to let the fluid inside your ear canals settle down.

3. Walk the Plank. Experience how the lobster feels after it has molted and has temporarily lost its sense of balance.

ITEMS NEEDED

six-foot-long piece of two-by-four

blindfold

PROCEDURE

1. Lay the board on flat ground or on the floor.

2. Have a partner blindfold you and help you step onto the board.

3. Try to walk the full length of the board without falling off. You can try to walk either the four-inch or the two-inch edge of the board. Do you have trouble putting one foot in front of the other? Does the board feel higher off the ground than only a few inches?

4. You were off balance only for the time you were blindfolded. What do you think would happen to the lobster if it had no statocysts and had to spend its life not knowing which way was up?

The Living Lie

Near the shore I found two sharply defined grooves in the sand; my index finger could have measured their span. Between the grooves was a faint, irregular line. Step by step, I was led out across the flat by the tracks; finally, at the temporary end of the trail, I came upon a young horseshoe crab, heading seaward.
—Rachel Carson

MORE THAN TWO FEET LONG AND EQUIPPED WITH TEN PINCER-TIPPED legs, a hard shell, and a long daggerlike tail, it looks fierce. Yet it's harmless to people and to most of the creatures that share its habitat. It's named after Polyphemus, a one-eyed giant of Greek mythology. But it has nine eyes. And, to complete the deception, this many-legged, multi-eyed, well-armed creature—the Atlantic Horseshoe Crab—isn't even a crab but is related to spiders and scorpions. As a result, scientists prefer to call the "crab" by its Latin name, *Limulus polyphemus*, rather than by its common one.

Limulus ("sidelong") and *polyphemus* ("many-eyed") describes the creature's visual equipment. The nine eyes don't work together to focus on a given object, as our eyes do, so the horseshoe crab can't make out sharp, clear images. Each of the two oval compound eyes, one on each side of the creature's shell, has eight hundred lenses sensitive to slight variations in visible, ultraviolet, and polarized light that allow the animal to distinguish between land and water. Two small eyes at the center front of the shell seem to be sensitive to ultraviolet light only; they may serve to warn the horseshoe crab of overexposure to the Sun's rays and cause it to burrow deeper into the sand to wait for night or for high tide. Finally, five photoreceptive organs, also located on the rim of the shell, see only visible light and work in conjunction with the ultraviolet-sensitive pair to give the horseshoe crab the ability to see shapes and shadows underwater.

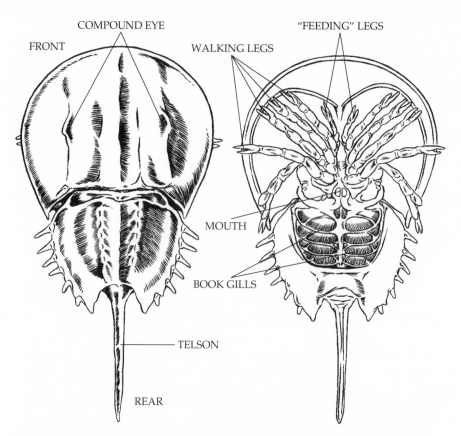

COMPOUND EYE
FRONT
"FEEDING" LEGS
WALKING LEGS
MOUTH
BOOK GILLS
TELSON
REAR

First described as the "horsefoot crab" in 1508, the creature has been studied for centuries to determine where it fits in the animal hierarchy. Biologists still disagree about how to classify the crab that isn't a crab, but most call it by the scientific name Limulus polyphemus.

Fortunately, the horseshoe crab has few natural predators; only occasionally does a large crab, sea turtle, or shark make a meal of it, and only once in a while does a lucky raccoon come upon one that hasn't made it back to the safety of deep water. In reality, the horseshoe crab is defenseless. Its claws are weak, and that swordlike tail, or telson, is useless as a weapon. It's simply a lever that the animal uses to right itself when a passing fish or a wave turns it onto its back. The creature's only defense from natural predators is to burrow into the mud to protect its soft underparts. Despite its clumsy, nonstreamlined shape, a horseshoe crab in shallow water can glide quickly to safety; the mucous coating on its shell helps reduce friction. When it detects a predator in deep water, the animal simply digs deeper into the mud. Enemies find it impossible to grip the rounded shell to loosen it from the sand.

On land, on the other hand, the horseshoe crab is awkward. To walk, it first raises its body off the ground by perching on the front pairs of legs. The claws, which are too weak and flexible to serve as weapons, fan out to distribute the animal's weight. Then, pushing down and backward with the remaining rear pair, it lurches forward, leaving a wide furrow in its wake. Looking like narrow tire treads, these furrows crisscross beaches along the mid-Atlantic shoreline each spring.

On a warm night during a Full or a New Moon, hundreds of thousands of male horseshoe crabs swarm the Atlantic shoreline, and wait. But not for long. Almost immediately, throngs of females, much larger than the males and laden with up to one hundred thousand eggs each, join them in the shallow water. As each female passes through the stag line of waiting suitors, a male uses his claws to grasp her shell and tail and is towed to the water's edge. His claws are strong nippers; if he's picked up by his tail, he and the female can be lifted as one.

Once ashore, the female digs a hole eight inches deep in the sand and lays from two hundred to four thousand pale, gray-green, gel-covered eggs, each with a diameter of about one-eighth inch (4 mm), in the depression. The female makes several nests in this way,

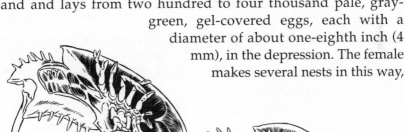

The Horseshoe Crab
uses its tail not to defend itself
but to turn itself right side up.
To turn over, the animal arches
its body and pushes its telson into
the sand, rocks from side to side,
and then flips over onto its belly.

During Full Moons in late spring and summer, Atlantic Horseshoe Crabs crawl ashore by the thousands to lay eggs in the sand.

and the male fertilizes the jellylike cluster of eggs in each of them. Then the creatures slowly return to the deeper water as the tide falls. In Delaware Bay alone, more than a million horseshoe crabs plod ashore and mate each May.

As dawn breaks, fish, eels, shrimp, gulls, terns, and shorebirds gorge themselves on the eggs, some of which have been carried, unlaid, back to the shallow water. Too impatient to probe for eggs in nests, the larger birds attack the crabs, flipping them over and striking at their unprotected underbellies to get at the eggs underneath. For birds migrating from South and Central America north to their Arctic breeding grounds, the feast of eggs refuels them for the rest of the journey.

Waves cover the surviving eggs with sand, protecting them from predators, heat, and rain. Because the eggs were laid during a Full or a New Moon, and therefore when the tide was high, the water line won't reach the nests and wash the eggs out to sea until the next high tide. The egg grows. As it swells, its covering splits, revealing a tiny transparent "pea" that contains a baby horseshoe crab, complete with gills, legs, and eyes, but no sword tail. The creature molts four times in this stage.

When it's about twenty-eight days old—at about the time of the next Full Moon—the embryo rubs against the sand to burst its protective covering. The sand-colored larva that emerges is only one fourth inch (8 mm) long. It is caught in the next high tide and is carried to the sea, where it uses its legs and leaflike gills to paddle in a zigzag pattern to escape predators. It swims upside down because its shell is so heavy. Now that it has survived the egg stage, the little creature is again a potential victim of fish, eels, shrimp, and seabirds.

After spending three weeks in the larval stage, it drops to the bottom of the ocean, where it molts. After the first larval molt, it has its tail, or telson. The larva remains buried in the sand until its shell, or exoskeleton, hardens. The Atlantic Horseshoe Crab molts its shell as it grows, and during each molt, the creature burrows into the sand to protect itself. After several years and several molts, the animal is about eight inches (20 cm) long, including the tail. A twelve-year-old female may measure thirty inches (76 cm) from the tip of the snout to the tip of the tail and weigh ten pounds.

Although harmless, in past years the horseshoe crab was considered an economic threat. In reality, the creature feeds on the major predators of shellfish and thus provides a service to commercial fishermen. For example, the Oyster Drill, a snail that makes a neat round hole in the shells of oysters to reach the meat inside, can destroy 60 percent of an oyster bed if left to reproduce at will. The horseshoe crab does a lot to keep Oyster Drill populations in check.

Although not valuable as a human food source, the horseshoe crab has become important for other reasons. For the past century, researchers have studied the creature's visual system and its blood in hopes of finding cures for human diseases. Knowing how different types of eyes perform certain functions provides researchers with a better understanding of how the human eye perceives borders, lines, and contrasts. This knowledge may lead to cures for partial or total blindness caused by degenerative eye diseases.

In 1885 researchers discovered that the bluish white blood of the Atlantic Horseshoe Crab doesn't tolerate bacteria. Fever-causing bacteria give off a toxin, which, when present in blood, causes a substance made from horseshoe crab blood to clot around the bacteria, isolating them and stopping them from spreading. Scientists now extract blood from horseshoe crabs to test for the presence of the bacteria that cause meningitis and venereal disease in humans. Taking the crab's blood seems to do the creature no harm, and using it to detect the presence of bacteria in humans leads to prompt treatment of potentially fatal diseases.

The horseshoe crab has made the journey from alleged scavenger to true lifesaver. Yet new threats face the animal. Because its numbers seem abundant and they are easy to net, when they come ashore to lay and fertilize their eggs, the peaceful creatures are caught to be chopped into pieces and used as fertilizer and lobster bait. In addition, the eggs themselves are used as eel bait. When a million horseshoe crabs gather along a mile of beach in one peak night in June to lay millions and millions of eggs, harvesters gather the females and chop them up to bait eel traps. The eels are exported to countries where they're considered gourmet fare. Unfortunately, people gather the eggs by cracking open the females and leaving them to die. Shorebird researchers in Delaware Bay and other primary horseshoe crab mating areas warn that about every two years, the horseshoe crab population is reduced by 50 percent. No species can survive long under such conditions.

In Nature's reproduction formula, horseshoe crab males have consistently outnumbered females by a ratio as high as eleven to one, probably to make it more likely that most of the hundreds of thousands of eggs laid during the mating season are fertilized. Since many of the eggs become food for coastal fish and birds, and since fish and other sea creatures eat countless larvae after they've reached the ocean, millions of eggs must be laid to ensure that a relatively few horseshoe crabs grow to adulthood.

The practice of killing thousands of females to get the eggs each summer is threatening the existence of the Atlantic Horseshoe Crab as a species. Sometimes the simplest creatures have the most to offer, but by the time we appreciate that fact, they may be gone.

Notable wildlife
Atlantic Horseshoe Crab, *Limulus polyphemus*
Oyster Drill, *Urosalpinx cinerea*

DISCOVERY

1. Castoffs. The Atlantic Horseshoe Crab molts its shell regularly.
PROCEDURE
1. Search for molted horseshoe crab shells, or casts, on an East Coast beach. The casts often are washed up onshore or left after egg laying when an adult horseshoe crab becomes the victim of a bird, eel, or fish.

The Crustacean with the Custom Home

A castle after all is but a house—the dullest one when lacking company.
—James Sheridan Knowles

A HOUSE-HUNTING HERMIT CRAB WILL KILL A WHELK JUST TO TRY ON ITS shell. Then the persnickety predator is just as likely to move back into its old shell as it is to keep the new one. A hermit crab also will pull another hermit crab from a coveted shell to claim it for a home. Some hermit crab species prefer certain snail shells over others, and two crabs occasionally argue over which gets that one perfect home. Accompanied by high-pitched whirring and chirping sounds, two tiny Long-clawed Hermit Crabs, for example, may compete for the same periwinkle shell. These feisty little crabs congregate in groups of hundreds of thousands. When you pick one up by the shell, it doesn't withdraw but struggles to get away, hanging out of its shell and in some cases abandoning the shell in favor of escaping. Or a pair of large Red Hermit Crabs may battle for the same heavy shell of the Queen Conch. The winner struts away on tiptoe, with its antennae outstretched in victory.

The hermit crab is unique in the world of crustaceans. Most crustaceans, such as shrimp, lobsters, and other crabs, grow their own shells. A few, such as slugs, do not need shells. But unlike its fellow crustaceans, the hermit crab compromises: It needs a shell to survive, but it doesn't produce one, so it appropriates one.

As do other crustaceans, the hermit crab outgrows its hard outer skin, the exoskeleton, as it grows. So periodically, the hermit crab molts its too-small exoskeleton while lying in damp sand. The crab eats the calcium-rich cast-off covering, absorbing the minerals it contains to carry on life processes, including building a new outer skin. The new covering hardens in a few days.

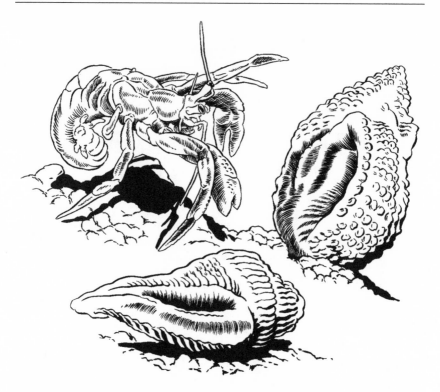

This unprotected hermit crab needs to find a well-fitting shell or it will die. It may try on several before finding the perfect one.

After each molt, the hermit crab goes in search of a new snail shell. Because the hermit crab's soft abdomen (the rear end of its body) coils to the right, and because almost all snails are right-hand twisted, the crab has little difficulty finding a perfectly fitting shell. The shell provides protection from predators and keeps the crab's abdomen from drying out. In a "three bears" kind of scenario, some shells are too small, others are too large, and still others are just right. A too-small shell leaves part of the crab exposed and vulnerable to hungry gulls and other crabs. A too-large one invites bacteria to enter and grow, eventually killing the animal. But a well-fitting shell provides protection from all such dangers.

Yet some species of hermit crabs aren't satisfied with merely finding a shell that's the right size, shape, and weight. For example, some hermit crabs abandon their plain shells in favor of more ornate ones. Other crabs place various kinds of sea anemones on the shell, transplanting the anemones when it outgrows the shell. Still another crab carries sea anemones only on its big front claw—and this species of anemone is never found anywhere else.

A perfect fit keeps out predators and disease-causing bacteria. Notice how the crab uses its claw as a door.

The reddish-and-brown-striped Cloak Anemone lives only on shells occupied by hermit crabs. Although this colorful anemone can be found on several species of hermit crabs, it seems to prefer the shells of hermit crabs that remain in deeper water. Therefore, because it can't endure long periods of exposure to the drying effects of air, the Cloak Anemone has a symbiotic relationship with the big, hairy Red Hermit Crab, which may carry as many as twenty Cloak Anemones.

Not content with a plain shell, this hermit crab has adorned it with flowerlike sea anemones. In return for providing camouflage, the anemones are allowed to share some of the crab's dinner.

In experiments conducted with octopuses and one of their favorite meals, hermit crabs, marine biologists proved that a undecorated hermit crab has a far greater chance of being eaten than does one that carries anemones. When hermit crabs without anemones were put in tanks with hungry octopuses, the octopuses made as many as twelve attacks in 6 hours. None of the crabs survived longer than 89 hours. But when hermit crabs with Cloak Anemones were available to the octopuses, the octopuses still attacked but were unsuccessful. When these experiments ended 150 hours later, these "cloaked" hermit crabs were still alive and the octopuses were still hungry. What made the difference? The stinging cells of the anemones had kept the octopuses from chomping down on the crabs.

In return for camouflaging the crab and protecting it with its stinging tentacles, the anemones feed on bits of food that float upward as the crab eats or on tiny creatures that the crab stirs up as it scoots along the ocean floor. Sometimes an impatient anemone stretches over the crab and snatches the food before its host gets even a taste, but in general the situation is balanced, for the crab is just as likely to gobble down all the food if the anemone doesn't react quickly enough to grab some for itself.

Once inside its home shell, the crab grips the inner wall of the shell with special appendages called rasps. The creature holds on so firmly that it can't be forcibly removed without injury. It uses its distinctive foreclaw as a tight-fitting door over the opening of the snail shell.

Hermit crabs should be left in their natural habitats, where you can observe them in shallow water. You can pick one up, rest it in the palm of your hand, and wait patiently for the little animal to come out so that you can examine the eyes on the ends of stalks, the legs, and the front claws to try, with the aid of a field guide, to identify it. But you shouldn't take it home as a pet. A hermit crab in captivity usually remains inactive and quickly dies. Enjoy this creature where it thrives, along the ocean shores.

Notable wildlife
Striped Hermit Crab, *Clibanarius vittatus*
Long-clawed Hermit Crab, *Pagurus longicarpus*
Red Hermit Crab, *Petrochirus diogenes*
Queen Conch, *Strombu gigas*
Cloak Anemone, *Calliactis tricolor*

DISCOVERY

1. Hermit Crab Race. Even if you don't win, this game will leave you laughing.

ITEMS NEEDED

two cardboard cartons large enough to get under

PROCEDURE

1. Mark a starting line and a finish line. Place the cardboard boxes at the finish.

2. You and a friend should sit on the floor or lawn with your backs toward the finish line.

3. At the signal "Go!" walk backward on your hands and feet, face up with your backs raised and parallel to the ground.

4. Whoever gets a new shell (gets under the box) first wins. (All four edges of the box must be resting on the floor, and the player must be completely hidden.)

Variation: This game can also be played as a relay race. As each team member reaches the finish line, he or she gets under the box, then stands up and runs back to the waiting players and touches the next person, who should be sitting and ready to assume the position of a scurrying crab.

Living Skeletons

*In other parts of the sea are seen sponges of various
magnitude, and extraordinary appearances,
assuming a variety of fantastic forms like large
mushrooms, fonts, and flower-pots.*
—Oliver Goldsmith

THE JAPANESE TRADITIONALLY PRESENT A LACY SKELETON OF THE
Venus's-Flowerbasket Sponge to newlyweds. The custom developed because of the lifestyle of a sponge-dwelling shrimp. A mated
pair of deep-sea shrimp enters the flowerbasket when the shrimp
and the sponge are small. The shrimp live on the food that enters
the sponge's digestive system, and as they grow, they become
imprisoned. The three creatures spend their lives together. The
remains of the two shrimp encased forever in the glistening skeleton symbolize eternal love and devotion.

Biologists were stumped for decades about how to classify the
sponges in the scientific system of plants and animals. The things
looked like plants and, consigned to spend their lives anchored in
one spot, acted like plants. But even with no head, mouth, or internal organs, they ate, breathed, and reproduced, characteristics usually attributed to animals. Finally, in the late nineteenth century,
John Flemming, a professor of natural history at King's College in
Edinburgh, studied sponges carefully enough to determine that
each of the world's hundreds of species was one of a class of
Earth's most primitive multicelled animals.

Sponges live in all the world's seas and belong to the phylum
Porifera, meaning "pore bearer." Water flows into the sponge
through openings called ostia. The ostia lead to a system of internal
canals that in turn lead to a central chamber called the spongocoel.
Tiny hairs, or cilia, line each spongocoel. As the threadlike cilia
whip around, they help to push the water through the sponge.
Cells in the spongocoels absorb oxygen and microscopic plants and

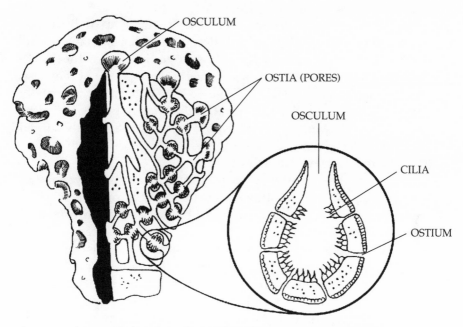

Spongocoel magnified to show the hairlike cilia lining the inner walls.

animals from the water. The sponge must process a ton of water to gain an ounce of weight. The filtered water is ejected through outgoing canals, collecting body wastes as it flows through, and is eventually expelled through the large opening called the osculum.

Each sponge is capable of two methods of reproduction, one plantlike and one animal-like. Like a plant, a sponge may develop buds that break off and grow into new sponges. Like some animals, the same sponge may be a hermaphrodite, both male and female, producing both eggs and spermatozoa. The eggs remain attached to the body until they're fertilized by the spermatozoa. A free-swimming larva the size of a pinhead and covered with cilia emerges from each mature egg and is swept through the canals to the outside, where it drops to the bottom of the ocean, attaches itself to a solid surface, and remains there to develop into an adult sponge.

Like most simple animals, the sponge has remarkable regenerative powers, so it can easily replace lost parts. In addition, if a full-grown sponge is cut into small pieces, each piece also becomes a full-grown sponge within about five years.

Sponges are divided into three main classifications: Hexactinella, Calcarea, and Demospongial. The Hexactinella are the glass sponges, deep-water creatures that are most abundant at three thousand feet below sea level. They're made up of distinctive six-rayed needles of glass called siliceous spicules that take several forms, including those of the Glass-Rope Sponge of the North Atlantic Ocean and the Venus's-Flowerbasket Sponge of the western Pacific Ocean. The Glass-Rope Sponge consists of unusually long spicules that twist and spiral as the sponge grows along the ocean floor. The Venus's-Flowerbasket grows into a slightly curved column fifteen inches (38 cm) high. Its latticework skeleton is often cleaned and displayed as an ornament.

Despite their tendency to take over their watery habitat, sponges are valuable to other sea creatures. They provide food for angelfish, filefish, and sea slugs and home bases for brittle stars and anemones. In addition, tiny fishes like gobies, cardinalfish, toadfish, and blennies find safety in the sponge's canals and chambers. Shrimp, immature lobsters, barnacles, crabs, clams, and sea worms also find temporary havens or make permanent homes, complete with water-driven room service, inside sponges. One crab, the Sponge-dwelling Hermit Crab, can be found only inside the Hermit Crab Sponge. The fuzzy little crab strains plankton from the water flowing through the sponge. And the Hermit Crab Sponge grows over other species of hermit crabs, including the Flat-clawed Hermit Crab and Long-clawed Hermit Crab of the Atlantic coast. Sometimes these little crabs carry so many sponges that they have difficulty moving about on the sand. Other species of hermit crabs prefer to attach camouflaging pieces of sponge of their own choosing to their backs.

Researchers have found that the sponge can contribue to human healing. For example, the Fire Sponge, which lives off the coast of Florida and causes skin irritation when touched, yields eight antibiotics; other species produce substances that kill bacteria and inhibit cancer. But for most of us, what makes sponges useful is the capacity of some to soften as they absorb water.

The Common Loggerhead Sponge, which grows at a depth of up to 650 feet off Florida's west coast, Key West, the Bahamas, and Cuba, is the sponge that we know commercially. A member of the Demospongiae class, the Loggerhead can grow to be three feet in diameter and consists of dark purple fibers that form a dense network of canals. To harvest this large sponge, fishermen may dredge the ocean bottom or, working in teams of two from a glass-bottom boat, collect them by using a long, hooked pole. In the latter case, one person spots the sponges through the bottom of the boat and guides his pole-wielding partner's hook to them. The collected sponges are spread out until the soft parts disintegrate, then the skeletons are bleached and dried. They are hard to the touch when dry, but their canals and chambers readily fill with water and their fibrous skeletons soften when wet. They can be used for anything from bathing babies to washing automobiles.

Notable wildlife

Venus's-Flowerbasket Sponge, *Euplectella speciosissima*
Glass-Rope Sponge, *Hyalonema sieboldii*
Hermit Crab Sponge, *Xestospongia halichondrioides*
Sponge-dwelling Hermit Crab, *Paguristes kubliskii*
Flat-clawed Hermit Crab, *Pagurus pollicaris*
Long-clawed Hermit Crab, *Pagurus longicarpus*
Fire Sponge, *Tedania ignis*
Loggerhead Sponge, *Spheciospongia vesparium*

DISCOVERY

1. Testing Absorption. Find out for yourself if all sponges are created equal.

ITEMS NEEDED

natural sponge   two one-cup measures
cellulose sponge

PROCEDURE

1. Cut the cellulose sponge the same size as the natural one.

2. Pour one cup of water in each of two bowls.

3. Place one sponge in each bowl.

4. Without squeezing, remove one sponge. Squeeze the water it holds into a measuring cup. Repeat with the other sponge.

5. Which sponge holds more water? Which sponge feels softer when it's wet?

2. Get to Know a Sponge. It's easy to see how small sea creatures can live in a sponge's canals.

ITEMS NEEDED

natural sponge
scissors

PROCEDURE

1. Pull or cut apart the natural sponge to expose the canals.

2. Can you follow one to a spongocoel? Does the sponge have an opening that seems larger than the others and therefore may be what's left of the osculum?

Snails Dextral and Sinistral

The snail, which everywhere doth roam,
Carrying his own house still, still is home.
　　　　—John Donne, "To Sir Henry Wolton"

MOST SNAILS ARE RIGHT-HANDED; THAT IS, THEIR SHELLS TWIST IN A clockwise direction as seen from the top. When you hold a snail with its aperture, or opening, facing you and with the apex, the pointed end, at the top, the opening is on the right. This design leaves room for the heart and other internal organs on the left.

Nine out of ten people, or 90 percent, are right-handed, or dextral; the rest of the population is left-handed, or sinistral. But the odds of finding a left-handed representative of a normally right-handed species of snail are one in a million. There are, however, a few North American snails that are naturally sinistral. Triphoras, a group of left-handed horn shells, are common on the Atlantic and Pacific coasts of North America; all of these are slender and one-fourth inch (.8 mm) or less tall (snail shells are measured in terms of height, not length). And Lightning Whelks, also known as Left-handed Whelks, which live in shallow coastal waters of South Carolina, Georgia, and Florida, range in height from seven to ten inches (17.5–25 cm). A matching pair of Lightning Whelk shells, one left-handed and one a rare right-handed specimen, may bring several hundred dollars from a collector.

The snail is a soft-bodied animal that's protected by a shell of its own making while it creeps along on a single flat foot. It fits into the larger classification of shellfish called mollusks, the group that includes clams, scallops, mussels, oysters, slugs, squids, and octopuses. What distinguishes it from the other mollusks is that it has just one shell, or valve, so it's sometimes called a univalve. Depending on the species, it can live from two to twenty years and may eat only vegetation, only meat, or a combination of both.

The single shell of a snail, unlike the double shell of a bivalve,

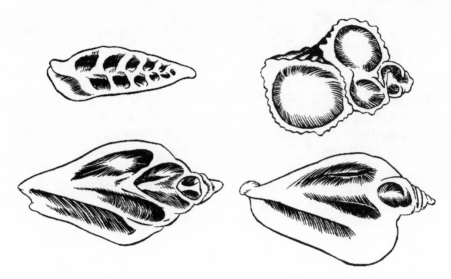

Cross sections of snail shells from the side (left) *and the top. Was this snail right-handed or left-handed?*

winds around itself, enclosing the animal inside. The snail extends and retracts its soft body through the shell's opening, or aperture. When threatened by an enemy or by the drying effects of full sun, the snail shuts itself up tightly within the spiral shell by pulling a hard plate, the operculum, over the aperture. When the tide is out, the air bubble trapped inside the shell provides oxygen for the animal.

All snails produce shells in much the same way, yet each species has its own distinctive shape, size, and combination of color, pattern, and texture. Cone-shaped limpets, rounded cowries, and coronetlike conchs are all snails, as are tiny periwinkles and huge whelks and murexes. The snail extracts shell-building minerals from its food. The minerals enter the bloodstream and are carried to the mantle, a thin fleshy tissue inside the shell.

The mantle contains an assortment of specialized glands. The glands along the edge of the mantle secrete the outer and inner layers of the shell; those distributed on the entire outer side of the mantle produce the inner layer of the shell. In some snails, the shell-making glands evenly deposit calcium carbonate, or lime, to form a smooth outer shell. In others, the glands deposit the calcium carbonate unevenly, resulting in a shell that's ridged, beaded, or spiked. Some glands secrete liquid lime, and others produce a quick-acting hardener. Spikes, ridges, and rows of beadlike knots often form lines of demarcation between new growth and old.

Excess lime forms a thick outer lip along the aperture in some species and creates long, thin spines in others.

As the lime is deposited, color glands secrete coloring agents. If the snail continuously adds color from one gland, the shell has one stripe. If color is secreted simultaneously from three glands, the shell has three stripes. If the color flow is intermittent, the shell is patterned with bars. And if the glands spurt shots of color, the shell is spotted. Some shells get their distinct patterns when several types of ducts from the glands operate at the same time. At other times, the ducts go off and on in a well-orchestrated sequence of colors and intervals, producing bands as well as spots.

Snails can be found almost anywhere: in fresh water, in salt water, on land, and even in trees. Freshwater snails live along the edges of ponds, streams, swamps, and ditches. Some have gills and take oxygen from the water; others have lungs and must surface occasionally to breathe. Freshwater species are generally omnivorous, feeding on water plants as well as on dead animals. One freshwater species, the Apple Snail, is important to an endangered bird species called the Snail Kite. The kite feeds almost exclusively on these two-inch (5 cm), brown, globular univalves, which live on the plant life growing in the marshes and canals of southern Florida's Everglades. But much of the Apple Snail's habitat is being filled in to provide more land for development. As the Everglades ecosystem shrinks, the supply of snails is diminishing and the kite's survival is threatened.

Marine snails, which live in salty coastal waters, have gills. They eat seaweed or drill through the shells of other mollusks to get a fresh seafood dinner. A few marine snails are parasites, living on starfish or in coral.

Land species generally live in damp environments under leaf litter, stones, and the bark of rotting logs, although a few southern species live in trees. To avoid the drying effects of the Sun, land snails typically venture out only at night, when they feed on plants, including those in flowerbeds and vegetable gardens.

Regardless of the variety of the shapes of their shells and where they live, all univalves share several physical characteristics. Each has a distinct head equipped with a pair of tentacles, a pair of eyes on the ends of stalks, and a tongue with tiny teeth. Land snails use these teeth to tear vegetation, freshwater snails to scrape algae from rocks, and saltwater snails to drill holes into the shells of prey such as oysters. And almost all snails use a strong muscle called the foot to creep along the ground, move along the ocean floor, or slowly climb plant stems and tree trunks. The animal's scientific classification, Gastropoda, means "one that walks on its stomach" and describes the way the snail moves from place to place. A gland located behind the foot of a land snail secretes a slimy mucus to lay a slick path for the creature to follow. After laying its track, the snail easily glides forward with a backward rippling motion of its foot.

The habits of snails are just as varied as their colors and patterns. The limpet, for example, establishes a home base on a rock. It leaves to forage for food, then returns to the same spot, where the action of its muscular foot wears a smooth place on the hard surface. The limpet attaches itself so firmly to this place that no amount of pushing or pulling can remove it. Only a knife blade slipped between the shell and the rock can dislodge the snail. Since it has no switchblade-carrying natural enemies, it has only to hang on tightly to protect itself. The Common Slipper Shell also attaches itself to a rock, but it usually ends up as part of a "totem pole" formed by as many as a dozen of its kind piled on top of one another. The larger, female slipper shells form the base of the stack, where they lay their eggs. Hermaphrodites are in the middle of the stack as they change from male to female, and males form the top.

There's nothing unusual about the home life of the Florida Fighting Conch, but its means of escape is unique. Not at all aggressive, despite what its name suggests, this four-inch (10 cm) conch occasionally challenges another of its species in a territorial dispute. But the Florida Fighting Conch prefers to somersault away from danger.

Notable wildlife
> Apple Snail, *Pomacea paludosa*
> Snail Kite, *Rostrhamus sociabilis*
> Lightning Whelk, *Busycon contrarium*
> Limpets, Families *Acmaeidae, Calyptraeidae*
> Common Slipper Shell, *Crepidula fornicata*
> Florida Fighting Conch, *Strombus alatus*

DISCOVERY

1. Have a Snail Race. In a new twist on an old theme, you win this race by going *slower* than anyone else!
> ITEMS NEEDED
>> chalk or stick
>> bicycles

PROCEDURE

1. On a driveway or other smooth surface away from car traffic, draw a starting line and a finish line at least twenty feet apart.

2. Then, on bicycles, see who can ride the slowest without touching the ground with a foot. In this race, the slowest rider wins. (By the way, the average speed of a snail is two inches [5 cm] a minute. How did your speed compare?)

2. Celebrate International Left-handers Day. Even though it falls on August 13, you can do this anytime.

ITEMS NEEDED

piece of rope, or a scarf

PROCEDURE

1. Have someone tie your dominant hand, the one that you use to hold a pen or a fork, behind your back for an hour—or a day, if you're really adventurous.

2. Do what you normally would do in the course of the day.

3. Did you feel clumsy? Did you adapt? Do you think that you could ever train yourself to become ambidextrous (able to use both hands equally well)?

3. Make a Collection of Snail Shells. See how many different snails you can identify, and learn some Latin in the process.

ITEMS NEEDED

bucket

egg cartons or plastic ice cube trays

field guide to shells

PROCEDURE

1. Walk on a beach and collect snail shells in your bucket.

2. Identify them by using a field guide to shells.

3. Store the shells in egg cartons or ice cube trays, labeling each compartment with the shell's common and scientific (Latin) name.

4. Mollusk Mobile. Put your collection to practical use. This mobile makes a much better souvenir of your trip to the beach than a painted sand dollar does! IMPORTANT: Adult supervision is needed for this activity.

ITEMS NEEDED

bucket

field guide to shells

three- to four-inch-diameter plastic lid from margarine tub

four-pound test weight clear
fishing line
assorted small seashells
craft glue
paper punch
drill with sixteenth-inch bit

PROCEDURE

1. Walk the beach and collect univalve and bivalve shells.

2. Identify them using the field guide.

3. Now make a mobile. With the paper punch, punch four or five holes in the plastic lid about one-fourth inch from the edge. This is the bottom of the hanger. Then punch a hole in the top center.

4. Ask an adult to drill holes in the tops of several of the shells.

5. String the shells on fishing line. Vary the strands of shells by using different lengths of line and by tying two or three shells along some strands and only one on others. Then tie the strings of shells to the holes in the lid. Put a drop of craft glue on the knots to reinforce them.

6. Loop a long piece of fishing line through the hole at the top of the hanger, and tie the ends together to double it. Reinforce the knot with glue.

7. Spread craft glue liberally on one side of the lid. Cover the lid with small shells. Let dry.

8. Spread glue on the other side of the lid, and cover with shells. Let dry.

9. Hang your ornament in a window.

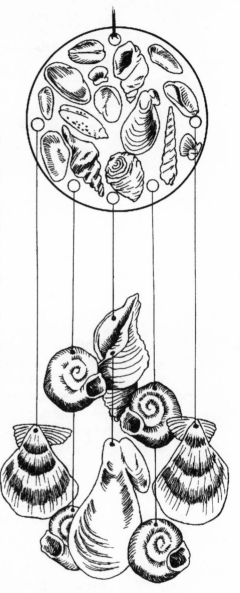

Of Gills and Air Bladders

Ocean: A body of water occupying about two-thirds
of a world made for man—who has no gills.
  —Ambrose Bierce, *The Devil's Dictionary*

ANYONE WHO TRIES TO HOLD HIS BREATH FOR ONLY A MINUTE QUICKLY finds out just how short a time sixty seconds really is. To stay underwater longer than that short minute, a diver must carry an external air supply. But the human respiratory system, which fails us underwater, certainly works well on land.

An adult human uses about twenty-three thousand gallons of air every day. Men draw in and expel air an average of 17,300 times a day, while women breathe an average of 28,000 times. When a person is working strenuously or is excited, the breathing rate increases; the rate slows down during inactivity and sleep.

With each breath, air taken in through the mouth or nose passes through the larynx, or voice box, and enters the trachea, a column of elastic tissue also called the windpipe. The trachea is attached to the lungs. Inside the lungs, it divides into two bronchial tubes. These bronchial tubes branch again into thinner and thinner tubes called bronchioles. The structure inside the lungs looks very much like an inverted oak or maple that has lost its leaves, and as a result, it is referred to as the bronchial tree. At the ends of the thinnest bronchioles are clusters of air sacs, or alveoli, rich with minute blood vessels called capillaries. The capillaries absorb oxygen from the air and release carbon dioxide as a waste product.

At the bottom of the chest cavity, below the lungs, is a thick sheet of muscle called the diaphragm. The diaphragm, not the lungs, does the real work of breathing. To take air into the body, the diaphragm moves down to allow the ribs to spread and make space for the lungs to expand. Air rushes in. Then, as air is expelled, the diaphragm moves up so that the ribs come together again and push the air out of the lungs.

As underwater creatures, fish rely on a completely different method of breathing. Most of the world's twenty-one thousand fish species have four feathery breathing organs called gills; these are located in gill chambers behind the back of the mouth, on each side of the head. Each gill is formed of a double row of flexible, closely spaced filaments attached to a support called the gill arch. Lamellae, thin plates of tissue, range along each filament.

To inhale, the fish opens its mouth and closes its gill covers. The gill cover is a flap of bone or skin. Almost simultaneously, the fish expands the walls of its mouth, an action that creates suction and draws in water. When its mouth is full of water, the fish closes it again. Then the fish opens its gill covers, presses the walls of its mouth together, and forces the water into the gill chambers. As the water passes over the gills, blood vessels in the lamellae absorb about 75 percent of the available oxygen from the water.

Most fish species are also equipped with an air bladder, or swim bladder, a saclike organ that provides buoyancy. To rise to a higher depth, the fish uses gases produced by the blood to inflate the bladder; to swim deeper, it deflates the bladder. When the fish is at rest or is in deep water, where water pressure increases, the amount of gas in the air bladder is automatically regulated by the nervous system to keep the fish at a constant depth. A variation of this air bladder concept is used by submarines. To dive, the sub's ballast tanks, located between the inner and outer hulls, are flooded with water; to surface, compressed air is blown into the tanks, forcing the water out and allowing the ship to rise.

Just as a human must keep his or her arms and legs constantly moving in order to tread water, a fish without an air bladder must

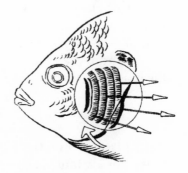

Left: *With gill covers closed, the fish expands the sides of its head and takes water into its mouth.* Right: *Then the fish closes its mouth, compresses its "cheeks," and forces water out through the gills.*

By using its air bladder as a lung, the lungfish can travel over land.

move constantly to keep from sinking. Swimming not only propels the fish but also keeps it afloat. For that reason, rays, sharks, hagfish, and other bladderless species generally remain in deep water.

The air bladder may also serve additional functions. Some fish species use it to produce sound. Others use it as an auxiliary air supply—like having built-in scuba (self-contained underwater breathing apparatus) gear. The most unusual function of the air bladder is seen in the lungfish. In these freshwater fish of Australia, Africa, and South America, the bladder is an air-breathing lung. To breathe, the lungfish goes to the surface to take in air through its mouth. The air goes into the air bladder, which has an abundant supply of blood vessels to absorb oxygen and release carbon dioxide. A few North American fishes—gars, bowfins, and catfish, for example—have rudimentary lungs on the gills and are able to take oxygen from the air if the oxygen content of the water is low. But the lungfish—unique in the fish world—breathes only air.

DISCOVERY

1. Hold Your Breath. Experienced divers routinely hold their breath for a minute or more. Can you?

    ITEMS NEEDED

        stopwatch or watch with second hand

PROCEDURE

1. Take a deep breath, and have a friend time how long you can hold it.

2. Practice until you can hold your breath for a full minute on land.

3. Try to hold your breath for just as long underwater. Does water pressure seem to affect how long you can hold your breath?

2. To Float or Not to Float. Find out for yourself what buoyancy is.

ITEMS NEEDED

stone, at least two inches in diameter

balloon

cork

PROCEDURE

1. Fill a sink with water.

2. Blow up the balloon

3. Gently place the inflated balloon, the cork, and the stone on the surface of the water.

4. What happens? The degree of buoyancy that an object has depends on the amount of air it contains. Which of the three objects is most like a fish's air bladder?

3. Bladder Buoyancy. How does a fish's air bladder work? See for yourself.

ITEMS NEEDED

small glass jar with lid

PROCEDURE

1. Fill a sink with water.

2. Fill the jar about half full of water and put on the lid.

3. Put the jar in the water in the sink. What happens?

4. If the jar sank to the bottom, pour out some water. If it floated to the top, add some.

5. Adjust the amount of water in the jar until it stays submerged just under the surface of the water.

6. The jar represents a fish, and the air in the jar acts as the air bladder. You had to use trial and error to perfectly adjust the balance of air and water. The fish does this automatically!

Bubbles

A soap bubble is the most beautiful thing, and the most exquisite, in nature.
—Mark Twain

BUBBLES ARE LIGHT AND BOUNCY. BUBBLES BEND LIGHT INTO BEAUTIFUL, iridescent rainbows. Bubbles make taking baths and washing dishes fun. Bubbles can be caught on a finger or scattered in a breeze. Do you agree with all those descriptions of a bubble? Here's another: Animals of many kinds use bubbles for protection, transportation, food collection, and habitation.

The froghopper is an insect that lays its eggs on plant stems in spring and summer. The eggs hatch the following spring. The larvae of some froghopper species make bubbles to create a climate-controlled environment; those that do so are called spittlebugs. The spittlebug positions itself head downward and tail upward on the plant stem. As digested waste is excreted from the hind end of the insect, it runs down the stem and underneath the abdomen of the spittlebug, where it mixes with a sticky substance secreted by special glands. Overlapping plates on the spittlebug's abdomen form a chamber into which the insect draws air and then expels it. The action of the plates whips the liquid mixture and air into a foamy mass that covers the larva's body. The spittlebug spends its early days hidden inside the gooey froth where, protected from the drying rays of the Sun, it sucks plant juices. Spittlebugs that are removed from the foam quickly die. Their skin must stay moist if they're to survive; without their bubble "cocoon," their bodies rapidly dehydrate.

The Water Spider of Europe and Asia uses bubbles to construct its home. The creature first spins a slightly curved web underwater, attaching it to water plants growing in ponds and lakes. Then it fetches an air bubble by swimming to the surface of the water, grasping a bubble close to its body between its hind legs, and car-

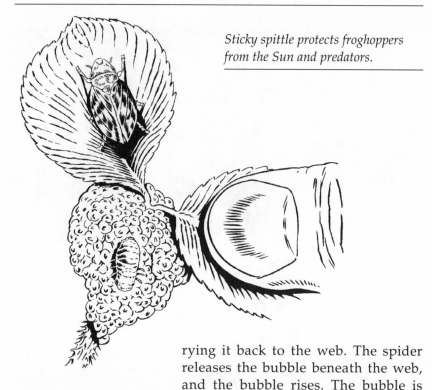

Sticky spittle protects froghoppers from the Sun and predators.

rying it back to the web. The spider releases the bubble beneath the web, and the bubble rises. The bubble is caught by the web, causing it to form a greater curve. Bubble by bubble, the spider's accumulating oxygen supply increases the size of its nest until the web becomes bell shaped.

The Water Spider breathes through book gills. As they move oxygen into the spider's lungs, these thin sheets of tissue look and act like the pages of a book being turned by an invisible finger. As the spider uses up the stored oxygen, it collects more air bubbles to replenish the supply. Carbon dioxide exhaled by the spider is released into the water, where it disperses.

The male Siamese Fighting Fish, or betta, also uses bubbles to make a nest. First, this two-and-a-half-inch-long deep red or deep blue fish finds a quiet spot sheltered by plants. Then he swims to the surface of the water to gulp air. Finally, he swims under the chosen spot and releases the air bubble. Each bubble is covered with mucus to provide strength and to allow it to stick to the others. The finished nest is round and flattened, about two inches (5 cm) in diameter and one-half inch (16 mm) thick.When he completes the nest, the male waits for the female.

When the female arrives, the pair mates. Soon the female begins to lay eggs in the water. As the eggs begin to sink to the bot-

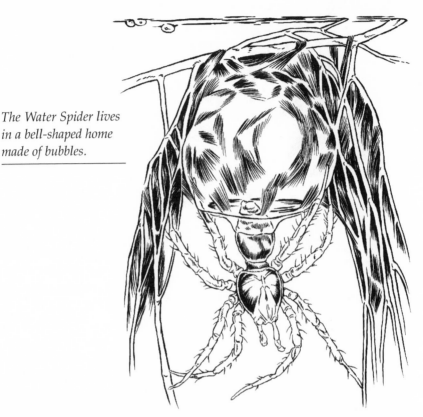

*The Water Spider lives
in a bell-shaped home
made of bubbles.*

tom, both parents catch them in their mouths and carry them to the
nest. The eggs stick to the bubbles until they hatch a few days later.

During incubation and after hatching, the male is the sole pro-
tector of the eggs and young. He drives away the female (which
would eat the newborns if allowed to stay) and all other fish predators; carries eggs and newborns, a few at a time, in his mouth to
give them fresh oxygen; retrieves fallen eggs and straying hatch-
lings; and replaces bubbles as they break. When the young fish are
able to care for themselves, the male Siamese Fighting Fish relin-
quishes all responsibility for his children and, in a queer twist of
nature, will eat them if they don't swim away.

Violet snail, purple sea snail, and raft shell are all names for the
five *Janthina* species, snails that have thin, fragile, globular shells
ranging in color from lavender to purple. These snails are hermaphrodites; that is, each is both male and female.

Unlike other sea snails, which crawl from place to place on a
muscular footpad, the violet snail floats by holding on to a raft
made of hundreds of air bubbles. A newly hatched larva weighs

almost nothing and readily floats on the surface of the ocean. But as it grows, the animal inside the delicate shell soon becomes heavy. Without a life raft, the snail would sink to the bottom and die. So the snail pushes the front part of its footpad along the surface of the ocean to collect an air bubble. It holds the air in a special cup at the tip of its foot, where glands secrete a mucous coating to make the air bubble strong and sticky. Bubble by bubble, the snail builds its raft at the rate of three or four bubbles a minute. When the raft is several inches long, the snail attaches itself to the underside and spends the rest of its life riding upside down.

Living at the mercy of wind and water, hundreds of thousands of violet snails are blown ashore by ocean storms. When that happens, miles of Atlantic or Pacific coastline are covered with shells, rafts (which feel very much like the packing substance called bubble wrap), and purple dye. Live snails washed up on the sand cannot crawl back to the ocean. The footpad that's so well adapted to bubble collecting and raft building is useless as a means of locomotion on land.

The Humpback Whale is another creature that uses bubbles to its advantage. This whale can grow to be fifty feet (15 m) long and forty-five tons (41,000 kg). Its body is black, except for the white throat, chest, undersides of the fluke (or tail), and long, narrow flippers. A roll of fat on the back gives the whale its name.

Whale species are divided into two categories: toothed and toothless, or baleen. Like most of its fellow large whales, the Humpback is a toothless whale. Hundreds of long, thin, flexible fringed strips of whalebone, the baleen, hang down in two rows from the roof of the whale's mouth. To eat, the whale swims along

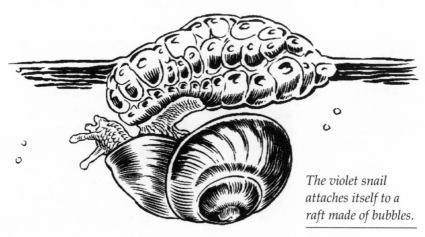

The violet snail attaches itself to a raft made of bubbles.

Whales blow small bubbles to net small fish and large bubbles to net large ones.

with its enormous mouth open, taking in huge quantities of water. When the giant cavern is full, the whale closes its mouth, lifts its great tongue, and strains out the water. Then it swallows the tiny shrimp and other crustaceans left behind.

When the Humpback wants more to eat than tons of tidbits, it creates a bubble net to catch fish. One or two Humpback Whales swim in circles beneath a school of fish. As the whales swim, they blow a constant stream of bubbles by expelling air through their blowholes. The bubbles form a curtain that rises to the surface. While they are blowing, the whales spiral upward, swimming in tighter and tighter circles. Soon the bubble net completely surrounds the fish. Because fish instinctively flee from anything flashing in the water, they move away from the sparkling bubbles and congregate in the center of the net. The whales need only to lunge upward through the bubble net to fill their mouths with food.

Here's another fact about bubbles: The entire Solar System is enclosed in a gigantic bubble, between ten and twenty billion miles across, called the heliosphere. The heliosphere is shaped like a teardrop, with the Sun lying at the larger end. The skin of the space bubble is formed by the outer limit of the electromagnetic radiation of the Sun. During periods of heavy sunspot activity, when the Sun is spewing great amounts of electromagnetic radiation, the heliosphere swells. When the Sun's surface is relatively calm, producing very few sunspots, the bubble shrinks. Beyond the border of the heliosphere is interstellar space, space beyond the outer limits of the Solar System.

A bubble is defined as a space filled with a gas and enclosed in a liquid, a transparent solid, or some other type of skin. A phenomenon called surface tension forms a "skin" around an air bubble. In a soap bubble, the air-filled space is enclosed in a "skin" of detergent.

A cluster of soap bubbles may look like a haphazard jumble, but mathematicians have discovered that, depending on the number of surfaces that are connected, bubbles form one of only two possible angles when they join, 109 or 120 degrees.

Mathematicians define the bubble as a sphere, a shape that has no corners or edges. Each point on the surface is the same distance from the center as every other point. Because the sphere has a single continuous surface, it's the strongest shape in nature. The impact of a thump on part of the surface is easily and immediately absorbed without destroying the sphere. As a result, if you drop a plastic ball on a hard surface, it may bounce and ricochet, but it'll hold together. On the other hand, if you drop a plastic block on that same surface, there's a good chance that it'll land on an edge or a corner, and crack.

The oil industry has taken advantage of the strongest structural design by building spherical gasoline tanks. Early man-made communications satellites were built as 135-foot spheres so that radio signals beamed from Earth to the satellite would bounce off the structure. And on the island of Sumi, off Greece, a water-distillation system built in the form of a hemisphere, or dome, evenly collects the Sun's heat to condense seawater, separate the salt, and produce fresh water.

Notable wildlife
   Froghoppers, Cercopidae family
   Water Spider, *Argyroneta aquatica*
   Humpback Whale, *Megaptera novaeangliae*
   Violet snails, *Janthina* spp.
   Siamese Fighting Fish, *Betta splendens*

DISCOVERY

1. I'm Forever Blowing Bubbles. David Stein holds the world's record for the largest bubble, a fifty-foot-long one produced on June 6, 1988. Now you try. IMPORTANT: Adult supervision is needed for this activity.

ITEMS NEEDED

  one-half cup of dishwashing liquid (Dawn works well)
  one and a half cups of water
  one cup of glycerine (from pharmacy)
  drinking straw
  two-liter plastic bottle
  sharp knife or hacksaw

PROCEDURE

1. Mix the dishwashing liquid, water, and glycerine. (The glycerine slows evaporation, which thins the bubble skin.)

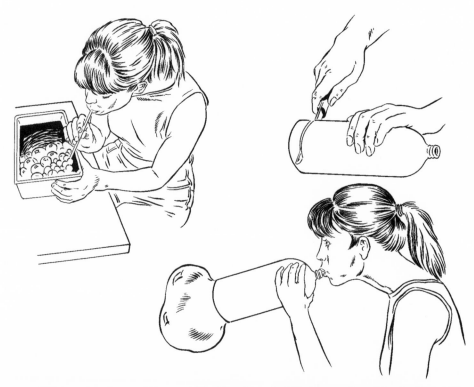

Can you top the world's record by blowing a bubble longer than fifty feet?

2. Dip one end of a drinking straw in the mixture, then lift and blow through the dry end.

3. For huge bubbles, ask an adult to cut the base off a two-liter plastic bottle. Dip the end of the bottle into the bubble mixture, lift, and blow through the neck to make gigantic bubbles.

4. For winter fun, blow bubbles when the temperature is thirty-two degrees Fahrenheit (0 degrees C) or lower and watch them freeze.

2. The World's Not Flat. Or did you already know that?

ITEMS NEEDED

paper

pencil or pen

PROCEDURE

1. List all the things in nature you can think of that are either spherical or hemispherical (dome shaped). You can begin your list with fish eggs.

2. How long does it take you to list one hundred items?

The Eyes Have It

Birds of a feather will gather together.
—Robert Burton

YOU'RE AN ORNITHOLOGIST, AN EXPERT IN BIRDS, AND AS YOU STROLL along the beach, you hear something that's different from the raucous cries of the gulls and terns and the high notes of the shorebirds . Even though it's difficult to home in on the faint cheeping, you eventually follow it to its source: a baby Herring Gull sitting among broken eggshells in a grassy nest on the ground. You hide behind a rock and watch the nest for a while, until it becomes evident that the mother won't be back.

You know that this fuzzy chick will soon be a meal for another gull or for a passing cat if you don't do something fast. Raising this chick will be easy; gulls aren't fussy eaters at any age. So you take the chick home and offer it food. But it refuses. Okay, it's not hungry right now. An hour passes and you try again. The baby still refuses the food. Hour after hour passes. The baby, which still won't eat, is getting steadily weaker.

Suddenly, you remember the red spot on the bill of the adult Herring Gull. Could that spot have something to do with the problem that you're having? Since anything's worth a try at this point, you dab some red paint on your thumb and show it to the baby gull. The chick takes one look at that spot, hits it with its little beak, opens its mouth wide, and swallows all the food that you can stuff down its throat.

The red spot on the yellow beak of some gulls signals young birds to feed. When a foraging adult returns with a crop full of food, the nestling reaches up to tap the red spot on the parent's beak. Then, when it's full of food, the chick stops tapping the dot. The tapping instinct is so strong that if the young bird doesn't tap that red spot, its parent won't regurgitate food. And if the hungry

The Herring Gull chick must poke the red spot on its parent's bill to be fed.

nestling doesn't see a red spot to tap, it won't eat and could starve with plenty of food available.

Throughout their lives, gulls pay more attention to the colors of the bill and the skin around the eye than to the color of the feathers. The color of the bills and eye ring have a wide range—greenish yellow, clear yellow, orange, bright red, dark red, black—and they dictate which mates the males choose and which chicks the females feed. For example, the Herring Gull has a yellow beak with a bright red spot on the lower mandible, and pink legs and feet. The Ring-billed Gull has a yellow beak with a black ring around the end, and greenish legs and feet. And in the West, the very common California Gull has a yellow beak with both a black ring and a red spot, and yellowish legs and feet. Through these variations, the gulls can differentiate not only among species but also among individuals within a species. The small differences that may not seem apparent to humans are important to gulls in maintaining pair bonds when mating and when raising their young.

The fact that it's so hard to differentiate among four kinds of gulls that nest side by side in northern Canada led scientists to wonder how the birds can select a mate from the same species. All four species are approximately the same size and color, right down to their bright yellow bills with red spots on them. How, then, could a male Herring Gull distinguish his mate from a Glaucous, Iceland, or Thayer's Gull? Easy! By the color of her eyes.

When a male Herring Gull goes courting, he looks for a mate with a yellow iris and a ring of orange skin around the eye. A yellow iris and yellow skin around the eye (Glaucous Gull), a brown iris and dark red skin around the eye (Thayer's Gull), or even a yellow iris and dark red skin around the eye (Iceland Gull) just isn't acceptable. To test the importance of eye color, an ornithologist captured some mated female Herring Gulls and painted their orange eye rings yellow. Their mates would have no more to do with them and chose new females that had the right color irises and eye-rings.

Notable wildlife

Herring Gull, *Larus argentatus*
Ring-billed Gull, *Larus delawarensis*
California Gull, *Larus californicus*
Glaucous Gull, *Larus hyperboreus*
Iceland Gull, *Larus glaucoides*
Thayer's Gull, *Larus thayeri*

DISCOVERY

1. The Eyes Have It. Take a survey of the eye color of your family members and find out what color, if any, predominates.

ITEMS NEEDED

paper
pen or pencil
ruler

PROCEDURE

1. List the following colors across the top of the paper: brown, blue, green, hazel.

2. List the names of your family members down the left-hand side of the paper.

3. Use the ruler to draw lines between the horizontal rows and the vertical columns to make a matrix.

4. Check off the eye color of each person. Are there more brown-eyed people than blue? More blue than hazel?

5. Take a survey at school. Do the results match the ones you got with your family? Why do you think they do—or don't?

2. Gull Identification. Start with a few gulls that are easy to identify in adult plumage and you may get hooked on birding, the activity of identifying birds.

ITEMS NEEDED

   stale bread

   binoculars

PROCEDURE

1. Go to the seashore or a lake.

2. Break the bread into one-inch pieces, and toss them into the air for the gulls.

3. As they gulls fly in for the food, try to identify a few of the common ones. The brown ones are immature birds and are difficult for beginners to sort out. Adult birds are easier, however. Copy the illustrations on page 179 to make your own mini field guide. Then go out and find a living example of each gull species. The sizes given are approximate measurements from bill tip to tail tip.

   • Herring Gull (*Larus argentatus*). Our most common gull can be found on the Atlantic and Pacific coasts and inland along lakes, on farmlands and fields, and at dumps. Be sure to look for the red spot on the bill. 26 inches (65 cm).

   • Ring-billed Gull (*Larus delawarenis*). This common gull is similar to the Herring Gull but is much smaller and the black ring around the bill is easy to see. The eyes are yellow. 19 inches (48 cm).

   • California Gull (*Larus californicus*). Although at first glance this gull of the Pacific coastline looks like the Ring-billed, it has a dark eye and red and black spots on the lower bill. 23 inches (58 cm).

   • Greater Black-backed Gull (*Larus marinus*). Like the Herring Gull, this gull has a red dot on its bill, but the black back and wings of this species of the Atlantic coast and Great Lakes region make it easy to identify. 31 inches (78 cm).

There's No Such Thing as a Sea Gull

Stranger to the land, they light,
A quiver of silver, black, and white
To pluck the grain the need for flight.
—Grace Noll Crowell
Sea Gulls Far Inland

DURING THE YEARS 1848 TO 1850, MILLIONS OF BLACK FIELD CRICKETS threatened the crops in Utah. And all three years, thousands of California Gulls appeared to devour the insects. About sixty years later, during the growing seasons of 1907 and 1908, Nevada's alfalfa farmers faced the danger of losing their crops to field mice. Again, California Gulls moved in by the thousands, fed on the pests, and saved the crops.

Luckily, gulls aren't fussy about food. For the most part, they're scavengers, and as such, they are fond of the dead fish and other sea creatures that wash up on the beach, and they follow boats to pick up the scraps of fish bait thrown overboard. Gulls also love garbage, so they find banquets in our garbage pits and landfills. Once in a while a gull gets fresh food by picking up a lazy starfish or an unprotected seabird egg. If the time is right, it gluts itself on the eggs of Atlantic Horseshoe Crabs that breed along the Atlantic coastline. But most of the time, gulls take the easy way out, eating whatever's available and thus providing an essential service by acting as a worldwide cleanup crew.

One gull feeding habit regularly aids farmers. In the prairie and coastal states, flocks of gulls follow tractors, much as they follow fishing boats on the open water. As the farm machinery scares up insects and small mammals that feed on crops, the gulls pick them up and eat them.

Calling all the big white birds at the beach "sea gulls" would be like calling all small brown birds in trees "sparrows." There are lots of big white birds by the sea that aren't gulls, and many gulls are abundant inland, along rivers and lakes, on farmlands, and at garbage dumps.

Of the forty-five species of gulls in the world, about twenty-five can be found in the United States and Canada. They range in size from the Glaucous Gull of the Arctic, a bird that measures thirty-two inches (80 cm) from the tip of its bill to the tip of its tail, to the eleven-inch (27-cm) Little Gull.

In terms of feather color and feather pattern, gulls are among the most variable of all bird groups. Most are predominantly white, with the position and number of dark accents distinguishing each species. But every species passes through several years of dramatic plumage changes that complicate the enjoyable task of identifying them. First-year birds look nothing like their parents, and second-year birds often look nothing like either first-year birds or adults. Some species go through eight or nine different plumages as they mature. When they finally reach adult plumage, they fluctuate between the breeding plumage of summer and the nonbreeding plumage of winter.

Left to right: *Great Black-backed Gull, Herring Gull, California Gull, Ring-billed Gull. Note their similarities and differences, even in this black-and-white illustration.*

In addition to the many plumage changes of maturing birds, there are regional variations in adult birds as well. For example, the dark backs of Western Gulls are darker on the California birds than on the Washington ones. To confuse their identity even further, Western Gulls hybridize, often breeding with other species of gulls. When this dark-backed species breeds with the light-backed Glaucous Gull, which it often does, the offspring can be any shade of gray, from light to dark. As a result, a birder often must be content with having seen a "gull species"—not a satisfying identification.

Notable wildlife
   California Gull, *Larus californicus*
   Glaucous Gull, *Larus hyperboreus*
   Little Gull, *Larus minutus*
   Western Gull, *Larus occidentalis*
   Atlantic Horseshoe Crab, *Limulus polyphemus*

DISCOVERY

1. Taking Flight. You may feel a little silly doing this, but it really works!

PROCEDURE

1. Find a flock of gulls on the beach or on any other flat, open area, such as a mud flat or a field.

2. Stand far away from the flock but in full view of it. If you can see them, they can see you.

3. Jump up and down. What happens?

4. If you've traveled in a car, honk the horn and slam the doors. What happens?

5. Now face the flock, stand up straight, and while holding your arms straight out from your sides, begin to raise and lower them in slow, "stiff-winged" beats. Now what happens?

6. Within a short time, you'll see the results of your action. First one gull, then another, and finally the whole flock will take to the air. Theoretically, the faraway flock sees you as a distant flapping gull (gulls flap several times before taking off). And flapping means one of two things to gulls: food or foe. So the gulls take flight to see what your flapping's all about.

2. Build a California Gull. Utah's farmers were so grateful to the birds that had saved their crops that they built a monument to them in Salt Lake City. If you can't visit the monument, you can make your own California Gull by following the directions below.

ITEMS NEEDED

ruler	scissors
manila folder	paper punch
two sheets of white	string
construction paper or	yellow, red, black,
lightweight poster board	and gray crayons
pencil	

PROCEDURE

1. Enlarge the pattern to twice its size.

2. Trace the pattern onto the white paper

3. Draw in the details and color the parts according to the illustration.

4. Cut out the parts, making slots where indicated.

5. Put the bird together, punch a hole in the body, and hang it from a string.

6. Make a flock of California Gulls and you'll never have to worry about crickets or mice invading your room!

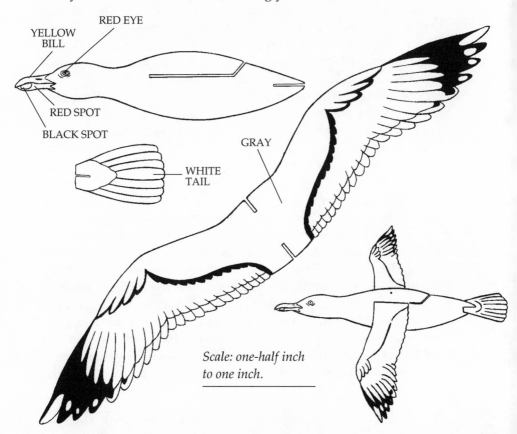

RED EYE
YELLOW BILL
RED SPOT
BLACK SPOT
GRAY
WHITE TAIL

Scale: one-half inch to one inch.

Big Birds with Special Bills

It is not only fine feathers that make fine birds.
—Aesop

FOUR SPECIES OF LONG-LEGGED WADING BIRDS BRIGHTEN THE SHORES OF the Gulf of Mexico. Among flocks of white egrets and gray herons, the American Flamingo, the Lesser Flamingo, the Scarlet Ibis, and the Roseate Spoonbill provide accents of color ranging from pale pink to blood red. But as striking as their feathers are, their bills also demand a second look.

The American (Greater) Flamingo, found on salt flats and in shallow lakes and lagoons, stands forty-six inches (117 cm) high. An immature flamingo can be pale gray to white, but an adult bird is rose pink with black feathers in the wings. Its bill is pink with a black tip, and its legs are also pink. In flight, the bird's five-foot (152-cm) wingspan, long extended neck, and long trailing legs make it a sight not soon forgotten. The noticeably smaller Lesser Flamingo is a much brighter pink, has a proportionately shorter neck, and has a carmine red bill.

Flamingoes once ranged throughout Europe, Asia, Africa, South America, and North America, but plume hunters killed the North American populations of these timid birds faster than the birds could breed and raise young. The flamingoes that we now only occasionally see along the Atlantic and Gulf coasts of North America have wandered here from the West Indies.

The flamingo's bill is sharply bent, looking very much like a large nose with a bump. The upper part of the bill is small and functions as a lid; the lower part is large and acts as a trough. Both parts of the bill are lined with comblike structures called lamellae. Inside the mouth, the flamingo's tongue is thick and spiny. When the flamingo feeds, it holds its bill upside down in the water, using its tongue as a piston to suck water and mud into its mouth. As the muddy water flows past the lamellae, bits of food are caught and larger particles of mud filtered out.

The American Flamingo is carnivorous. It uses its small webbed feet to stir up the bottom of the lagoon, fills its bill, then strains out algae and microscopic animals, leaving the small snails and shrimp. The lamellae that line its beak are coarse and toothlike. The Lesser Flamingo, on the other hand, is a vegetarian. Its lamellae are so tiny that they prevent particles larger than $1/50$ of an inch (0.5 mm) from entering the bill. Even finer lamellae filter out particles larger than $1/1,250$ of an inch (0.02 mm). The bird swallows the microscopic, protein-rich algae that remains.

Flamingoes are monogamous; that is, they take one mate. And that bond may last from one year to the next. Both the male and female of the pair use their bills to scoop mud into a mound with a hollow on top in which one large, white egg is laid. They build their nest mound about twelve inches (30 cm) high to protect the egg from washing away during high tides. When the chick emerges, both parents feed the hatchling with a milky fluid secreted from glands in the crop and dripped into the baby's mouth. Although flamingos nest in colonies, parents seem to have no difficulty identifying their own chicks.

The Scarlet Ibis is another colorful bird that may wander to the Gulf states, this time from South America. It's a very bright red bird with a long, thin, dark curved bill; long, red legs; and black wingtips. The Scarlet Ibis is twenty-five inches (65 cm) tall and has a three-foot (91-cm) wingspan.

Like the Flamingo, the Scarlet Ibis also feeds along coastal marshes and lagoons, but it does so in a completely different way. Using its bill, it probes the soft mud to feel for prey. When it finds a slow-moving shrimp, snail, or small fish, it snaps it up in its bill. The ibis supplements its diet with frogs and insects.

The Scarlet Ibis may be a race of the White Ibis of the southeastern United States. White Ibis incubate Scarlet Ibis eggs placed in their nests, and there's evidence that the two species mate and produce offspring.

Unlike the American Flamingo, Lesser Flamingo, and Scarlet Ibis, the Roseate Spoonbill is a native of North America. This pale pink bird with blood red shoulders is thirty-two inches (80 cm) tall. The skin on its featherless head is greenish gray, and its legs are bright pink. Ranging from the Gulf states south to Chile and

Unique beaks. The flamingo (left) *strains its food from a beakful of water, the spoonbill* (center) *snaps up its snacks, and the ibis* (right) *probes for prey in the mud.*

Argentina, it feeds in coastal marshes, lagoons, and mud flats, and nests in mangrove trees.

Like the Scarlet Ibis, the Roseate Spoonbill feeds by touch. Sensitive receptors under the horny covering of its spatulate bill signal when it has come in contact with a shrimp, snail, or other small animal. Whereas the ibis probes the mud, the spoonbill holds its bill open as it swings its head from side to side to stir up the muddy bottom. Then its uses its long, broad, flattened bill to snap up prey in a fraction of a second. By relying on touch, both the spoonbill and the ibis have the advantage of being able to feed in muddy water and in water clogged with plant life.

Notable wildlife

American (Greater) Flamingo, *Phoenicopterus ruber*
Lesser Flamingo, *Phoenicipterus minor*
Scarlet Ibis, *Guara rubra*
Roseate Spoonbill, *Ajaja ajaja*

DISCOVERY

1. Be a Flamingo. And learn patience and balance.
ITEMS NEEDED
   bowl of clear soup
   fine strainer or slotted spoon
PROCEDURE
1. Eat the soup with the strainer or spoon.
2. Stand on one leg, as flamingoes often do to rest their legs, one at a time. How's your balance? How long can you stand that way?

2. Be an Ibis. Still hungry from your flamingo experience? Try this method.
ITEMS NEEDED
   raisins   cooked oatmeal or other hot cereal
   nuts   large blunt tapestry needle, knitting
   bowl   needle, or nut pick
PROCEDURE
1. Put the raisins and nuts in the bowl, then pour the cooked cereal on top.
2. Use the needle or nut pick to probe for the raisins and nuts.

3. Be a Spoonbill. *Still* hungry? Here's one more method to try.
ITEMS NEEDED
   bowl of vegetable soup
   spaghetti tongs or sugar tongs
PROCEDURE
1. Eat the soup with the tongs.
Consider how lucky we are that the fork was invented. This utensil was first brought to America in 1630 by John Winthrop, governor of the Massachusetts Bay Colony. He considered it so precious that he carried it with him in a specially made velvet-lined leather case!

Otters: Streamlined and Friendly

All of the animals, excepting man, know the principal business of life is to enjoy it.
—Samuel Butler

NEWBORN RIVER OTTERS DON'T TAKE TO WATER NATURALLY. THE PUPS have to be tricked into entering the water for the first time. Sometimes the mother uses a crayfish to lure them in; other times she carries them piggyback into deep water and drops them, and it's "sink or swim." The babies quickly learn to paddle around and are soon diving and frolicking on their own.

The two or three pups born in spring are born blind and open their eyes about thirty days later. During the first few months of their lives, the mother guards them from all danger, forbidding even their father to go near them. When they're a few months old, the father once again joins the family unit, and the task of teaching the babies to swim begins.

Watching a River Otter, you can't help but be convinced that this animal enjoys life to the fullest. Agile and strong, this member of the weasel family shoots rapids that an experienced canoeist would hesitate to attempt. Families of otters join in the fun, taking turns down the bank with the father in the lead. Tucking its legs back and throwing itself down in a belly flop, the otter slides headlong down a riverbank, wearing a slippery trough into the mud. In winter, the otter turns its mudslide into a ski slope, using the snow as its playground. Shooting down the snowbank into the lake or stream at the bottom, the otter then swims under the water or the ice to appear as far away as a quarter mile (0.4 km), because this aquatic mammal can remain submerged for as long as four minutes. Long, course guard hairs cover and protect the soft, thick

The River Otter's life certainly isn't one of all work and no play.

underfur. The underfur traps air to keep the otter dry and warm in the icy water.

Contrary to what some sports fishermen believe, the River Otter is no threat to game fish, such as trout and salmon, because even as the fastest-swimming land mammal in the world, the River Otter can't swim fast enough to catch them. In addition, as research has shown, a steady diet of fish will kill an otter, so it sticks to a healthy variety of crayfish, frogs, water snakes, insects, turtles, mussels, and slow-moving fish.

The River Otter speedily escapes predators in the water, but the animal is clumsy on land. The River Otter has a long, slender body, up to forty-eight inches (120 cm) long and twenty-five pounds (11.2 kg) in weight. It has short legs and webbed feet. Its streamlined shape and paddlelike feet serve it well in water but become handicaps on land, where it so fiercely defends itself that it can fight off an attacking eagle or kill a hungry wildcat or striking snake. What it can't do is outrun an enemy, so occasionally an otter becomes a meal for a hungry wolf or bear.

The Sea Otter, slightly longer and bulkier than its freshwater cousin, may grow to be fifty inches (124 cm) long and as much as eighty-five pounds (38.2 kg). It often floats, feeds, and swims on its back, keeping to the kelp beds and rocky shores of the Pacific coastline. The Sea Otter brings sea urchins, fish, crabs, abalones, and other shellfish to the surface of the water, then it flips onto its back and uses its chest as a table. Sometimes the otter also brings up a rock from the ocean floor to use to break open shells.

A Sea Otter often eats while floating on its back, using its chest as a table.

Researchers wondered for years how a fifty-pound otter could pry an abalone or other firmly attached shellfish from a rock when it was often impossible for a man three times its size to do so. While looking at three-dimensional X rays of the Sea Otter's bone structure, marine biologists recently discovered an extra bone in the otter's wrist that gives the animal additional leverage. The X rays also revealed why old Sea Otters often die of congestive heart failure. Over time, the otter's habit of using its chest as a chopping block causes the bones to cave in and put pressure on the heart.

The female Sea Otter is an attentive mother. When danger threatens, she tucks her pup under her foreleg and dives to safety, surfacing frequently to allow the baby to breathe. Although the adult otter can stay underwater for about four minutes, the pup must breathe more often. A Sea Otter mother shows affection by kissing and hugging the pup, and shows disapproval by spanking it.

The Sea Otter ranges from the Aleutian Islands to California; it's most likely to be seen off Amchitka Island, Alaska, and Point Lobos, California. Once abundant, by 1911 the species had been hunted so extensively for its fur that a four-nation agreement to place severe restrictions on killing Sea Otters was signed by the United States, Russia, Japan, and Great Britain. In spite of this precaution, however, by 1920 some naturalists were certain that the animal had vanished forever from California's shores. Its fur, warmer than sable and more durable than mink, seemed to have sealed its fate. But in 1938 a herd of about three hundred Sea Otters was spotted off the California coast, and from those few hundred individuals, the population has steadily increased to number several thousand.

New dangers now threaten the Sea Otter, however. A lush forest of Giant Kelp grows to depths of 130 feet along California's coast and provides hundreds of marine species with protection and food. At the base of the plants, rootlike structures called holdfasts anchor the kelp to the ocean floor. The kelp provides a habitat for more than 175 marine animals, including the sea anemones, brittle stars, and abalones favored by Sea Otters. At the surface of the water, the otters secure themselves during storms by wrapping several strands of kelp around their bodies. Adult otters also use the kelp to tie up their young while foraging for food.

But within the past ten years, several occurrences have threatened the existence of the kelp beds. First, huge numbers of kelp-eating sea urchins overwhelmed the kelp beds; as the sea urchin population increased, acres of kelp died. Marine biologists intervened, and millions of sea urchins were harvested in order to allow the kelp beds to recover.

The kelp beds also suffered as a result of El Niño, the phenomenon in which the abnormal warming of tropical oceans causes unusually warm ocean currents farther north. As the icy Arctic waters were displaced, the resulting rise in water temperature killed nutrients needed by the kelp as well as by the animals that lived among its fronds. At the same time, severe storms hit the area, tearing kelp from the ocean bottom. Untreated sewage dumped into the ocean water further threatened the kelp's survival. Nothing can be done to stop the flow of ocean currents and storms at sea, but environmentalists have worked to stop the dumping of untreated sewage into the fragile ecosystem. If the kelp recovers, the Sea Otters living off the coast of Southern California have a good chance of survival.

In the North Pacific, however, oil spills pose another threat to the Sea Otter. On March 24, 1989, in the most recent spill, ten million gallons of crude oil poured from the Exxon *Valdez*, an oil tanker that ran aground on Bligh Reef in Prince William Sound. In addition to killing seabirds and marine life, the oil was responsible for the death of thousands of Sea Otters. Oil reduced the insulation and buoyancy of their fur, so many froze to death in the extremely cold water. Others were poisoned when, trying to clean their fur, they swallowed lethal amounts of oil. Even after cleanup efforts, much of the oil still remains in the water and along the shores of the sound.

The Sea Otter was once hunted to near extinction but, when given a chance, began to repopulate West Coast waters. It's hoped that the animal's determination to survive will once again rescue it from continuing natural and man-made dangers.

Notable wildlife
River Otter, *Lutra canadensis*
Sea Otter, *Enhydra lutris*
Giant Kelp, *Macrocystis pyrifera*

DISCOVERY

1 River Otter Slide. This activity will keep you cool on a hot summer day.
ITEMS NEEDED
sheet of heavy plastic, such as an old plastic shower curtain or tablecloth
hose hooked up to water source
bathing suit
PROCEDURE
1. Lay the sheet of plastic on flat ground.
2. Position the nozzle of the hose at one end of the plastic sheet.
3. Turn the water on.
4. Run, jump, and slide on the slippery surface.

2. Sea Otter Snack. Can you float and eat at the same time? IMPORTANT: Adult supervision is needed for this activity.
ITEMS NEEDED
banana ("sea urchin")
nut ("abalone") and nutcracker ("rock")
PROCEDURE
1. Fill the bathtub and get in.
2. While floating on your back in the bathtub, see if you can balance the banana, nut and nutcracker on your tummy and chest. You don't have to use a rock to crack the nut—and sit up when you decide to eat your snack.

Hide-and-Seek Bird

*There are many times and circumstances in life when
our strength is to sit still.*
—Tryon Edwards

WHEN DANGER, SUCH AS A PROWLING HAWK, THREATENS, THE AMERICAN
Bittern doesn't fly away. Instead, it faces its adversary, stretches its
neck upward, points its beak toward the sky, flattens its feathers
against its body, and freezes. In this position, the bird blends in
perfectly with its surroundings.

The American Bittern shares several features of its heron family
members: It lives in marshes, bogs, and reedy lakes; has long legs
for wading through water in search of prey; and uses its long neck
and beak to reach for and capture water insects, snails, crayfish,
snakes, fish, and frogs. But instead of the striking plumage that
characterizes most herons and egrets, the bittern has blotched, drab
coloring—just what it needs to protect itself. Its pale throat, neck,
chest, and abdomen are vertically streaked with dark brown feathers. The dark vertical stripes formed by its dark feathers look
exactly like dark reeds; the pale ones, like sunlit reeds. Because it's
difficult to distinguish the shape of a mottled bird against a mottled background, the color, shape, and posture of the rigid bittern
make it almost impossible to see, even when its location is known.
On a still day, the bittern remains motionless; on a windy one, it
sways back and forth, mimicking cattails blowing in the breeze.
The bittern keeps up its act as long as danger remains.

If the threatened bittern fails to deceive its attacker, it extends
its spearlike beak and walks deliberately toward the adversary. If
it's forced to defend itself further, the bittern hurls itself at its
attacker, jabbing with its beak at the eyes of the enemy. That usually does it.

The American Bittern also has an unusual voice. In fact, bird-
book authors struggle with the task of successfully describing the

American Bittern's song. One writer offers *oonk-a-lunk,* while another suggests *oong-ka' choonk,* both repeated several times in succession. Some authors avoid trying to duplicate the sound by settling for descriptive words and phrases, such as "pumping," "booming," or "the last scream of a drowning man." "Plum pudd'n" converts the phonetic imitations to a more familiar term. And folk names for the American Bittern—stake-driver bird, barrel maker, and thunder pump—are picturesque comparisons between the bird's song and the sound of a hammer driving a stake or nail or of an old-fashioned pump handle. The explosive song of this secretive bird certainly guarantees that the bittern is more often heard than seen.

To produce its song, the bittern swallows several gulps of air, swelling its throat until it looks like a bird with the mumps. When it has taken in all the air it can hold, the bittern constricts its strong neck muscles and expels the air to produce the booming sound that can be heard a quarter mile away. The American Bittern is polygamous, and the song is intended to attract several females.

Notable wildlife
American Bittern, *Botaurus lentiginosus*

DISCOVERY

1. Hide a Bird. Color the illustrations on the following pages to hide a bittern in the reeds. These pages may be photocopied so that the book does not have to be cut. You may want to make copies so that a number of children can take part in the activity.

ITEMS NEEDED
   illustration of bittern and reeds
   tan, medium brown, and dark brown crayons

PROCEDURE

1. Using only the three colors listed, color the reeds and the bittern in the drawing. Be sure to leave some white areas to represent sunlight showing through the reeds.

2. Cut out the bittern and place it where indicated over the grassy background.

3. Can you see how well the bittern blends in with its surroundings? How easily do you think you could find one in tall marsh grass?

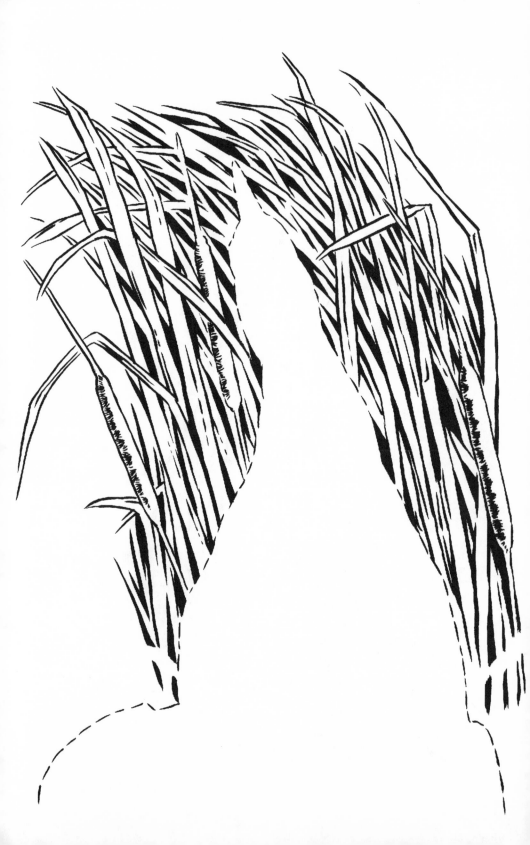

The Animal That Somersaults

I cut off the heads of the one that had seven, and after a few days I saw in it a prodigy scarcely inferior to the fabulous Hydre of Lernaea. It acquired seven new heads. . . . But here is something more than legend dared to invent: the seven heads that I cut off from the Hydre, after being fed, became perfect animals. . . .
—Abraham Trembley

IN 1744, ABRAHAM TREMBLEY, A RESEARCHER WORKING IN THE NETHER-lands, carried out a series of experiments that he had hoped would determine the true nature of this tiny freshwater creature. With the aid of a microscope, Trembley cut individual hydras into a hundred minute pieces, then watched them regenerate new parts to become complete new animals. He grafted two or more hydras together and watched as they functioned in multiheaded harmony. And he turned their cylindrical bodies inside out and watched them carry on as if nothing were unusual.

Later, German naturalist August Roesel von Rosenhof crushed several hydras into a pulp, then let the gooey stuff sit. Would mixing up the essence of several hydras put a stop to their regenerative powers? Nope. Within two weeks, active, healthy, complete hydras, exactly the same number as had existed originally, emerged from the pulp.

The mythical Hydre of Lernaea that Trembley referred to in the quote above was a nine-headed reptile said to guard the entrance to the Underworld. According to the myth, eight of its heads grew back as soon as they were cut off. The other was immortal. Hercules finally killed the beast by cutting off all the eight regenerative heads, sealing the eight necks, and then chopping off and burying the immortal head.

The real hydra looks like a tiny, translucent palm tree growing underwater in lakes, ponds, streams, and rivers. But the hydra also

*The hydra may be gray, tan,
brown, or, when algae live
in the cells of the body
wall, bright green. The
animal anchors itself to a
solid surface, then waves
its tentacles to find food.*

acts like an animal by
capturing food and mov-
ing from place to place. As a
result, Carolus Linnaeus, the
Swedish botanist and naturalist
who developed the system of plant
and animal classification still in use
today, compromised by calling the
hydra a flower-animal.

The little creature that can be taken
apart and put together in new ways is
the only freshwater representative of
the coelenterates, the group of animals
that includes sea anemones, corals,
sponges, and jellyfishes. It has a three-
layered body wall, a single body cavity
with only one opening, and stinging tentacles. That simple structure allows the hydra to survive the investigative chopping and
grinding of curious researchers. In fact, current studies indicate
that the hydra's tissue flows out and is replaced at the rate of one
millimeter a day. The creature replaces all its body cells every two
weeks, so, theoretically, a hydra can live forever.

The hydra's tubular body is about as thick as carpet thread and
only one-fourth to one-half inch long. One end is attached to a
stick, stone, or plant. The other end is equipped with a mouth,
which serves as an entrance for food, water, and oxygen, as well as
an exit for waste products. Five to seven tentacles surround the
mouth. The hydra's body design classifies it as a polyp, a creature
with a simple, saclike body.

The hydra's body and tentacles are covered with a network of
nerve cells. When fishing for water fleas, its primary food, the
polyp anchors itself to a firm base, extends its body, and sways back
and forth while waving its tentacles. Nematocysts, threadlike sting-

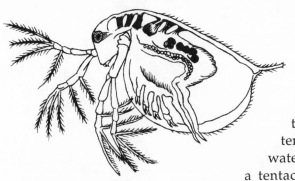

The water flea (greatly magnified) is the hydra's favorite food.

ing organs, are kept tightly coiled in the tentacle walls. When a water flea swims against a tentacle, a nematocyst is fired. The nematocysts of some hydras spin like rifle bullets as they are ejected (spinning gives them straighter flight). When the nematocyst makes contact, it pierces the flea and poisons it. Other nematocysts consist of sticky threads that acts as lassos, reeling in the water flea. Each nematocyst is fired once, then replaced. When the hydra has captured the water flea, it uses its tentacles to stuff the food into its mouth. The hydra's mouth leads directly into the digestive cavity, and undigested food is expelled through the same opening.

Like the flower-animal that Linnaeus recognized, the hydra has two distinct ways of reproducing. In spring and summer, when pond water is warm and food is plentiful, the hydra develops buds that grow into smaller but self-sufficient replicas of itself. Each small hydra gets nourishment from the parent until tentacles form; then it breaks off and becomes independent. A single hydra can produce twenty-five thousand offspring in this way during one summer.

Buds can't form when the weather turns cooler, however. As fall approaches and the air temperature cools, the temperature of the water also cools and food becomes scarce. Under these conditions, the hydra develops eggs, which it also fertilizes. The eggs, encased in a hard shell, drop to the sandy bottom to await warm spring weather to hatch.

The hydra typically stays in one spot, although it will sometimes seek a place with more light, more oxygen, or a more suitable temperature. Just as it has a choice in methods of reproduction, the hydra has more than one way to move. The hydra may simply let go of its foundation and float upside down, letting the current take it to a better spot. Or it may take a more active role by somersaulting to another location.

To somersault, the hydra contracts the cells of the outer wall along one side of its body. This action shortens that side and, as a

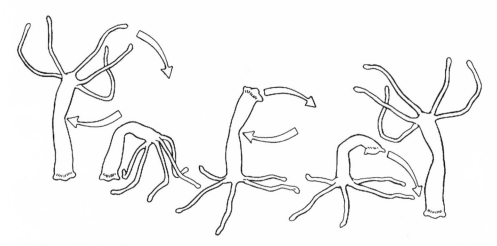

By contracting the outer cells of its simple body, the hydra can slowly flip end over end to a new feeding area.

result, bends the body. Then the hydra places its tentacles on the lake or river bottom, lifts its trunk until it's standing on its head, contracts the opposite side of its body, and sets itself upright. The hydra continues to turn head over heels very slowly until it finds a place to its liking.

DISCOVERY

1. Be a Hydra. Then decide how much you would like flipping head over heels through life.

PROCEDURE

1. Choose a shady tree or a sunny rock as your goal, and see how fast you can somersault to it. Or simply somersault until you're tired. Somersault to your limit every day for two weeks. Were you able to do more somersaults on the fourteenth day than on the first?

2. Stage a contest with your friends, competing to see who can somersault the fastest or who can do the greatest number. If there are lots of you, form teams. The team with the highest average score of speed or number of somersaults wins.

3. Have a somersaulting relay race.

4. Play softball and somersault around the bases. Aren't you glad that you don't have to somersault everywhere? What do you think would happen to the hydra if it didn't have this ability?

Air, Sky, and Space

Fireworks in the Sky

Thunder is good, thunder is impressive; but it is the
lightning that does the work.
—Mark Twain

A CURIOUS AIRLINE PILOT FLEW HIS PLANE INTO THE CENTER OF A THUN-
derhead. Caught in the fury within the cloud, the aircraft bounced
around like a kernel of popcorn in a popper. After several minutes,
the plane was tossed out of the thunderhead, upside down and
almost completely destroyed. The pilot parachuted to safety, but
his curiosity had almost killed him.

It's difficult to imagine the amount of raw power contained in a
thunderstorm. Meteorologists tell us that the energy released by an
average thunderstorm is equal to the force discharged by the
explosion of ten atomic bombs. Approximately forty-four thunder-
storms occur every day on Earth; almost two thousand are occurring at any given moment.

A thunderstorm starts with a massive cloud formation called a
thunderhead. When warm, moist air rises from Earth's surface, it
cools into a mass of millions of water droplets floating in the air.
The hotter the air, the faster it rises, until it reaches very cold air
and condenses into rain, snow, or hail. As the precipitation begins
to fall to the ground and meets the still-rising warm air, it creates a
whirlwind within the cloud.

Scientists don't completely understand the process that causes
lightning, but they believe it goes something like this: Everything is
made of atoms, which in turn are formed of smaller particles,
including protons and electrons. The conflagration going on in the
center of a thunderhead shears electrons from the water drops that
form the cloud and carries them to the top of the cloud; the protons
that are left behind are picked up by the falling raindrops, snow, or
hail. When the violent activity within the thunderhead continues
for some time, an enormous number of free electrons accumulate

A thunderhead forms when cold air pushes under a mass of warm air. A thunderhead may hold more than 150,000 tons of water, which will be released in a downpour.

and, as a group, speed to another part of the thunderhead, to another cloud, or to Earth in search of proton partners.

When lightning streaks, light waves and sound waves are simultaneously set in motion. We experience lightning and thunder as two separate events because sound travels much more slowly than light does. Light races to our eyes at a speed of 186,000 miles per second, but sound lags far behind, traveling to our ears at the rate of about 1,000 feet, or one fifth of a mile, per second. The streaks may be no larger than the diameter of your finger, but they may be several miles long.

The downward stream of electrons is called the downstroke. This downstroke is answered by an upward stroke from any available conductor, such as a lightning rod, a club in a golfer's hand, or the water on a person standing in the rain. Lightning is measured as electricity is, in units of energy called amperes. When the downstroke and upstroke meet, the result is an ultrapowerful upstroke from the ground to the cloud carrying an average of thirty thousand amperes traveling at half the speed of light and heating the air on its course to 60,000 degrees Fahrenheit (33,315 degrees C). That's five times the temperature of the Sun's surface. The stream of electrons in the upstroke causes the air to glow in the phenomenon we call lightning. The resulting heat expands the air at supersonic speeds; we hear this as a sonic boom called thunder.

Lightning not only heats the air on its path to Earth; once it hits land, its intense heat may also ignite deadly fires. In the western United States, lightning is responsible for more than 9,000 forest fires every year. This area of quick-burning evergreens and little rainfall is like a tinderbox waiting for a spark. One year 1,488 lightning fires were counted just in the forests of Montana and Idaho; one thunderstorm alone ignited more than 100 fires.

With all its potential for destruction, though, it's somewhat surprising that only about one hundred people in North America are killed by lightning each year. Yet even though the chances of being struck and killed are low, your life may someday depend on how you react to being caught outdoors in a thunderstorm. One thousand lightning-caused deaths were studied to determine where people are safest in a lightning storm. The following are places where you should *not* be: in an open space, under a tree, in or near water, near tall or metal objects, inside small sheds or small barns, near large appliances or electrical fixtures, talking on a telephone, or in front of a fireplace or an open door or window.

To be safe, you should be in a large building, especially one that's protected with lightning rods. The larger the building or house, the better. An enclosed automobile (not a convertible!) is also good protection.

If you happen to be out in the open when a lightning storm overtakes you, quickly get into a gully or ditch that's lower than ground level but isn't filling with water. If the ground is dry, no

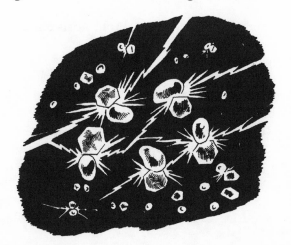

Lightning occurs when the molecules in water droplets collide with each other and produce sparks of electricity.

rain is falling, and no gully is available, lie flat on the ground; however, if the ground is wet or if it begins to rain, squat down and tuck your head between your knees. If you're in the woods, find a clump of low bushes that you can get to quickly and take cover in the clump—but don't lean against even the smallest trunk.

Lightning isn't all bad. It provides the nitrogen that green plants need to stay healthy. Although a few plants can take nitrogen directly from the air, others cannot extract it unless its atoms are attached to oxygen atoms. Lightning changes the nitrogen so that it can combine with the oxygen in water as rain falls. Then plant roots absorb the nitrogen from the ground.

DISCOVERY

1. Faraway Fireworks. Calculate the distance of a thunderstorm. If a real thunderstorm isn't handy, have one person flash a light to represent lightning and another slam a door to represent thunder.

PROCEDURE

1. Since sound travels at a speed of about one thousand feet per second, start counting seconds as soon as you see a lightning flash. The instant you see the flash, begin to count "one-thousand-one, one-thousand-two, one-thousand-three," and so forth until you hear the thunder. It takes one second for the sound of thunder to travel each thousand feet of distance between you and the flash, so, for example, if five seconds pass between the flash and the sound, then the storm is about five thousand feet, or close to a mile, away.

2. How far away is your storm? Keep counting for a several lightning flashes. Does the storm seem to be moving away from you or toward you?

2. Make Lightning. Well, not really, but you *can* duplicate its effect.

ITEMS NEEDED

two long, narrow balloons

PROCEDURE

1. Blow up the balloons.

2. At night, turn off the lights in a room.

3. Rub the ends of the balloons—both at the same time—against your clothes, the carpet, or a piece of upholstered furniture.

4. Hold the balloons parallel to the floor and bring the ends together until they're almost touching.

5. What happens?

The Sun: Our Closest Star

The sun, with all those planets revolving around it
and depending upon it, can still ripen a bunch of
grapes as if it had nothing else in the universe to do.
—Galileo Galilei

THE SUN—THAT GREAT HOT BALL OF FIRE—IS ONLY A MEDIUM-SIZE STAR. It appears brighter to us than any other star because, even at a distance of ninety-three million miles (149,600,000 km), it's much nearer than the next closest star, which is twenty-five trillion miles from Earth.

The Sun is a huge ball of gases consisting of about 75 percent hydrogen, the most abundant element in the universe, and about 25 percent helium. Within the core, thermonuclear reactions are continuously taking place. As constantly moving hydrogen atoms crash into each other, they combine to form helium atoms. This fusion of atoms releases energy in the form of intense heat. Because heat normally flows from a hot place to a cooler one, the heat produced by the atomic reactions occurring in the Sun's core moves to the cooler surface of the photosphere, where it's released as light and heat. In terms of wattage, the Sun shines with the brilliance of 380 septillion (380 million million million) watts. Light bulbs, by the way, are usually no more powerful than 300 watts.

Giant magnetic storms sometimes occur in the turbulence of the boiling gases of the photosphere. Following a cycle of about eleven years, these magnetic storms originate approximately halfway between the Sun's equator and its north and south poles. Then the storms move slowly toward the equator, where their activity peaks. Because they prevent light from escaping and appear as dark blotches on the Sun's surface, the storms are called sunspots. At each peak in the cycle, as many as one hundred large sunspots may be observed. The last peak in the eleven-year cycle occurred in 1991; the next will be about 2002.

Sometimes the magnetic storms carry burning gases with them. When this happens, the gases flare upward, like geysers. Called prominences, these streams of hot gases arch at speeds approaching two hundred miles (320 km) per second. Many prominences are more than one hundred thousand miles (1,600,000 km) long and three thousand miles (4,800 km) thick. Some loop back to the surface; others disappear into space. Active prominences erupt rapidly, lasting only a few hours; quiescent prominences burn more slowly and may last for months.

When the magnetic forces in the sunspots explode, they create flares that can last from ten minutes to one hour. Radiation from these flares hits Earth in the form of high-speed radioactive electrons and protons. At the peak of the eleven-year cycle, magnetic compasses spin wildly and electronic components in communications satellites fry.

The charged protons that result from sunspot activity give us one of Nature's most beautiful phenomena, the auroras. When the protons come in contact with Earth's upper atmosphere, they're attracted to the magnetic poles. As the particles move, they collide with other atomic particles in the atmosphere, change their electrical charges, and release energy as glowing light. In the Northern Hemisphere, this glowing light is called the aurora borealis, or northern lights; in the Southern Hemisphere, it's known as the aurora australis, or southern lights.

One hundred miles (160 km) above the photosphere, the temperature cools to about 8,000 degrees Fahrenheit (4,400 degrees C). Then, beyond the coolest region, the temperature again rises to 50,000 degrees Fahrenheit (27,800 degrees C) in the middle area of the atmosphere called the chromosphere. The chromosphere is usually impossible to see because of the bright glare of the Sun's surface, but it does become visible during a solar eclipse, when the Moon comes between the Sun and Earth. During an eclipse, the chromosphere appears as a pink halo around the dark Moon. Above the chromosphere is the corona. Floating above the Sun's atmosphere, the corona has no definite outside perimeter. The temperature of the corona reaches 3,000,000 degrees Fahrenheit (1,670,000 degrees C). The Sun uses about four million tons of hydrogen every second, yet it still contains enough of that element to continue shining for about another five billion years. The fact is that if the Sun didn't release its energy, it would get hotter and hot-

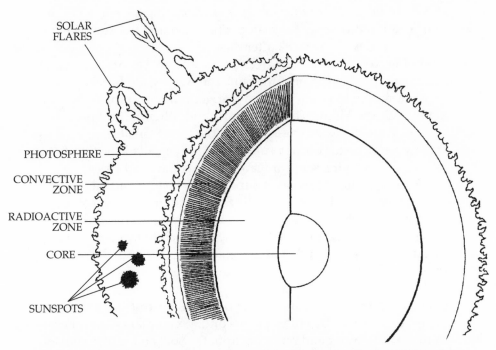

SOLAR FLARES

PHOTOSPHERE

CONVECTIVE ZONE

RADIOACTIVE ZONE

CORE

SUNSPOTS

The center of the Sun, the core, has a diameter of 100,000 miles (160,900 km) and a temperature of 27 million degrees Fahrenheit (15,000,000 degrees C). Surrounding the core is a radioactive zone that extends through about the middle of the Sun's interior. The temperature of the radioactive zone is 4.5 million degrees Fahrenheit (2,500,000 degrees C). The convective zone surrounds the radioactive zone. It begins about two-thirds of the way from the core, ends a few hundred miles below the surface, and has a temperature of 2 million degrees Fahrenheit (1,100,000 degrees C). The photosphere, or surface, is a sea of boiling gases 200 miles (320 km) thick with a temperature of 10,000 degrees Fahrenheit (5,500 degrees C). The outside diameter of the Sun is 865,000 miles (1,392,000 km), almost 110 times greater than that of Earth.

ter until it exploded. The Sun's release of energy guarantees not only life on Earth but its own as well.

Sun worship was an important part of the lives of early Egyptians, Babylonians, Persians, Greeks, and others. For example, the Egyptians called their sun god Re, or Ra, and considered him "the creator of all that is good and not yet, the father of fathers and the mother of mothers." The Greeks called their sun god Helios. He lived in a majestic palace in the east. When he arose each morning,

Helios drove his chariot through the sky, carrying the sunlight with him. The Teutons, early Germanic tribes, honored the Sun by naming the first day of the week after the god.

In the New World, the Aztecs, Incas, and Mayas of Central and South America also revered the Sun. The Aztec god Huitzilopochtli served a dual role as sun god and war god. In Inca culture, the Sun, along with the Moon, Thunder, Stars, and other natural phenomena, was one of several assistants to the Great Creator, as well as the divine ancestor of Inca rulers. The Maya called the Sun "our father," much on the same order as the Egyptians did Re.

Although the Sun is not a supernatural being and has no creative power, it is the center of the Solar System and the source of light and heat that keeps us warm and illuminates our world. It's not difficult to imagine why, then, when ancient farmers realized that there was some kind of direct relationship between the Sun and the success of their crops, they regarded the Sun as a god. Today we understand this relationship. We know that all life on Earth depends on the Sun. As our planet orbits its nearest star at a speed of eighteen and a half miles per second, green plants take energy from the Sun, water and nutrients from the soil, and carbon dioxide from the air to make food. The green plants give off oxygen, which we inhale; when we exhale, we release carbon dioxide back into the air to be used again by the plants. Green plants also provide food for animals and people. In turn, some of those animals also become food. More directly, the Sun lights Earth and warms it.

Although Ptolemy was one of the greatest astronomers of the ancient world, he firmly believed that Earth was motionless. Because Earth had a gravitational pull directed toward its center, he further concluded that Earth was the center of the universe and that the Moon, Sun, and planets, held by gravity, orbited around it. He compiled his views in a thirteen-volume work titled *Mathematike Syntaxis* or (*Mathematical Composition*) and was considered the authority on matters of outer space from about A.D. 150 until 1543, when the Polish astronomer Nicolaus Copernicus revived the theory that the Sun was center of the Solar System.

DISCOVERY

1. Following the Sun. Watch a sunflower follow the Sun.
   ITEMS NEEDED
      packet of sunflower seeds

PROCEDURE

1. Following the directions on the seed packet, plant one or more sunflower seeds in full sun.

2. Keep the soil moist.

3. When the plant blooms, you can watch the flower turn to keep the Sun full in its face.

2. Made in the Shade. See for yourself how much green plants depend on the Sun.

ITEMS NEEDED

brick or dark plastic bag

PROCEDURE

1. Lay the brick or bag (weighted down so that it won't blow away) in a sunny spot of your lawn, and leave it there for a week.

2. When the week's up, lift it. What do you see?

3. Charting Daylight. Do days gradually get longer and shorter as the year goes by, or does the change happen all at once?

ITEMS NEEDED

daily newspaper for   pen
    June and December   ruler
two sheets of paper

PROCEDURE

1. Head one sheet of paper June and one December.

2. Make two columns on each sheet: Sunrise and Sunset.

3. Check the newspaper for daily times of sunrise and sunset every day for the month of June, and fill in the times in the appropriate columns. Then do the same for December.

4. Compare the times of the two months. Earth, as well as all the planets in the Solar System, rotates around the Sun. Because of the way in which Earth tilts, during the summer months it's facing the Sun more directly than during the rest of the year. As Earth turns, or revolves, on its axis, the number of hours of daylight changes from day to day.

4. How Hot Is Hot? The temperature of the Sun's corona reaches 3,000,000 degrees Fahrenheit (1,670,000 degrees C). It gets pretty hot some places on Earth. The hottest day on record is 136.4 degrees Fahrenheit in Al'Aziziyah, Libya, on September 13, 1922. In the United States, record-breaking Fahrenheit temperatures include 134 degrees in Death Valley, 113 degrees in Dallas, 110 degrees in Los Angeles, 106 degrees in New York, 98 degrees in Miami, and 90 degrees in Juneau. Where does your state fit in?

ITEMS NEEDED

graph paper (eight squares to the inch)	pencil ruler

PROCEDURE

1. Mark the graph paper in increments of 5 degrees Fahrenheit, beginning on the left with 0 degrees and ending on the right with 200 degrees.

2. Plot the all-time high temperatures of the cities listed above. Be sure to label each dot with the name of the city.

3. Call the National Weather Service to find out the record-breaking high temperature in your state and plot that on the graph.

4. Are you glad that you live where you do? Or would you like to live in a cooler or warmer place?

The Moon:
Stepping-Stone to Space

. . . the art of flying is only just being born; it will be perfected, and some day we will go as far as the moon.
—Bernard Le Bovier de Fontenelle

ON JULY 20, 1969, ASTRONAUTS NEIL ARMSTRONG AND EDWIN "BUZZ" Aldrin fulfilled that prophecy when they became the first humans to walk on the Moon. Their footprints left half-inch-deep (16-mm) depressions in the lunar surface, and Armstrong's words, "That's one small step for man, one giant leap for mankind," have become historic. Armstrong and Aldrin spent two days traveling to and from the Moon, two and a half days in the spacecraft when it landed on the surface, and two hours and twelve minutes outside the spacecraft.

What Armstrong and Aldrin stepped onto was a lunar surface that Aldrin described as "magnificent desolation." The surface is pock-marked with craters and ridges and littered with rocks—all gray. The samples of lunar rocks that the astronauts brought back to Earth show that lunar rocks and Earth rocks contain many of the same elements, such as silicon, iron, magnesium, aluminum, titanium, and calcium, but that these elements combine differently. And although water constitutes 1 to 2 percent of Earth's rocks, Moon rocks contain no water. Most of the Moon rocks are like glass, attesting to the fact that a great deal of the Moon's surface is made up of fine glassy particles and fused glassy rocks formed by an intense volcanic heat that occurred thousands of years ago.

Not content merely with analyzing the chemical composition of lunar material, scientists experimented with lunar soil—which, naturally, is made of the same stuff as the rocks. For example, they mixed some of it with Earth soil and planted several species of plants in the mixture. Curiously, although some of the plants withered, others grew lush and full. Yet no plant life grows on the Moon.

For centuries, the Moon's changing shape was a significant factor in mankind's daily life. Some North American Indians measured time in numbers of "moons." Jews and Christians used the Moon to establish the dates of religious holidays. And farmers in North America and England planted and harvested their crops according to the phases of the Moon. They planted underground vegetables, like potatoes, carrots, turnips, and beets, on moonless nights but planted and harvested aboveground crops, such as corn and wheat, during a Full Moon.

The same Moon that served as a helpful guide for planting crops was blamed for births, deaths, famines, and wars, depending on its phase or if it was being blotted out by the Sun's shadow during an eclipse. Some people even believed that sleeping in moonlight caused insanity. This superstition is reflected in the word *lunatic*, which comes from the Latin word for Moon, *luna*, and literally means "moonstruck." Since about 2200 B.C., observers predicted and recorded lunar eclipses and phases in order to prepare themselves for the dire circumstances that they believed the Moon's changing shape could cause.

Several North American Indian tribes believed that the Sun and Moon were sister and brother gods but that the Moon was the more powerful of the two, perhaps because it overpowered the darkness of night. The Moon actually has no light of its own. Its brightness is reflected sunlight. In the phase called the New Moon, the Moon is between the Sun and Earth; its sunny side, the far side, is turned away from Earth. A thin crescent appears on the Moon's east side on the following day. The Moon is now waxing, and in seven days, during the First Quarter, we see half of the Full Moon. The Full Moon appears seven days after the First Quarter and fourteen days after the New Moon. Now Earth is between the Moon and the Sun, so we see the entire sunlit side. Seven days after the Full Moon, the Moon is waning as it enters the Last Quarter, when it shines only on the west side. In seven more days, the cycle begins again with the New Moon.

The Moon's easily seen surface features also fueled early mankind's imagination. For example, the Moon is covered with broad, flat plains that appear as dark patches when seen from Earth. As telescopes became more powerful, and lunar probes sent back photographs of the Moon's surface, knowledge replaced folk-

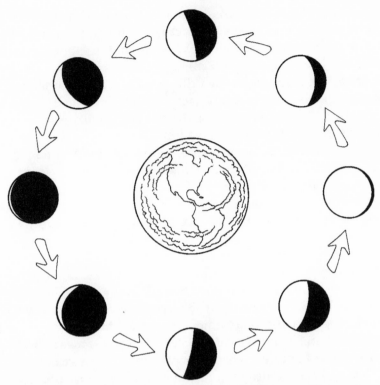

Since the Moon always shows the same side toward Earth, and since the plains on that side form an image like a face, the legend of how a man has been imprisoned in the Moon as punishment for breaking the Sabbath exists in several countries.

lore. Before Aldrin and Armstrong's historic landing, scientists knew that the Moon's landscape was covered with craters ranging in size from microscopic to several hundred miles wide. Most range from five to ten miles (8 to 16 km) in diameter, but the Ibrium Basin, which is the largest crater on the Moon and forms one eye of the "Man on the Moon," is approximately seven hundred miles (1,126 km) wide.

The photographs also proved that the far side of the Moon is nearly all highlands and craters, whereas the near side, the side we see from Earth, is primarily composed of flat plains. (These plains are called maria (singular, mare), meaning "seas" in Latin, because the Italian astronomer Galileo believed that they were bodies of water.) The craters are scars left by the impacts of meteoroids, asteroids, and comets. The highlands, or mountain ranges, are the broken rims of the larger craters. Some of these rims are almost as high as the highest peaks on Earth. Earth's highest mountain, Mount Everest, is 29,028 feet (952 m) high; the Moon's Leibnitz Mountains are 26,000 feet (792 m) high.

Long, narrow valleys called rills crisscross the lunar landscape. These snakelike depressions were probably formed when the Moon's crust cracked under extreme heat. Narrower winding channels may be the result of lava flow.

In addition to changing shape, sometimes the Moon seems to change size. The Moon appears to be huge when it's close to the horizon because of the visual effect caused by its relative size to nearby objects. For example, when the Moon shines between two trees, the relative difference between it and the trees is great. When that same Moon is high in the sky, surrounded by nothing but a dark background, it seems to be its "normal" size.

There's another reason why the Moon looks larger on some nights than on others. The Moon revolves around Earth in an elliptical, or oval, orbit. As a result, at some points in its orbit, the Moon is closer to Earth than at other times. When the Moon is nearest Earth, it looks larger. Six months later, when it's farthest away, the Moon appears to be 12 percent smaller, a noticeable difference in size.

The Moon may also seem to vary in size because of the variation in its perceived brightness. For example, the Moon seems smaller in summer when it's viewed through the haze caused by humidity, or moisture in the atmosphere. In addition, because its path is lower in the sky in summer, the Moon shines through a denser atmosphere and takes on an amber cast from atmospheric particles. In winter, however, the Moon shines through dry air and follows a higher path in the sky, one that's nearer the Sun; under these conditions, it seems brighter and, therefore, larger.

The Moon is 238,900 miles (384,400 km) from Earth, although it moves away from our planet at the rate of about one and a half inches per year. It has no atmosphere, no weather, and no water. Its gravity is six times weaker than Earth's. Its surface temperature has a monthly variation from a high of 225 degrees Fahrenheit (110 degrees C) during the day to a low of minus 274 degrees Fahrenheit (-170 degrees C) during the night. As our nearest neighbor in space, the Moon has been the source of fables, as well as the scene of humankind's first opportunity to walk on the surface of a celestial body other than Earth.

DISCOVERY

1. Waxing and Waning. Can't remember which is which? Try this method.

PROCEDURE

1. Cup your right hand. When the Moon's crescent fits that shape, it's waxing.

2. Cup your left hand. When it fits the shape of your cupped left hand, it's waning—and a waning Moon shows what's "left."

2. Chart the Moon's Phases. The regularity of the phases of the Moon are something we can count on.

ITEMS NEEDED

paper

pen

calendar showing Moon's phases

PROCEDURE

1. Using the calendar to get you started, draw a circle and label it Full Moon. (Although starting with the Full Moon means that you are beginning in the middle of the twenty-eight-day cycle, it's much easier to identify this phase than a New Moon.)

2. Then each night, draw the shape that you see. Label the Last Quarter, New Moon, and First Quarter drawings.

3. Menus on the Moon. Even Moon Men have to eat. But how do you plan for a picnic in space?

ITEMS NEEDED

paper

pen

calorie chart

PROCEDURE

1. Using a basic calorie chart found in a cookbook or diet guide, keep track of what you eat every day for a week. A calorie, by the way, is a measure of the energy content of a given food. A candy bar has a lot more calories than an apple.

2. Add up each day's calories, and divide the week's total by seven to get your average daily calorie requirement.

3. Make up a list of high-nutrition, nonspoiling, lightweight foods that you might take on your space flight.

4. Follow your menu for the next week.

Between Earth and the Sun

Touch a scientist and you touch a child.
—Ray Bradbury

WHEN ANCIENT GREEK ASTRONOMERS STUDIED THE NIGHT SKY, THEY grouped the four thousand visible stars into constellations. Astronomer means "one who arranges the stars," and the Greeks did just that, connecting the stars with imaginary lines, as children connect dots, to form forty-eight images in the sky. The Greeks noted that as the stars moved through the sky, they remained in the same position with respect to each other. Polaris, the North Star, could always be found at the tip of the handle of the constellation called the Little Dipper. In fact, every star forming the Little Dipper could be counted on to always be part of the Little Dipper. And as they moved west through the night sky, the stars stayed on schedule, rising and setting about four minutes earlier each day. A star chart was a reliable calendar of the seasons for farmers and a map of the sky for seafaring navigators.

Early stargazers noted that five bright "stars" didn't abide by the rules governing the others. The five renegades changed position against the background of the other, "fixed," stars, and they didn't keep to the four-minute-a-day timetable. They also roamed from constellation to constellation, and they didn't twinkle, as the other stars did. The Greeks called the five odd stars *planetes*, or wanderers, and named them for their gods. We now use the Roman equivalents of those names.

Today, we know that stars generate their own light and are many billions of miles from Earth, a distance measured by the speed of light and not by mere miles or kilometers. Planets, on the other hand, shine with the reflected light of the Sun. And in terms of distance, Pluto, the farthest planet from Earth, is only a few bil-

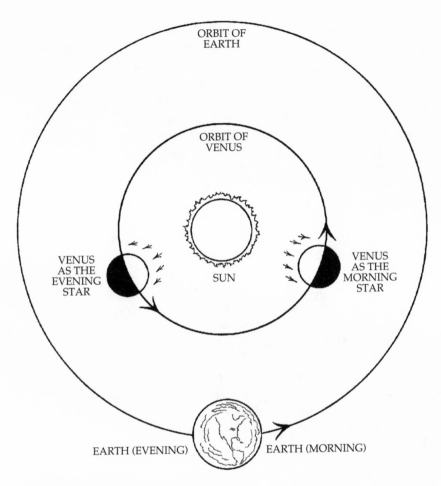

Early Sumerians determined that the morning star and the evening star were actually one planet: Venus. At some points in its orbit, the planet can be seen in the early evening, and at other points, in the early morning.

lion miles from Earth. Beginning with Mercury and Venus, let's take a look at the planets in the Solar System to see how they're like each other and how they're different.

MERCURY

If you were leaving the Sun to visit all the planets in the Solar System, the first one you'd come to is Mercury. And if you could hop a photon freighter traveling at the speed of light, it would take you just over three minutes to cover the thirty-six-million-mile (58,000,000 km) distance. That might be enough time to learn the following facts:

• Mercury is hot. It has the highest surface temperature of all nine planets—1,090 degrees Fahrenheit (605 degrees C)—not only because it's closest to the Sun, but also because it lacks an atmosphere to absorb and deflect some of the Sun's heat.

• Mercury has no atmosphere. Its lunarlike surface is covered with craters and high cliffs called scarps, evidence of the asteroids that continually bombard the planet. If you were standing on Mercury, you'd never know when another incoming asteroid would crash into the surface, sending up a splash of dust and boulders. And with no atmosphere to conduct sound waves, you wouldn't even hear the whoosh and thud of the asteroid.

• Mercury has a mystery: It is surrounded by a weak magnetic field, but it shouldn't be. In order for a planet to have a magnetic field, it must have a liquid core to conduct an electric current, and it must rotate fast enough to make that liquid spin. Although Mercury may very well have a liquid center, the planet rotates too slowly to set up a magnetic field, even one that's only one-hundredth as powerful as Earth's. Yet it has one that is 35 percent that of Earth's, thereby creating a puzzle for astronomers.

• Mercury is one of two planets, along with Pluto, that have an elliptical, or egg-shaped, orbit. The other seven planets have circular orbits.

• Mercury is about three thousand miles (5,000 km) in diameter; only Pluto is smaller. And it spins on an axis that is exactly perpendicular to its orbital path; that means it's not tilted and thus doesn't have seasons as we know them.

• Mercury has a slow rotational speed. It takes six Earth months for Mercury to turn from one day to the next, and a Mercury week lasts for three and a half Earth years.

• Mercury has a fast revolutional speed. Moving along its orbital path at more than one hundred thousand miles (160,000 km) an hour, it is the speediest planet in the Solar System, circling the Sun four times in less than one Earth year. If you were growing up on Mercury and counted years as we do, you would be four times as old as you are now.

Because of its speed of revolution, early Roman astronomers named the planet after the winged messenger of the gods. Mercury, the son of Jupiter, also was the Roman god of commerce and travel; the guardian of thieves, gamblers, and ambassadors; and the guide for souls of the dead on their journey to the Lower World.

VENUS

The second planet from the Sun is Venus, about sixty-seven million miles (108,000,000 km) from the Sun. Traveling at the speed of light, it would take you just under six minutes to zip to Venus. You might want to know the following facts before visiting, though:

• Ancient Greek and Roman astronomers believed Venus to be two separate stars. As the evening star, it was the first and brightest to appear in the sky, always rising in the west and visible no later than three hours after sunset. As the morning star, it appeared in the east no earlier than three hours before sunrise. The Greeks called the evening star Hesperos Aster, a direct translation of "evening star"; they called the morning star Phosphoros, meaning "light-bringer." The Romans carried on the tradition by naming the evening star Vesper, for "evening," and the morning star Lucifer, for "light bearer."

• Venus goes through phases like the Moon's as it revolves. (Mercury also exhibits phases, but most of the time Mercury's reflected sunlight is overwhelmed by the direct light of the Sun. The planet's distance from Earth and the overpowering light of the Sun combine to make Mercury difficult to see at any time.)

• Venus has a cooler surface temperature than Mercury, only 890 degrees Fahrenheit (465 degrees C). That's still hot enough to melt lead and tin.

• Venus's atmosphere is dense. In fact it's ninety times as dense as Earth's, ranging from one-and-four-fifths to two-and-a-half miles (3 to 4 km) thick. And, composed of 96.6 percent carbon dioxide, the atmosphere is poisonous to animal life as we know it. In addition, Venus is covered with a layer of clouds. Droplets of sulfur in the clouds give the planet its yellowish appearance. Small drops of sulfuric acid, a highly corrosive compound used on Earth in making dyes, paints, and explosives, float above the main cloud layer.

• Venus's surface is made up of plateaus, mountain ranges, volcanoes, and canyons scattered with wide, flat rocks measuring about twelve inches (30.5 cm) across.

• Venus is contrary. Astronomers use Earth's North Pole as the point of reference to describe the motions of the planets. They know that all the planets, including Venus, revolve around the sun in a counterclockwise, or prograde, direction. In addition, eight of the nine planets also spin, or rotate, in a prograde direction. But because of the way in which its axis tilts, Venus is the only planet that rotates clockwise, in a retrograde direction. That means that if you could stand on Venus and look through the thick atmosphere, you would see the Sun rise in the west and set in the east.

• Venus is unique because its period of rotation, 243.09 Earth days, is longer than its period of revolution around the sun, 224.7 Earth Days. The rate of rotation, then, is only 4.06 miles (6.54 km) per hour, the rate of a brisk walk for a human. That means that if you were on Venus and walked eastward at a speed of 4.06 miles per hour, you would see the Sun at the same spot in the sky day after day.

• Venus is about seventy-five hundred miles (12,000 km) in diameter.

The Sumerians, who first realized that Venus wasn't a star, showed their appreciation for the planet's brightness by naming it Ishtar, after their goddess of love and beauty. The name of the planet later became Venus in honor of the Roman goddess of love and beauty.

DISCOVERY

1. Why Isn't There Life on Mercury and Venus? They're hotter than you think!

ITEMS NEEDED

   pan of water
   pan of sand

PROCEDURE

1. On a warm day, put a pan of water and a pan of sand in bright sunlight.

2. After about an hour passes, lay the palm of one hand on the surface of the sand, and lay the palm of the other hand on the surface of the water. Which feels hotter?

3. Now lay the palm of your hand on a sidewalk or paved driveway. Does it feel hotter than either the sand or the water? Which surface has accumulated more heat?

4. You've learned that some surfaces absorb more heat than others. Mercury and Venus are essentially big rocks, and they're

closer to the Sun than Earth is. Do you understand why when you're at the beach the water is cool, the sand is warm, and the parking lot surface burns the soles of your feet? Do you also understand why Mercury and Venus can't support life?

2. Make a Model of Mercury or Venus. This activity lets you play with goo and learn at the same time.

ITEMS NEEDED

flour	board or heavy cardboard
table salt	medium gray poster paint
water	paintbrush
bowl	

PROCEDURE

1. Make a mixture of two parts flour to one part salt, plus enough water to form a thick paste. To keep it from drying out, cover the clay and put it in the refrigerator when you take a break.

2. The surfaces of Mercury and Venus look much like the landscape of parts of our Southwest. Using the board as a base, make a model of the craters, mountains, and lava seas of the Mercurian or Venusian landscape.

3. Let the clay dry.

4. Paint the model with gray paint. Does this look like a friendly place to live?

Three More Bright Stars

*A good scientist is a person in whom the childhood
quality of perennial curiosity lingers on. Once he gets
an answer, he has other questions.*
—Frederick Seitz

THE TWO PLANETS NEAREST THE SUN, MERCURY AND VENUS, HAVE SUR-
face temperatures hot enough to melt lead and tin. But beyond
Earth, many millions of miles farther from the Sun, are six planets
that represent the opposite extreme, temperatures far below freezing. Three of those planets, Mars, Jupiter, and Saturn, reflect
enough of the Sun's light to have been visible to ever-curious early
astronomers.

MARS

Skipping Earth (because we know it so well), our next stop on our
celestial journey is Mars. Moving at the speed of light, you can
cover the distance of 142 million miles (228,000,000 km) in about
thirteen minutes. When you get to the red planet, you will discover
the following:

• The diameter of Mars is about forty-two hundred miles (6,800
km), slightly more than half the diameter of Earth; only Mercury
and Pluto are smaller.

• Traveling at a speed of forty-eight thousand miles (77,000
km) per hour, Mars orbits the Sun in 687 Earth days, almost two
Earth years. If you lived on Mars and counted the years as we do,
you would be half your age.

• Mars rotates from one sunset to the next in twenty-four hours
and thirty-seven minutes, Earth time. So a day on Mars is almost
the same as it is on Earth. Your biological clock would operate normally there.

• Mars is inhospitable, however. With an average surface temperature of minus 80 degrees Fahrenheit (−62 degrees C), it's freezing cold. And the atmosphere, which is composed of carbon dioxide and water vapor, contains almost no oxygen. Life as we know it cannot exist under such conditions. There are no large plants or animals, either living or in fossil form, on the planet, and there is no evidence of microscopic life-forms in the soil. The soil contains silicon, oxygen, iron, and magnesium, but no carbon, the basic component of life on Earth. Each grain of soil appears to be covered with rust, giving Mars its reddish color.

• Mars has a metal core composed mainly of iron. Dry, desert-like regions make up two-thirds of the planet's surface. The northern part of Mars is relatively smooth, but the southern areas are covered with deep craters formed when meteors bombarded the planet, and with huge volcanoes. Lava from the volcanoes pooled into greenish and bluish gray "seas" called maria (one such pool is called a mare).

• Mars has polar ice caps that increase and decrease in size according to the Martian seasons. During spring in the northern hemisphere (when the northern hemisphere is closer to the Sun), the polar cap almost disappears while the southern cap grows. During spring in the southern hemisphere, the process is reversed. The ice caps are made primarily of frozen carbon dioxide, or what we call dry ice.

• Mars has two moons. Phobos, the closer and larger moon, has a diameter of fourteen miles (22 km) at the equator. The diameter of Deimos, the other moon, is about six miles (10 km). When seen through a telescope, both moons look like tiny bright jewels shining in the sky; however, photographs have revealed two potato-shaped, crater-scarred chunks of icy rock.

In Roman mythology, Mars was the son of Jupiter, the king of the gods. Originally the god of agriculture and fruitfulness, Mars later became the god of war, so the blood red planet was named for him. The month of March, also named to honor Mars, was the first month in the Roman year.

JUPITER

The next stop on your space trek is Jupiter. Leaving the Sun and traveling at the speed of light, you would cover 486 million miles (778,000,000 km) in about forty-three minutes. Approaching the planet, you will notice the following:

• Jupiter is huge! With an equatorial diameter eleven times larger than Earth's and a mass that accounts for two-thirds of the solid matter in the Solar System, Jupiter is the largest and heaviest planet, about ninety thousand miles (143,000 km) in diameter. Compare that with Earth's eight thousand miles (12,700 km).

• Jupiter is the fastest-spinning planet. A day on Jupiter lasts only nine hours and fifty-five minutes. And because the planet has a core of molten metal to conduct an electrical current and rotates so fast, it has a strong magnetic field. Yet even though the planet rotates so fast, its orbital path around the Sun is slow. Moving at a speed of twenty-nine miles (46,000 km) per hour, it takes Jupiter almost twelve Earth years to revolve around the Sun. If you were twelve years old and lived on Jupiter, you would have just celebrated your first birthday.

• Jupiter has no solid surface. The planet's core is surrounded by layers of gas hundreds of miles thick. Composed of about 90 percent hydrogen and 10 percent helium, methane, water vapor, and ammonia, Jupiter's atmosphere is certainly toxic to life as we know it.

• Jupiter has a ring system shimmering above its surface. In 1979 *Voyager 1* discovered rings of dust encircling Jupiter about 30,000 miles (48,000 km) above the planet's surface. The rings are too dim to be seen from Earth, but photos show a main ring extending from 32,250 to 36,000 miles (52,000 to 58,000 km) above the planet, a thin inner halo, and an outer "gossamer" ring that extends outward from the main ring until it diffuses into space.

• Jupiter's cloud layer has a upper temperature of minus 202 degrees Fahrenheit (-130 degrees C). Although the planet's surface temperature hasn't yet been measured directly, the thick clouds hold hot hydrogen vapor near Jupiter's surface to maintain a temperature estimated to be 1,768 degrees Fahrenheit (1,000 degrees C) or higher. Winds of superhurricane force move upward to keep the clouds in motion, creating an ever-changing pattern of colorful dark belts and light zones. Spots along the belts and zones are whirling windstorms.

• Jupiter has an enormous red spot. For more than three hundred years, astronomers have been speculating about what they have labeled the Great Red Spot. Spanning twenty-five thousand miles (40,000 km) from east to west and eight thousand miles (13,000 km) from north to south, this oval, swirling concentration of gas covers an area equal to 175 million square miles (453,250,000 square km). The Great Red Spot moves slowly around Jupiter, spinning at the rate of once every six Earth days. Unlike the other windstorms, which come and go along the planet's belts and zones, the Great Red Spot is always present in some form, its color deepening and fading in response to some unknown chemical reaction.

• Jupiter has at least seventeen moons orbiting around it. The four largest of Jupiter's moons are called the Galilean satellites, after Galileo, the astronomer who in 1610 first viewed them with a telescope. Callisto and Ganymede, the two moons farthest from the planet, are giant chunks of ice and rock. Europa, second closest to Jupiter and smallest, has a core of rock and a surface of ice. When a meteor strikes Europa, water under the icy layer fills in the scar and freezes, so no craters form.

Io, the Galilean moon closest to Jupiter, has no ice but instead has ten active volcanoes that spew sulfur. As the sulfur cools, it fills in any craters that may have formed on Io's surface and gives this moon its yellow color. Evidence indicates that Io's surface may be solid only down to about ten miles. As the crust buckles under the stress of violent volcanic activity, molten rock inside the planet is forced upward to the surface at the rate of about 0.039 inches (1 mm) a year. At the same time that molten material is churned upward from Io's interior, surface material is stirred into the moon's lower depths. As a result, scientists describe Io as the moon that, given enough time (about two billion years) turns itself inside out.

Smaller moons ranging in size from 12 to 105 miles (19 to 169 km) in diameter travel beyond the orbits of the Galilean satellites. Even smaller moons, unknown until discovered by probes, travel inside Io's orbit.

In keeping with the planet's size and mass, Jupiter was named for the king of the gods in Roman mythology. Jupiter overthrew his father, Saturn, a cruel ruler. As the new king, Jupiter created the seasons and served as god of thunder, lightning, and rain. Jupiter gave Pluto control of the Lower World and Neptune control of the seas. Mercury and Mars were his sons.

SATURN

Saturn, the sixth planet from the Sun, comes next. Traveling at the speed of light, it would take you one hour and twenty minutes to cover the distance of 893 million miles (1,400,000,000 km) from the Sun to Saturn. Like Jupiter, Saturn has no solid surface, so you would have to hover in space to observe the following:

- Saturn, with a diameter of seventy-five thousand miles (121,000 km), is the second-largest planet in the Solar System.
- Saturn has a core of molten rock surrounded first by a relatively thin layer of water and ammonia, then by a much thicker layer of liquid hydrogen. The atmosphere, composed primarily of hydrogen, is 620 miles (1,000 km) thick.
- Essentially an orb of gas only 70 percent as dense as water, Saturn should float on water. But because the planet has no solid surface to hold its shape and because it spins so quickly, once every ten hours and thirty-nine minutes, centrifugal force causes the planet to bulge at the equator. As a result, Saturn is shaped like a flattened ball.
- Saturn revolves around the Sun relatively slowly, completing a revolution once every 29.4 Earth years at a speed of twenty-two thousand miles per hour. If you were growing up on Saturn and counted time as we do, you'd be a lot younger. If you're ten years old now, you'll have to wait another 19.4 Earth years to celebrate your first birthday.
- Saturn's most distinguishing feature is its beautiful ring system. When Galileo first discovered the rings in 1610, he saw only two faint knoblike projections, one on each side of the planet, and called them "ears." In 1656, equipped with a stronger telescope, Dutch astronomer Christian Huygens identified the projections as a continuous ring encircling Saturn. In 1675 Italian astronomer Giovanni Cassini noted a gap in the ring. The outer half, known as the A ring, and the inner half, the B ring, were separated by what became known as the Cassini Division. In 1850 a faint ring, called the C Ring, was discovered. Over the next 130 years, four more rings became distinguishable as optical equipment got more powerful. And in November 1980 data collected by *Voyager 1* revealed that there are actually thousands of rings made of ice particles encircling Saturn.

The rings are arranged in six major bands that span 45,260 miles (73,000 km). The A and B Rings form one band, but each of the C, D, E, F, and G Rings is regarded as an individual band. The bands were labeled in order of their discovery, not in their arrangement relative to Saturn; therefore, starting with the outermost, the rings are labeled E, G, F, A, B, C, and D. The thousands of rings that make up the bands vary in color, probably because of differences in the size and chemical and mineral compositions of the individual particles that form them.

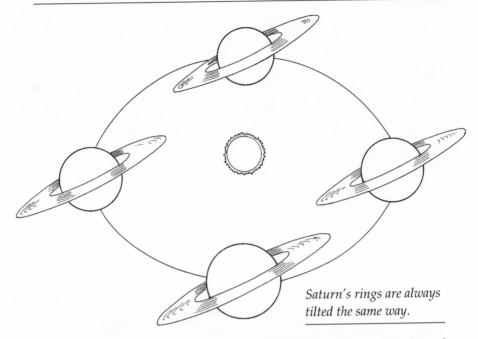

Saturn's rings are always tilted the same way.

• At least twenty-one satellites orbit Saturn at the outer edge of a faint blur called Ring E, the outermost band. Composed of water ice or a combination of ice and rock, Saturn's moons show the scars of their bombardment by meteoroids and asteroids. Titan, the largest of the moons, has an atmosphere that's almost completely composed of nitrogen, as is Earth's, with traces of argon, methane, and other gases. Scientists hope that by someday studying Titan's composition they'll learn more about Earth's geological history.

In Roman mythology, Saturn was the youngest son of Uranus (god of Heaven) and Gaea (the Earth goddess). Portrayed in art carrying a scythe, Saturn was the god of the harvest.

DISCOVERY

1. Start a Mobile of the Solar System. You'll get to use lots of math—for fun—in this activity. (You can complete the Solar System Mobile by doing Discovery 3 at the end of the next chapter.)

ITEMS NEEDED

pencil
drinking straws
fishing line
needle with eye large
    enough for fishing line

colored paper, in the
   colors listed below
compass, for drawing
   circles
scissors

PROCEDURE

1. With the compass, draw circles to represent the first six planets, using the following guidelines:

> Mercury: gray or lavender one-inch circle
>
> Venus: yellow one-and-a-half-inch circle
>
> Earth: blue one-and-a-half-inch circle
>
> Mars: red one-and-three-fourths-inch circle
>
> Jupiter: orange six-inch circle
>
> Saturn: gold six-inch circle, plus ten-inch circle with eight-inch in center to form a ring

2. Cut out the planets and the ring.

3. Use the needle to thread fishing-line through the straws.

4. Referring to the illustration as a guide, suspend the planets.

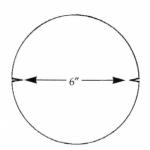

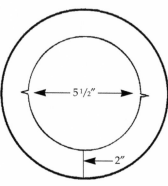

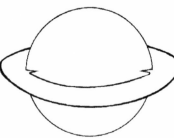

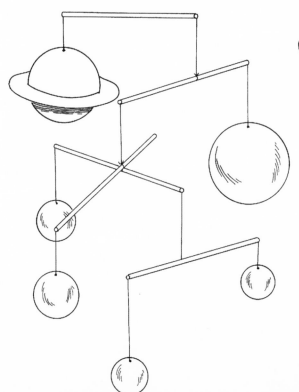

The Unknown Planets

The telescope makes the world smaller.
—G. K. Chesterton

URANUS WAS A MAJOR ASTRONOMICAL DISCOVERY. UNTIL THE LATE EIGH-teenth century, astronomers believed Saturn to be the outermost planet in the Solar System. Then on March 13, 1781, while studying the constellation Gemini, Sir William Herschel noticed a "star" that wandered across the background of the other stars. Herschel became the first person since ancient times to discover a planet. And since that planet was twice Saturn's distance from the Sun, its discovery doubled the expanse of the Solar System.

The discovery of Netpune provided the answer to a mathemat-ical question about the Solar System. Astronomers had noted that Uranus didn't orbit around the Sun at a consistent speed. Although they had no visual evidence, they theorized that the gravitational pull of an even more distant planet was causing Uranus's unex-plained variations in orbit, known as perturbations. In Uranus's case, the planet speeded up at some points in its orbit and slowed down at others.

By 1846 two astronomers working independently of each other calculated the orbit of the unknown body. In England, John Couch Adams came to the same conclusion as Urbain Leverrier in France. By looking at the area in the sky where such a planet should be according to its invisible influence on Uranus's orbit, they proved the existence of a planet more than one billion miles (1,500,000,000 km) beyond Uranus. Leverrier communicated his beliefs to Johann Galle at the Berlin Observatory, and on September 23, 1846, Galle looked for—and found—the new planet just where it was pre-dicted to be.

Pluto also was discovered mathematically. Like Uranus, Nep-tune didn't follow its projected orbit. The existence of a ninth planet pulling on Neptune, then, was a real possibility.

At the turn of the nineteenth century, Percival Lowell calculated the proposed orbit of what he called Planet X. Using his own
funds, Lowell had built an elaborate observatory in Arizona. Lowell died before he found the unknown planet, but by using his data,
Clyde Tombaugh first observed Pluto on February 18, 1930—right
where Lowell predicted it would be.

URANUS

Continuing on your journey through the skies, the next planet
you come to is Uranus. Traveling at the speed of light, it takes
about two hours and forty minutes to get from the Sun to Uranus, a
distance of about two billion miles (2,900,000,000 km). When you
arrive at Uranus, you would notice the following:

• Uranus, the third-largest planet in the Solar System, is about
thirty-two thousand miles (51,000 km) in diameter.

• Traveling at fifteen thousand miles per hour (24,000 kph),
Uranus takes eighty-four Earth years to orbit the Sun. That means
that if you were growing up on Uranus and counted years as we
do, you would have to live eighty-four Earth years before celebrat-
ing your first birthday.

• Uranus orbits the Sun on its side, so sometimes the north or
south pole of Uranus is pointed sideways, toward Earth. And
because Uranus's magnetic poles aren't lined up with its rotational
poles, its magnetic field is askew. If the same conditions were to
exist on Earth, our north magnetic pole, now located very near our
geographic North Pole, would be south of Los Angeles.

• Uranus has a core of molten rock and metal about the size of
Earth. This core, at approximately 12,660 degrees Fahrenheit (7,000
degrees C), is hotter than the surface of the Sun, and is covered by a
layer of scalding water and ammonia. Beyond that layer is an
atmosphere 4,960 miles (8,000 km) thick made up mostly of hydrogen. Methane in the upper atmosphere gives the planet its blue-
green color. This is not a place you'd want to live!

• Uranus has rings. Astronomers waited for Uranus to cross in
front of a star in an eclipse called an occultation. They hoped that
during the occultation, moons might be revealed. As they watched,
dips in the strength of the light of the star occurred before Uranus
passed in front of it. Bewildered, the scientists carefully noted the
interval between each dip and the duration of the fade-out. After

Uranus passed the star, five more dips of light occurred, in reverse sequence. Only rings, not moons, could create such a pattern.

When *Voyager 2* passed within 49,600 miles (80,000 km) of Uranus, a system of eleven main rings made of black boulders was observed. Because the rocks aren't coated with ice, as those in Saturn's rings are, they don't reflect light, and Uranus's rings remained hidden for two hundred years after the discovery of the planet. In keeping with Uranus's contrariness, the rings encircle the planet vertically, not horizontally as do Jupiter's and Saturn's.

• At least fifteen moons orbit Uranus. Studies of the five largest satellites show craters, mountains, deep valleys, and evidence of volcanic action. Of those five, Umbriel displays a bright circular shape in its atmosphere that scientists cannot explain but call the "fluorescent Cheerio." Most of the moons also have white markings of unknown origin on their otherwise dark surfaces.

In mythology, Uranus was the sky god and husband of Gaea, the Earth goddess. Provider of light, heat, and rain, he was Saturn's father and Jupiter's grandfather. Uranus and Gaea produced a mythical family of giants called Titans.

NEPTUNE

If you traveled the 2.8 billion miles (4,000,000,500 km) from the Sun to Neptune at the speed of light, the trip would take you four hours and ten minutes. The following facts about Neptune will tell you if the trip was worth the effort:

• Neptune is about thirty thousand miles (49,000 km) in diameter, making it the smallest of what astronomers call, along with Jupiter, Saturn, and Uranus, the four gas giants.

• Neptune has a core of molten material with a temperature of about 12,660 degrees Fahrenheit (7,000 degrees C) surrounded by a layer of hydrogen gas about 4,970 miles (8,000 km) thick. A layer of ammonia clouds separates the hydrogen layer from the methane atmosphere above. The upper atmosphere is composed primarily of hydrogen, with traces of methane, helium, and other gases at a frigid minus forty-two hundred degrees Fahrenheit (-200 degrees C).

• One day on Neptune equals about only eighteen Earth hours, but even traveling at the speed of 12,150 miles per hour, it takes Neptune almost 165 Earth years to orbit the Sun. This faraway giant won't return to the same position where it was first seen in 1846 until 2011. To be 12 years old on Neptune, you would have to live 1,980 Earth years. When Methuselah died at the age of 969, he was less than 6 Neptune years old!

• With its similar size, density, mass, and period of rotation, this twin of Uranus may also have a system of complete or partial rings.

• Two moons orbit the planet. But they don't act like the moons of any of the other planets. One follows an egg-shaped orbit that takes a full Earth year to complete. The other has a circular orbit and circles Neptune once every six Earth days, but it orbits backward—opposite the direction in which the planet spins.

Neptune was the Roman god of the sea, thought to control all water on Earth. He was also credited with having created the horse and emphasizing its usefulness. The brother of Jupiter, Neptune was worshiped by sailors and by people who raced horses.

PLUTO

Pluto is so far from the Sun and so small compared with the other planets that it may not be worth the five and a half hours it would take to cover the 3.7 billion miles (2.3 billion km), even traveling at the speed of light. But if you decide to take the journey, you'll find the following:

• Pluto is a ball of frozen ice about the size of Earth's Moon.

• Pluto takes 247 years to complete its huge orbit. The planet won't return to the spot in the sky where Tombaugh discovered it until 2178.

• Pluto has a huge moon. On June 22, 1978, James W. Christy noticed a bulge on Pluto. A closer look revealed that the bulge was actually a satellite. The moon, named Charon (pronounced KAIR-on), is large as moons go. Whereas most moons are a small fraction of the size of the parent planet, Charon is half as large as Pluto. Like Pluto, Charon seems to be made up of frozen methane with an average temperature of minus 370 degrees Fahrenheit (–225 degrees C). Charon is so close to Pluto that the planet's atmosphere extends from its moon. Atmospheric particles form a thin methane cloud around Pluto and its moon, creating a double-planet system and raising questions as to whether both Pluto and Charon actually are moons that escaped from Neptune's orbit to take up orbits of their own.

In Roman mythology, Pluto ruled the Underworld, the world

Charon is so close to Pluto that astronomers first thought it was a huge bulge on the planet.

of the dead. Few temples were built to honor Pluto, for although men worshiped Pluto as a just god, the knowledge that they would one day live with him curbed their celebration of his existence. Because silver and gold come from the earth, Pluto was also considered god of riches and wealth.

DISCOVERY

1. Weighing In. You can gain or lose weight quicker than any diet plan claims—just move to another planet!

ITEMS NEEDED

    pencil and paper, or calculator

PROCEDURE

1. Use the accompanying chart to determine what your height and weight would be on the other planets. Your height is determined by Earth's size as compared with the size of the other eight planets. Your weight is calculated according to the gravitational pull of each planet.

2. On which planet would you weigh the most? The least?

3. Where would you be the tallest? The shortest?

TABLE OF PLANETS

	Diameter at Equator	Rotation	Revolution	Avg. distance from Sun
Mercury	3,032 mi. (4,878 km)	58.65 Earth days	88 Earth days	35,900,000 mi. (57,900,000 km)
Venus	7, 520 mi. (12,104 km)	243.09 Earth days	224.7 Earth days	67,240,000 mi. 108,200,000 km
Earth	7,926 mi. (12,756 km)	23 hrs., 56 min.	365.26 Earth days	92,960,000 mi. (149,600,000 km)
Mars	4,212 mi. (6,778 km)	24 hrs., 37min	1.88 Earth years	141,680,000 mi. (228,000,000 km)
Jupiter	88,650 mi. (142,984 km)	9 hrs., 55 min.	11.86 Earth years	483, 700, 000 mi. (778,400,000 km)
Saturn	75,000 mi. (121,000 km)	10 hrs., 39 min.	29.46 Earth days	886,740,000 mi. (2,869,600,000 km)
Uranus	32,600 mi. (52,400 km)	16 hrs.	84.01 (Earth years)	1,783,170,000 mi. (2,869,600,000 km)
Neptune	27,700 mi. (44,600 km)	18 hrs., 30 min.	164.8 Earth years	2,794,190,000 mi. (4,496, 600,000 km)
Pluto	1,457 mi. (2,344 km)	6.39 Earth days	247 Earth years	3,706,780,000 mi. (5,965,200,000 km)

* Multiply your weight by this number. This gives you your corresponding weight on each planet.

** Multiply your height by this number. If you were the same size relative to the size of the planet, this measurement gives you your corresponding height on each planet.

† Estimated temperatures based on data collected to date.

Avg. Surface Temp.	Number of Satellites	Your weight on Planets*	Your height on Planets**	
1,090ºF (605ºC)	0	× 0.27	× 0.375	**Mercury**
870ºF (465ºC)	0	× 0.85	× 0.938	**Venus**
60ºF (16ºC)	1	× 1.00	× 1.00	**Earth**
−80ºF (−62ºC)	2	× 0.38	× 0.525	**Mars**
−200ºF† (−130ºC†)	17	× 2.64	× 11.088	**Jupiter**
−250ºF† (−160ºC†)	21, possibly 23	× 1.17	× 9.375	**Saturn**
−300ºF† (-185ºC†)	15	x 0.92	× 4.075	**Uranus**
−350ºF† (−210ºC†)	2	× 1.12	× 3.463	**Neptune**
−400ºF† (−240ºC†)	1	unknown	× 0.188	**Pluto**

2. How Far Is a Million Miles? It's a long trip—especially with no restroom stops along the way!

PROCEDURE

1. Count to one thousand miles at the rate of one mile per second. How long does it take you?

2. How long would it take you to count to one million by tens? By hundreds? By thousands?

Note: If you began to count miles at the rate of one per second and took no breaks, you'd count to one million in about eleven and a half days. To count to a billion, set aside thirty-one years of your life.

3. Finish the Solar System Mobile. This project completes the mobile begun in Discovery 1 in the preceding chapter.

ITEMS NEEDED

drinking straws   colored paper, in the colors
needle   listed below
fishing line   compass, for drawing circles

PROCEDURE

1. With the compass, draw circles to represent the remaining three planets, the Sun, and the Moon, using the following guidelines:

Uranus: green three-inch circle
Neptune: green three-inch circle
Pluto: gray or lavender three-fourths-inch circle
Sun: yellow two-inch circle
Moon: white two-inch circle

2. Cut out the circles.

3. Thread fishing line through the straws.

4. Suspend the planets, the Sun, and the Moon from the threads.

5. Hang the mobile from the ceiling in your bedroom.

4. Be the Solar System. Can you stay in a precise orbit?

ITEMS NEEDED

eleven kids in a large field
rope
stake
flour (for more lasting marks, use lime)

PROCEDURE

1. Put a stake in the ground. This is the position of the Sun.

2. Tie a loop in one end of the rope.

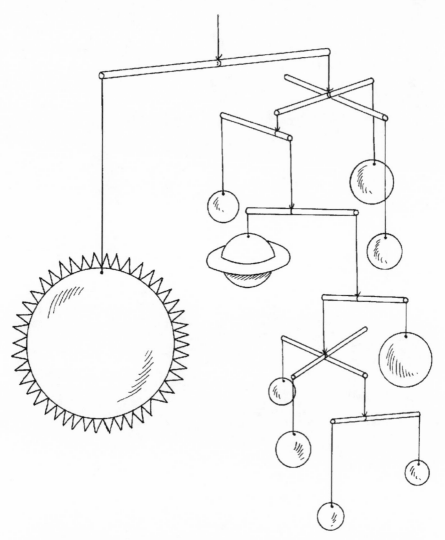

3. Put the loop over the stake so that the rope moves freely. This will serve as a compass for drawing circles.

4. Mark the orbits of the nine planets, at least six feet apart, around the Sun with flour or lime.

5. Position everyone in his or her designated orbit, with the Sun in the center.

6. Have the Moon orbit around Earth while the planets orbit around the Sun.

GLOSSARY

abdomen: in insects and crustaceans, the hind third of the body.

air bladder: a gas-filled chamber found in the bodies of most bony fishes; provides buoyancy and occasionally serves as a respiratory organ; also called a swim bladder.

allergy: a physical reaction to an irritant or poison, such as pollen or venom.

alveoli: air cells in the lungs of mammals.

amino acids: organic compounds that are the chief components of proteins and are synthesized by living cells or are obtained as essential components of the diet.

ampere: a unit used to measure electrical energy.

androconia: scent-producing scales on the wings of the males of some butterfly species.

antenna: a movable sensory organ on the head of insects and crustaceans (plural, antennae).

antennule: a small antenna.

anterior: toward the front end of the body of an animal.

anthocyanins: the red, rust, maroon, and purple pigments in leaves.

aperture: the open space in a univalve shell in which the animal lives.

apex: the closed pointed end of a univalve shell.

arthropod: an invertebrate, such as an insect, spider, or crustacean, with a jointed body and legs.

asteroid: one of thousands of small celestial bodies between Mars and Jupiter.

aurora: luminous bands or streamers of light that appear in Earth's polar regions.

baleen: whalebone.

calcium carbonate: the substance that makes up the shells of mollusks and crustaceans.

callow: a young ant.

cambium: the layer of cells, lying just under the bark, that produces all new cells for the tree.

carapace: the upper shell of a turtle or crab.

carbohydrate: sugars formed from the combination of carbon, hydrogen, and oxygen.

carnivore: a meat-eating animal.

carotenids: yellow, orange, or red plant pigments, such as the carotene in carrots.

chitin: the material that forms the external skeletons of insects, crustaceans, and other invertebrates.

chlorophyll: the green pigment in plant cells essential to photosynthesis.

chloroplasts: cellular parts in a plant that contain chlorophyll and are the site of photosynthesis.

chrysalis: the pupa of a butterfly, the form between larval and adult stages; the case itself.

cilia: hairlike outgrowths of some cells.

class: a major taxonomic group of related organisms, such as the class Mammalia (mammals); several orders form a class, and several classes form a phylum.

cloaca: in birds, reptiles, amphibians, and many fishes, body cavity into which the reproductive and excretory tracts empty.

clutch: a nest of eggs or brood of chicks.

cocoon: a case, usually made of silk, containing the pupa of moths and some other insects.

constellation: a group of stars that suggests a pattern or figure.

cotyledon: the tiny leaf in the embryo of a seed; dicotyledons, or dicots, have two, whereas monocotyledons, or monocots, have one.

crater: a depression in the surface of a planet or moon caused by volcanic action or the impact of a meteorite.

deciduous: plants, usually broad-leaved, that shed their leaves in fall.

diaphragm: in mammals, the muscle and tissue that separate the chest and abdominal cavities.

diurnal: active during daylight hours.

downstroke: the downward stream of electrons in a lightning strike.

eclipse: the total or partial obscuring of one celestial body by another.

ecosystem: a community of plants and animals in their environment.

egg: the reproductive cell that contains the nourishment necessary for the developing embryo.

egg tooth: hard, sharp prominence on the beak of an unhatched bird that is used to break through the eggshell.

elliptical: oval, egg-shaped.

embryo: an animal in the earliest stages of development before birth; the rudimentary plant contained in a seed.

endoskeleton: the inner skeleton of an animal, such as that of mammals and other vertebrates.

estivation: the sleeplike state that some animals enter to survive the heat of summer.

evergreen: plants, usually narrow-leaved, that retain their leaves all year.

excretion: the elimination of solid and liquid body wastes; also the body wastes themselves.

exoskeleton: the outer skeleton of an animal, such as that of a lobster or other invertebrate.

extinct: no longer in existence.

family: a major group of related organisms, such as the family Cricetidae (mice, rats, lemmings, and voles) in the order Rodentia (rodents); several genera form a family, and several families form an order.

fat: oily or greasy plant or animal tissue.

fertilization: the joining of male and female reproductive cells to produce another cell that develops into a new individual.

filter feeding: the method of feeding in which plant and animal organisms are strained from water; some mollusks, crustaceans, whales, and water birds are filter feeders.

flagellum: a whiplike thread used by some water creatures to catch prey (plural: flagella).

flower: the reproductive structure of a plant.

foot: the muscular organ that a snail uses for locomotion.

fossil: the remains of a long-dead organism preserved in rock or some other solid material.

fruit: the part of a flowering plant that contains seeds and, sometimes, a pulp.

fungicide: a chemical substance that destroys fungus or inhibits its growth.

genus: a major group of closely related organisms, such as the genus Neotoma (woodrats) in the family Cricetidae (mice, rats, lemmings, and voles); several species form a genus, and several genera form a family.

germination: in plants, the first stage of growth after fertilization.

gill: the external breathing organ of some aquatic and semiaquatic animals.

glucose: a sugar that occurs naturally in plants.

gravity: the attraction between objects, such as between Earth and the Moon, that causes them to be pulled toward each other; a force that tends to draw all bodies in Earth's sphere toward the center of the planet.

growing season: the annual period during which a plant actively grows.

guttation: the release of excess water on the surface of leaves.

habitat: the distinctive environment in which a plant or animal lives.

head: in insects and crustaceans, the anterior, or front, third of the body.

heliosphere: the teardrop-shaped bubble in which the Solar System is enclosed.

herbivore: an animal that feeds exclusively or primarily on plant material.

hermaphrodite: an animal that has both male and female reproductive organs, such as the hydra or the earthworm.

herpetology: the study of amphibians and reptiles.

hibernation: the sleeplike state that some animals enter in order to survive the cold of winter.

holdfast: rootlike structures that anchor kelp to the ocean floor.

hormone: a chemical secretion that regulates growth and reproduction, among other functions.

host: the plant or animal on which another plant or animal lives, sometimes in a symbiotic relationship.

humus: decomposing organic matter.

hybrid: the offspring of parents of different species.

ichthyology: the study of fish.

immunity: the ability to resist a specific infection or poison.

insectivore: an animal that feeds exclusively or primarily on insects.

instinct: inborn tendency to behave in a way characteristic of a species.

interstellar: located or taking place among the stars.

intestine: part of the digestive tract of an animal.

invertebrate: an animal without a backbone

lamellae: thin, flat scales or membranes such as those composing the gills of bivalve and univalve mollusks (singular, lamella).

larva: the immature stage of many animals, such as the caterpillar stage of moths and butterflies.

larynx: the voicebox.

lipids: fats and other compounds that are among the structural components of living cells.

locomotion: movement from one place to another.

lung: a breathing organ, usually internal and air filled.

mandible: jaw; the upper or lower segment of a bird's beak.

mantle: the skinlike organ in mollusks that produces the substance that makes the shell.

mare (pronounced *MARay*): an extensive dark area on the surface of the Moon or Mars (plural, maria).

membrane: thin, soft layer of animal or vegetable tissue serving as a covering or lining, as for an organ or part.

metamorphosis: the dramatic change that occurs in the development of some life-forms, such as the metamorphosis of a caterpillar to a moth or butterfly.

meteor: a meteoroid that burns with a white-hot light caused by the friction produced when an object enters Earth's atmosphere at great speed; a shooting star.

meteorite: a fallen meteor.

meteoroid: a small metallic or mineral body traveling through outer space.

mollusk: a soft-bodied animal, such as a clam, oyster, snail, or octopus. A mollusk with a one-piece shell, such as a snail, is a univalve; a mollusk with a two-piece shell, such as an oyster or clam, is a bivalve.

mucus: a slimy substance that consists mostly of water and is used by animals for protection (fish), locomotion (snails), bubble making (spittlebug), or other purposes.

native: a plant or animal that occurs naturally in a given area.

nectar: the sugary liquid produced by many flowers.

nematocysts: cells of some animals, such as of sponges and hydras, that contain tiny poisonous darts used to paralyze prey.

nephridium: an excretory organ found in earthworms.

nerve cell: a cell in animals that perceives subtle changes in surroundings, such as in light, temperature, and air currents.

nocturnal: active at night, such as bats.

nomenclature: a system of names. In nature, each distinct organism has a genus and species name according to the binomial system of nomenclature.

nymph: a young insect that resembles the adult, although in a smaller version and without the wings of the adult.

occultation: the interruption of light from a celestial body.

omnivore: an animal that eats both plants and animals.

operculum: the hard plate that covers the opening of some snails.

orbit: the regular path of a celestial object.

order: a major group of related plants or animals, such as the order Rodentia (rodents) in the class Mammalia (mammals); several families form an order, and several orders form a class.

organic: containing carbon.

ornithology: the study of birds.

osculum: in sponges, an opening through which filtered ocean water is ejected.

ostia: in sponges, openings that allow ocean water to flow into the animal to be filtered for food (singular, ostium).

outer space: the universe outside Earth's atmosphere.

ovulation: the process by which an egg is released in readiness for fertilization

perturbation: a disturbance in the regular orbit of a planet.

phloem: tubes that carry food from the leaves to the rest of a plant.

photon: a particle of light energy.

photoreceptor: a cell or organ that perceives light.

photosynthesis: the process by which green plants use sunlight, carbon dioxide, and water to manufacture food.

phylum: a major group of related plants or animals, such as the phylum Chordata (vertebrates), in which the class Mammalia (mammals) belongs; several classes form a phylum, and several phyla form a kingdom.

plankton: tiny plants and animals that float in rivers, lakes, and oceans.

plastron: the lower shell of a turtle or crab.

pollen: the powderlike male reproductive cells of plants.

pollination: the process by which pollen is transferred from the male part of a flower to the female part.

polyp: an animal with a mouth surrounded by tentacles at one end of a tubelike body, as a hydra or sea anemone.

posterior: toward the hind end of the body of an animal.

predator: an animal that kills other animals for food.

prey: the animal captured by a predator.

probe: a spacecraft used to collect data about celestial bodies.

prograde: the direction in which Earth revolves.

prominence: a cloud of gas that rises from the Sun's chromosphere.

protein: a combination of amino acids necessary for life.

pupa: the resting stage, usually spent in the protection of a cocoon or chrysalis, between the larva stage and the adult of some insects, including moths, butterflies, and ants.

pustule: a pus-filled pimple or blister.

queen: the only fertile female in a colony of social insects, such as ants.

respiration: the inhalation (breathing in) of oxygen and the exhalation (breathing out) of carbon dioxide.

retrograde: opposite to the direction in which Earth revolves.

rill: a long, narrow valley on the Moon's surface.

rotund: a honey-stuffed ant. Workers feed honey to other workers to use them as living storage vessels.

sap: a combination of sugar and other nutrients produced by plants.

sapling: a young tree.

scutes: external bony plates on a reptile, such as the pyramid-shaped scutes on the Wood Turtle's carapace.

social insect: an insect that lives in and performs a specific function in a colony, such as an ant.

species: a group of plants or animals that can produce fertile offspring but that usually cannot breed with other species. The species name generally refers to a physical characteristic or behavior of the plant or animal, or to its discoverer.

spermatozoa: sperm; male germ cell.

spinnerets: the organs in spiders and caterpillars that produce liquid silk.

spongocoels: in sponges, inner chambers that contain the cells that absorb oxygen and food from ocean water.

spp.: abbreviation for two or more species.

spore: reproductive cell of certain simple plants and animals.

statocyst: the sensory organ that affects balance.

stomata: pores on the upper and lower surfaces of a leaf.

sunspot: a dark spot on the Sun's surface usually visible only through a telescope.

symbiosis: a mutually beneficial relationship between two kinds of organisms.

tannin: an acid in the leaves of some deciduous trees, such as hickories, chestnuts, walnuts, and some oaks, that causes their brown coloration in fall; also tannic acid.

taxonomy: a system of classifying plants and animals.

telson: the last joint in the abdomen of a crustacean, such as the swordlike telson in the Atlantic Horseshoe Crab.

territory: an area occupied by and defended by one or more animals.

thorax: in insects and crustaceans, the second, or middle, of the three main body divisions.

tide: the alternate rising and falling of Earth's water surfaces.

trachea: the windpipe.

transpiration: the process by which leaves exude moisture into the air.

upstroke: the light-producing upward stream of electrons in a lightning strike.

valve: in animals such as snails and clams, one of the parts making up the shell (see also "mollusk").

vein: a thin-walled blood vessel that carries blood from the body tissues to the heart.

venom: the poison of some reptiles, amphibians, spiders, and insects, introduced into the body of the victim by bite or sting.

worker: a sterile female in a colony of social insects, such as ants.

xanthophyll: the yellow pigment in leaves.

xylem: tubes that carry water and nutrients from the roots to other parts of a plant.

yolk: the part of an egg that contains most of the nourishment for the growing embryo.